Endorsements

"When Laura Eisenhower speaks, Love listens... nudges that infinite source of Love in us all. Experie Frequency."——Cathy O'Brien, MK-Ultra survivor and

"Laura Eisenhower is an icon in the UFO field. She survived the infiltration & destruction of the 'UFO industry' over the past 7 years when most of the great researchers 'died mysteriously' in a short period of time. They were quickly replaced by bad actors, yet Laura stayed strong through all of it! She's been a refreshing face at the UFO events for more than a decade, delivering a true example of the Divine Feminine Human Soul. What makes her different is that she speaks & writes from her heart & she's honest. Unfortunately this is a rarity in the UFO field today. Laura exists in a different frequency than most people can imagine. She speaks the languages of Love & the stars through astrology as she guides people toward Ascension—rather than fear. She's delivered incredible wisdom about her Presidential family & memories of an invitation to the Mars Project, while tolerating rude, ignorant people denying her experiences over the years. She stayed strong through all of it because she knows the Truth. Yes, Laura Eisenhower knows more than most people about ETs, our multidimensional universes & President Dwight D Eisenhower's true intentions. I believe Laura's the real deal & I've been blessed to be her friend for many years. *Awakening the Truth Frequency* is a wealth of knowledge for those who hunger for the Truth, at a time when everything is upside down & backwards!"—Patty Greer, award-winning UFO filmmaker

"*Truth Frequency* is part guide to how to live your life in the most extraordinary way, part tell-all of our true human story and Mother Earth's (and beyond!) since the beginning, and part memoir of the most fascinating, courageous Warrior living in this world right now. Global Alchemist Laura Eisenhower shows you how to transmute and override negative frequencies and ride the truth frequency to both your own ascension and the rise of New Earth. A triumphant MUST READ for Light Warriors. Bravo Laura Eisenhower! I just love this book!"—Marisa Acocella, New York Times best-selling author of *The Big She-Bang, Cancer Vixen and Ann Tenna*

"*Among the infinite,* creational waters of our Universe and the infinite souls Divine Mother births, still Laura M. Eisenhower shines brightest. When choosing to read or listen to someone we look for honesty, integrity, and truth, and Laura is an embodiment of these divine qualities that at times seem scarce in this Matrix world. Her spoken words are poems which inspire and ignite what is awaiting to be reawakened within our souls. If you are ready to remember and grow through the reflection of the experience and wisdom Laura emanates, then this is the book for you. What we have been, and what we will be."—Rising Phoenix AuroRa, galactic historian, author, spiritual revolutionist and founder A.U.R.A Hypnosis Healing & Rising Phoenix Mystery School

Endorsements

"*A voyage into a new, living dimensional ecology.* A key insight in Laura's book states, 'A 'Light Life' is a higher intelligence energy form of 'Living Light,' they are 'Life'...Their Purpose? To BE the change on this world, standing side by side with those like yourselves that have been living under the rule of ignorance and deception without any intervention for so very long." [Chapter 5] Author Laura lets us the Reader know the core multi-dimensional secret: 'The military man and the one to enter the U.S. government was Dwight David Eisenhower, and the "Light Life" to come into the family still working today, no doubt, was me. I do have a hard time accepting such things. But knowing my mission was active at such a young age and that I came specifically for this mission, as did many others.' [Chapter 5] Now I know why, ever since 1958, when as a Secondary School Junior in Washington DC, I was invited to meet with Ike's Secretary of Labor for a debating team briefing, I so feel connected to Author Laura, to Ike, to the Eisenhower Family, and to the 'Living Light!' On one memorable night a couple of years ago I was seated alone at our Dining Room table, and a Voice came enveloping me and said: 'Alfred this is IKE! This is serious work you are doing with Laura! We are watching over you.' Or words to that effect!"—**Alfred Lambremont Webre, founder of omniversity.mn.co**

"*You CAN handle the Truth!* When we understand our history we can live and move in Divine Wisdom. Take this PowerFULL opportunity to dive in this beautifully written content and truly understand our history, propelling you to your HIGHEST now and beyond. Laura Eisenhower is literally my favorite conference speaker, researcher, writer and friend, and this book doesn't disappoint. She manages to weave and navigate several paths and streams of history into one activating tapestry of DIVINITY, TRUTH and LOVE. Explore the pages of this book and find yourself empowered to live a life of Sovereignty, PEACE and understanding. This IS Your Time to Upgrade Now! Thank you Laura!"—**Dr. Sharnael Wolverton Sehon, www.Swiftfire.org www.Drsharnael.com**

"*Laura has two voices* to me, the one of a kind wise friend that I have learned to trust. She has another voice that comes out on stage, when she seems to tap into a higher state of mind that is divine and often moves the crowd in a profound way. This book will introduce you to both. I am excited for her to have this book available to reach a broader audience of people that are in desperate need of her insight."—**Tony Rodrigues, author of *Ceres Colony Cavalier***

"*Thank you from the bottom of our hearts* dear Laura for all that you are, and all that you represent in global disclosure, you are an extraordinary being... Here you are today, holding the flame of truth and nothing can stop you. The divine energy that is an integral part of your whole being...a catalyst for a major global transformation of our times."—**Jean-Charles Moyen & Mélanie Charest, French-American Ultra Secret Space Program**

Awakening the Truth Frequency

INTO THE UNIFIED FIELD

LAURA EISENHOWER

Consortium of Collective Consciousness Publishing

www.CCCPublishing.com

Awakening the Truth Frequency: Into the Unified Field

1st edition

Into the Unified Field Series :: Volume I

Copyright © 2024 by Laura Eisenhower.

Published by the Consortium of Collective Consciousness™

Library of Congress Cataloging-in-Publication Data:

Eisenhower, Laura

    AWAKENING THE TRUTH FREQUENCY: INTO THE UNIFIED FIELD
    Laura Eisenhower
      p. cm.
    Does not include index

    ISBN 13: 9781888729948 (Pbk.)

1. Spirituality—Guidebooks. 2. Metaphysics—Astrology. I. Title

Library of Congress Catalog Card Number: 2022932955

10 9 8 7 6 5 4 3 2 1

DEDICATION

I dedicate this book to my great-grandfather's faithful service through pivotal times in our human history and his guidance in my life. My family's love and support throughout my journey and especially my children and Kevin for always encouraging me. To all the people of Earth as we experience a remarkable transformation. The Mother who has returned to awaken and nurture, and all those willing and fearless to explore their truth frequency.

Awakening the Truth Frequency

CONTENTS

CONTENTS

FOREWORD

by Brad Olsen

Most people instantly recognize the name Dwight David Eisenhower as the top general who helped end World War II in Germany, and as the popular two-term 34th President of the United States. In 1952, Eisenhower entered the presidential race as a Republican in favor of creating NATO and America taking a dominant role in foreign entanglements. Eisenhower won that election and the 1956 election both in landslides. In both elections he defeated Adlai Stevenson II. Eisenhower's main goals in office were to contain the spread of communism and reduce federal deficits. That's the textbook explanation. The esoteric side to the Eisenhower Administration was his instrumental role in establishing relationships with different extraterrestrial races and coming into contact with technology beyond our wildest dreams.

We have to remember Eisenhower's role as the Supreme Commander of the Allied Expeditionary Force in Europe going up against the most technologically-advanced armed forces in the history of warfare. The Allied Commanders were alerted to the "Wonder Weapons" of the Third Reich and their potentially destructive wrath. Because he achieved the five-star rank of General of the Army he would come to know what the Nazis were capable of, and how to gain this technology for the United States by bringing in top German scientists through Project Paperclip. Most World War II historians agree that if the war had dragged on for even another six months, the outcome could have been drastically different. Not only were German scientists on the verge of using atomic weapons, but they also had exotic anti-gravity craft with the potential of deflecting any fire, and the possibility of traveling off-planet.

BACKWARD-ENGINEERED TECHNOLOGY

The notion of Nazi Germany having anti-gravity spacecraft technology in the 1940s is supported by a 1952 CIA document describing "German flying saucers and the Canadian AVRO saucer." George Klein, a famous German engineer and aircraft expert, described the experimental construction of "flying saucers" carried out by him from 1941 to 1945 at the Škoda Works in Pilsen near Prague, in what is today the Czech Republic. This was the primary German Disc Testing facility that the Allies hoped to capture first, but the Red Army beat them there and absorbed Czechoslovakia into the So-

The Nazi Haunebu flying disc was the likely craft used in the Washington, D. C. flyover on July 19, 1952.

viet Union. The Škoda Works became nationalized and the captured German scientists began to work for the Soviets, Americans and British. Klein stated that he was present when, in 1945, the first piloted "flying saucer" took off and reached a speed of 1,300 miles per hour within 3 minutes. A German newspaper published an interview with George Klein before he passed away, who stated: "Though many people believe the 'flying saucers' to be a postwar development, they were actually in the planning stage in German aircraft factories as early as 1941." Klein said that he was also "present in Prague on 14 February 1945, at the first experimental flight of a flying saucer."

In 1958, in the waning years of the Eisenhower Administration NASA was created. If anti-gravity propulsion was developed several decades prior, which made the use of rocket propulsion as used today completely obsolete, then it becomes apparent that the heavily Nazi infiltrated NASA has always been a front which continues to make the public believe that rockets are the only method of overcoming the gravitational pull of our planet. This is also made apparent by the following statement from the head of Lockheed Skunkworks, Ben Rich, who said publicly in 1993:

"We already have the means to travel among the stars, but these technologies are locked up in black projects and it would take an Act of God to ever get them out to benefit humanity … Anything you can imagine, we already know how to do."

As a third generation descendent of Dwight D. Eisenhower, born into a prominent political family which also included the Richard M. Nixon family, Laura Eisenhower has had exposure to the esoteric side of the Eisenhower persona like no other person her age. From family memories to secrets told in private, Laura has an inside perspective most could only wonder about in fascination. It was this position in life she was born into, and also the reason she was recruited to be in the Mars Program. You see, the Eisenhower bloodline has a destiny with high technology and knowledge of outer-space travel.

SECRET SPACE PROGRAM

As the great-granddaughter of President Dwight D. Eisenhower, Laura Eisenhower is able to reveal exopolitical information about his administration including his connection with Val Thor and other star beings, that has been largely held in secrecy. The prophetic warning about the future of the Military Industrial Complex, delivered by President Dwight D. Eisenhower's Farewell Address in January, 1961, is regarded as one of the most famous speeches in American history, during which he stated:

> *"In the councils of government, we must guard against the acquisition of unwarranted influence, whether sought or unsought, by the military-industrial complex. The potential for the disastrous rise of misplaced power exists and will persist. We must never let the weight of this combination endanger our liberties or democratic processes. We should take nothing for granted. Only an alert and knowledgeable citizenry can compel the proper meshing of the huge industrial and military machinery of defense with our peaceful methods and goals, so that security and liberty may prosper together."*

Laura Eisenhower says there is more than meets the eye when it comes to her great grandfather's forewarning. Reading deeper into the speech it involves the emerging secret space program, and an insidious agenda by a global elite that has long been in contact with extraterrestrials with the singular goal of enslaving humanity in a neo-fascist technocratic government. As a patriotic president, Dwight D. Eisenhower formulated the resistance movement known as the White Hats, especially when he threatened to march the 1st Army into Area 51 after being denied access.

In her lifetime, Laura Eisenhower came to notoriety in the UFO community when she came forward in 2010 claiming she had been recruited to travel to Mars in 2006 with a man, whom she calls "Agent X." She became involved in a relationship with Agent X, whom she later learned was on a mission to enlist her and a friend for an interplanetary mission. She says the U.S. government established a colony on Mars through black budget programs, as a survival mechanism in the case of a catastrophic event on Earth known as Alternative 3.

Laura recounts how she was conscripted to join the Mars colony, due to her relationship to the Eisenhower bloodline. It is likely she would have never come back and thus would not play her part in the Great Awakening which she knew was coming as a child. Fortunately, she was able to avoid her recruitment

Dwight D. Eisenhower pictured as a West Point graduate. Could he have imagined he would become the Supreme Commander of the Allied Expeditionary Force in Europe during a World War, and then elected as the popular two-term 34th President of the United States?

and was awakened to the false matrix of reality, blinding her from seeing the truth behind the Military Industrial Complex's hidden agenda.

A NEW AWARENESS

The Eisenhower family story alone could fill the pages of this book, but in her extraordinary journey Laura has also broken ground in articulating an awareness into different realms. From a comprehensive understanding of the sacred union in our DNA, to the new awareness of Christ-Sophia Consciousness. This is the notion of consciousness in the role and mission of Jesus Christ born into the physical form and living a life of a man with all the passions and relationships in his life, and shedding light on the lost remembrance of the Mother Earth Sophia energy connected to the Magdalene. This book takes the 10,000-foot view—essentially what Laura's book is talking about is using more technical or otherwise terms pulled from Lisa Renee's material that was greatly inspired by a wonderful bond and alliance in their missions. Laura is also a master astrologer, and can derive cosmic truths from the knowledge of celestial movements. For example, the study of the Venus Transit can aide in self-correction, healing and transformation—and in fighting the global alchemy reset. Instead, we're made aware of a great awakening of humanity because the shift comes from within.

Laura Eisenhower shows us how to embody the living keys that have long been suppressed, that is, essentially guiding us to *Awakening the Truth Frequency* title of this book, which is being your authentic and true self that has always been in union with Source. She has an uncanny awareness of where humanity stands today. This is the information that needs to be grasped, understood and embodied for the next stage of our human ascension process. You will see in Laura's words it is all about existing beyond labels, coming together with love and respect, embracing our commonality and our return to Source beyond the illusion of separation.

This book articulates beautifully and simplifies what Laura is desiring to call out, as well as the personal mission Laura is on for the securing of the highest organic timeline and ascension mechanics which in our human form requires individual balancing of our masculine and feminine energies. This knowledge overrides the dark weaponry and liberates us from the inverted matrix. It enlightens our seven chakras as well as our Galactic Chakras, and ultimately illustrates the sacred physical union of male and female through sacred marriage/sexuality/hierogamic union to achieve what Laura refers to as the Diamond Sun, the Christ-Sophia embodiment. Where our bodies becomes the technology for ascension, and the ultimate light body embodiment while still physical on our path back to God Source.

ACKNOWLEDGEMENTS

I want to acknowledge the many inspirations and collaborations that helped produce this book. First, I deeply love my husband and children and appreciate their patience in helping me see this through. I am grateful to Brad Olsen for not giving up on me and for the incredible knowledge and service he provides humanity with his research, experiences, and publishing company that brought me on board. I am touched by Catherine Gentle's assistance and commitment to this effort while on her own mission and journey, supporting me through some heavy emotions around releasing this book while organizing and editing material that has been challenging to reassemble after many delays and the loss of a lot of it. I want to honor and thank many amazing friends, including Dr. Allison and William Brown, author of "The Origin Story," Journey to Truth, and Jenna Pennrose, as well as numerous clients and supporters who have remained connected with me over the years. My most profound learnings and realizations have bloomed through my client work and interviews, getting to the "heart" of people and their stories. I am deeply grateful to Lisa Renee for all the material she has brought to humanity, her amazing mission, and her loving support and friendship through some incredibly tough patches. Being drawn through synchronicity to discover her body of knowledge and their undeniable connection to my own realizations helped bridge many gaps and refined my explanation of complex concepts and ascension-related events. Our intimate and trusting exchanges are treasures that have greatly influenced much of the material I present. Lastly, thank you to all who have endorsed this book and continue to support its message.

I am inspired by the power of the human spirit that exists in all of us to overcome adversity and the challenges we face as a humanity. My intention in writing this book is that we know that however we are challenged, it is always an opportunity to discover and connect with our higher self, intuition and greater abilities in the face of it all and restore the fullness of all that we came here to be.

Awareness and knowledge are essential for humanity's liberation and growth beyond false limitations. As this book contains sensitive information that can be triggering to process, please proceed with caution and only when you feel guided.

Lead Editor: Catherine Gentle
Series Editor and Foreword: Brad Olsen
Cover Design: Carrie Toder
Contents Layout and Design: Mark J. Maxam

INTRODUCTION

"The supreme quality for leadership is unquestionably integrity. Without it, no real success is possible, no matter whether it is on a section gang, a football field, in an army, or in an office."

– Dwight D. Eisenhower

We live in a time when we as a human race are being tasked with awakening to our true potential, deeper origins and connection to this planet and cosmos, which helps us understand the multi-dimensional nature of all things. A more vast galactic picture is opening up, yet so much remains hidden. So to get to any truth requires us to dig deep, go way outside of our comfort zone and be open to letting go of what we may have learned or come to believe was reality.

Our planet has come to the time of the promised return of Christ-Sophia Consciousness. When I say this, I mean the recognition of our divine blueprint. We are in a time of many wanting briefings related to a Full Disclosure Event and The Great Awakening, and it is happening. The emphasis for me is in reminding people that we are the shift and that the higher Earth energies exist within our very own being. I have been on my journey to find this, and it has felt significantly interfered with even as I acknowledge, at times, getting in the way of myself. I have come to learn this is about continuing on and not giving up, being willing to overcome all obstacles and adversities while discovering myself more in the process, which is what I feel we can all do on the planet—find truth in the face of all threats and adversities that are constantly coming at us.

Having an open mind as you read these words, to take what resonates and leave the rest, is what I hope for. These times are challenging to navigate. They require embracing and living our inner truth to have clear discernment and feel empowered to say no when something feels off. Even though we might not all agree on what is truth, we must never let it divide us. We all go through our soul journey and day-to-day experiences that give us profound knowledge, wisdom, insights, information and answers. And though it cannot be precisely the same for everyone, some truths will connect us all—these serve to rebuild the architecture of our complete Diamond Sun DNA to recognize that we are all part of a great love story.

www.ujvilagtudat.blogspot.hu

A picture of me, Laura Eisenhower, the great-granddaughter of Dwight D. Eisenhower. I have always felt Ike was a spirit guide to me. Someone made this picture, and I love feeling that he is looking down at me, doing all I can to expose important truths to this world.

Our capacity to turn on what has laid dormant and our ability to come together in Unity Consciousness has everything to do with this. These dormant DNA strands and energy centers hold universal love, wisdom, sacred union and an energetic circulation that helps us to achieve natural heightened states of bliss and purification. As we awaken more to who we are, we realize and begin to grasp that we are the most advanced technology. When I say this, I mean that human beings have within them the potential and capabilities to co-create a beautiful future that goes beyond the script being handed to them by the outside world.

Each of us holds puzzle pieces for the other. Rediscovering and sharing all that has been lost or forgotten will help us retrieve what has fallen into unconsciousness, and by shining a light onto our unconscious, we can begin to remember ourselves as multi-dimensional beings with extraordinary abilities. We can expand our creative power to merge with the zero point unified field and have access to every dimension in between. Stepping through this process can deprogram us and reset the vibration of our physical, mental, emotional and spiritual bodies so we can release and transmute or neutralize toxicity, implants, programs and pathogens to bring harmony and balance back into our lives.

Whether we see it or not, betrayal, facades, hidden weapons and deceit surround us. Bad news is projected at us constantly—largely engineered with false narratives—and a dangerous form of misinformation bombards us daily. At the same time, there is a cover-up of the accurate news so that we don't hear how the power of the human spirit surfaces in our world when there is censorship for speaking what is true to your heart and mission or when the waging of severe crimes against humanity are brushed-off or labeled as "conspiracy theories." As a result, we are constantly stressed, confused, and uncertain about what or whom to believe or trust. As humans, we tend to seek anything that can relieve the discomfort we feel, sometimes making choices that aren't healthy for us and which only make matters worse.

Our physical body suffers if we aren't proactively processing and releasing things like grief, fear or anger. Conventional medicine doesn't consider the whole being and all the contributing factors to poor physical, emotional and mental health. Social engineering and mind control prevent us from accessing our healing powers, so we continually hand things over to someone else to fix. While it is valuable and important on our journey to have some assistance, it would be wise to remember that ultimately we can figure out how to be healers, redeemers and saviors to ourselves while allowing outside services to support this discovery as long as they appreciate our participation.

Deprogramming and treating PTSD and severe trauma is paramount, and expanding these services must be prioritized. By uncovering the profound truth of our reality, we can address some severe conditions with therapies that help us overcome what might seem incurable while empowering individuals to know how to maintain their health, wellness and balance instead of co-dependency.

Society today dictates how we should respond to an event or crisis that takes place and tries to influence what we should think. It becomes about picking a side or political party to polarize and divide us—to the point where the truth gets wholly ignored and horrific crimes against our children and humanity continue. We argue and create more distress amongst ourselves as we navigate our world and often become addicted to misery to avoid facing our deeper issues. This is similar to how the news works to distract us from the real issues, instead sharing celebrity scandals that seem to take center stage over anything more meaningful.

The boiling point has been reached where judgments, belittling, insults, toxicity and discord between those for and those against something are breaking up families and friendships. We must stop this madness and stay determined to overcome this level of divide-and-attack, not to let all that is sacred be destroyed. If we can maintain complete love, the rest stands a chance to correct itself and heal regardless of our decisions and differences.

We must be willing to see who the actual enemies of humanity are and help one another be brave. We need to listen to each other and communicate from the most genuine part of ourselves what we are feeling deep down instead of spewing mind viruses and being a product of harmful dark agendas. If we

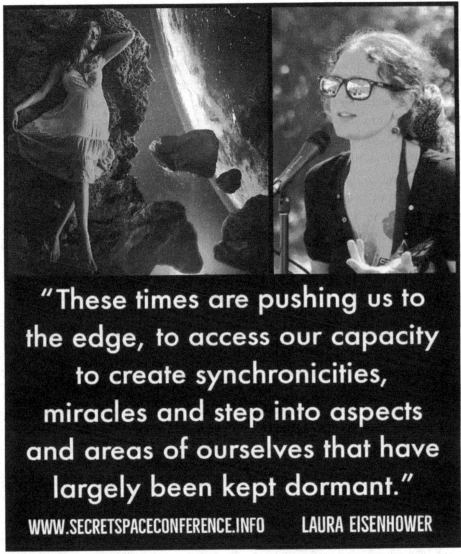

"These times are pushing us to the edge, to access our capacity to create synchronicities, miracles and step into aspects and areas of ourselves that have largely been kept dormant."

WWW.SECRETSPACECONFERENCE.INFO   LAURA EISENHOWER

I was a part of the Secret Space Conference hosted by the Journey to Truth Podcast. They created this meme from a quote they used. To me, it means that in order to stay out of survival and panic, we need to allow the current adversities in the world to push us into rediscovering our capacity to create positive change within ourselves and the world around us.

choose love, compassion, patience and kindness, their weapons will transform into tools we can use for higher growth. Instead of having a hold over us and breaking us down into a lower form of being, they will provide the necessary contrast to remind us what we should strive for.

Taking the higher road embodies the override frequency, as does choosing a more grand and profound love as bold as our imagination. Universal love holds neutrality, ensuring we don't absorb or take on too much. It helps us set appropriate boundaries and protects us while being an activating force that awakens others in the world. Being an empath can make it more difficult, but in that energy, one can release it to Source so that the pain you take on from others doesn't overwhelm you. We are starving for true love and deep connection in the human realm while losing trust in each other and letting outer forces steer us in our thinking and behavior that ultimately separates us from our intuition, higher awareness, integrity and ability to self-heal our ancestral lines, partners, children, future generations or the collective.

It is time to rise from under oppressive controller forces and what they are attempting to turn us into. They seek to keep us in a survival vibration so that we can't even think straight—this must stop. Instead, we can help one another alleviate the pain, confusion and shock from the constant turn of worldly events and access more of who we truly are!

When we shed all the layers that stand in the way of recognizing our divine blueprint and total DNA capacity, we change the script being forced upon humanity and open up the gateways to experience God Source more embodied. This allows a transformative and alchemical shift in our consciousness and physicality.

Restoring the Tree of Life is an initiatory process where gaining self-knowledge is the key. Many interpretations exist of the Tree of Life and the Tree of Knowledge mythologies. How they connect with our DNA is where so much is revealed. They uncover our hidden ancient and galactic history and how dark technology has impacted our evolution. Moving into these dormant levels also plays a vital role in dissolving the NET (Nibiru Electrostatic Transduction) field and frequency fences contained in our consciousness, our DNA and encircling the planet. In our lives this often manifests as facing a gatekeeper, major challenge or test. The test is, do we choose love? And are we willing to discover self-knowledge, our divinity and our ability to be a Christed embodied human in the face of the things that seek to invert us?

Most of what I write and share is not how my family raised me to think or believe. It has been a highly personal journey as I've been sorting out so much alone. Nevertheless, I am willing to be public because I feel some of my unique experiences, research and insights could be helpful to the collective. The things I and so many others talk about need a light shined on them so we can engage in a larger conversation with one another and open ourselves up to a greater truth very different from what we have come to know. If we don't, overcoming the immense challenges these times pose will be very difficult.

I wasn't born with the last name Eisenhower since this is on my mother's side of the family. My name was legally changed when I was 11 years old. When I

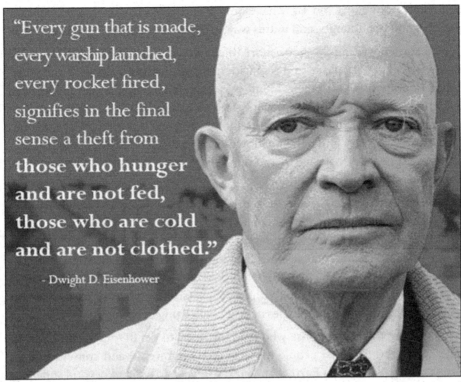

"Every gun that is made, every warship launched, every rocket fired, signifies in the final sense a theft from **those who hunger and are not fed, those who are cold and are not clothed.**"

- Dwight D. Eisenhower

From a speech given to the American Society of Newspaper Editors holding their annual convention in Washington, D.C.'s Hotel Statler on April 16, 1953. 8 years later would be his final speech. Known as the "Cross of Iron" speech, Eisenhower continues, "The cost of one modern heavy bomber is this: a modern brick school in more than 30 cities. It is two electric power plants, each serving a town of 60,000 population. It is two fine, fully equipped hospitals. It is some fifty miles of concrete pavement. We pay for a single fighter plane with a half million bushels of wheat. We pay for a single destroyer with new homes that could have housed more than 8,000 people. This is, I repeat, the best way of life to be found on the road the world has been taking. This is not a way of life at all, in any true sense. Under the cloud of threatening war, it is humanity hanging from a cross of iron."

was ready to share information about a Mars recruitment I experienced and had other important disclosure information to bring forward, I deeply meditated, and it became clear to me the importance of carrying the Eisenhower name and dropping my step-father's surname, Mahon. Some have criticized me for this, but I was willing to do whatever I could to help expose the many truths still hidden today.

As a public speaker, I discuss things held in secrecy before and during the Eisenhower administration. It seemed appropriate to carry this name, especially as I feel a deep bond with my great-grandfather. I could also sense that dark forces were attempting to rewrite history—the aspects of history I have become deeply familiar with so I felt compelled to bring it out in the open to prevent any distortion from going too far. I have only ever wanted to do what benefits the greater good of humanity, and in this way, I feel our missions are very connected.

I started writing this book more than a decade ago. So many things stood in my way of getting it out, and a considerable portion got deleted at one stage! I didn't do it, but it was "an accident" by someone helping me edit. It has been a challenge to get it going again, yet quite interesting to see where we are now and how much has changed. This version of my book is a mixture of information, stories, updates and personal downloads that I hope will assist in navigating these times. I also weave in and out personal stories and revelations to try and connect some significant dots.

With my connection and deep dives into the work of Lisa Renee and her Energetic Synthesis material[1], I am better equipped to explain the complexities of what is happening in the world and what took place in our galactic and Earth history. I also credit Ashayana Deanne's Freedom Teachings[2] and dictionary and the many other sources I bring forward in this book. I reference much of their material to assist in making sense of some of these concepts, although if you are new to this material, some of the terminologies may be challenging to wrap your head around.

I desire to activate those who read my book to get in touch with their divine birthright. To assist people in becoming empowered and conscious of all that is taking place on an Earthly and cosmic level and expand beyond suffering, limitation, fear and self-doubt. I seek only to share what serves the highest good for self, Earth and humanity. I hold this same intention for my mission on Earth. It is the time to step into the ascension energies within yourself and become the shift to advance your human vessel. Our true self is where the greatest cover-up exists—everything we have dealt with from birth through development until our death. Isn't it time we move on from this repeating time loop?

We need to step back and look objectively at the big picture with an open mind so that we can begin to refine it to something that works with us and for us rather than against us. Understanding the difference between Artificial Intelligence (AI) and Organic Ascension signals will only help us hold greater discernment with what we allow ourselves to align with. We are contending with nothing short of a war on consciousness. Trickery, lies, false flags and psychological operations are at an extreme to throw humanity off the trajectory of our divine potential, instead taking us into a New World Order (NWO) that many cannot see.

We are dealing with extreme censorship and low vibratory troll attacks, or just people who are freaking out and wanting to harm or smear well-intentioned people. I can't believe the level of trolling and attacks I have received. I know of websites and YouTube videos dedicated to making me look crazy, tarnishing and harming Eisenhower and everything about my message. Some-

I have done many interviews and conferences, and someone made this picture for me whose name I don't know. But I have been associated with this topic so much in wanting to bring a voice to these subjects and sort through what is truth versus disinformation. I listen to people's accounts first-hand, and that is where I have learned the most.

times it makes me not want to speak out, to contend with being lumped into categories and labels and even threatened. But I do it anyway—after all, truth stands on its own whether or not someone accepts it. I refuse to allow the bullies and disinformation that has infected people's minds to stop me from sharing all I have learned about Eisenhower, his administration, our galactic history and our incredible potential as divine human beings. My life's path has revealed all of this to me through synchronicities, deep soul work, in-depth research and incredible experiences that have proven to me without a shadow of a doubt what we can do to turn the madness around.

I don't claim to have all the answers, however. I'm not seeking a guru position or claiming to be a savior, expert, or anyone special. I am simply being true to myself, hoping it will ignite the truth within you. Spirit, Earthly and cosmic forces guide us through our intuition. Our pain body alerts us when something is stuck or not flowing or an aspect of us needs attention and unconditional love. The planets affect our nervous system, organs, glands, DNA, and chakra system, and these, in turn, are a part of the planetary grid network and multi-dimensional cosmos. Our bodies change as we evolve and become open to much more than we can imagine.

Though I understand astrology, the patterns, alignments and aspects they reveal are more like a map that guides us into the zero point unified field and

My website is Cosmic Gaia. Matthew Starseed made this funny picture and shared it with me. He felt this was very fitting to go along with the material I continually present on a wide range of topics.

our capacity to connect with a much more vast terrain. There are many systems of astrology, and though I don't use all of them, it sure has been a helpful tool in understanding the self more and the impact dark technologies have had on us, like reversal grids and the Saturn-Moon matrix. My life's work has been about understanding these dark agendas and meeting them face-to-face to expose what I have discovered as I am best able. The core goal has always been to ground into the Earth, embody sacred union, and activate the Diamond Heart and 13D Gateway to stop the descension and dark mother reversals that come from controllers who wish to feed on humanity and release the Earth and humans from their manipulations and misuse of power.

Not everyone will resonate with this, but I have found that with the 13th sign coming into the picture, it describes everything that I knew as a child— that there would come a time of a great shift that would be alchemical. It is why I chose to call myself a Global Alchemist. I want to give attention and voice to the fact that this is what is occurring. I am excited to use this book and others to dive deep into global alchemy concepts.

When our spiritual awareness and greater truth become a way of life, and we invite it into everything we do, we shift the physical density and raise the vibration by infusing it with our intentions, dreams and goals. We can unwind destructive patterns by being conscious and mindful of our thoughts, habits and words. Otherwise, our creative energy gets infected, and we mindlessly enable and manifest a future in which we do not want to exist. So don't let anyone own your thoughts—they are powerfully yours!

We can upgrade in the face of adversity and get to know ourselves so much more instead of being victimized and disempowered. Our greatest challenges can bring us closer to finding our lost treasures and help reinstate our full capacity to find balance, wholeness, peace and harmony. We all have this in common—remembering who we truly are gives us the upper hand to become the override frequency!

This is a picture taken of me by Frank Jacob, who is a documentary filmmaker. He did the documentary called "Packing to Mars." I was put in this film along with many others talking about what is happening there. I discussed an attempted recruitment to go off-planet. Here, you can see me in deep contemplation.

Laying the Foundation

"To succeed in your mission, you must have single-minded devotion to your goal."

– Abdul Kalam

To set the book in proper context, I'd like to walk through certain concepts and noteworthy events that are currently taking place. If this is a prophesied window period, what in reality is happening? Well, one of the most significant events in these times is the activation of the Mother Arc. She has returned and has been powering up the Earth's crystal core. More on this later.

Expanding upon the introduction, for as long as I can recall, I have intended to use my human vessel to serve humanity and do whatever is necessary to assist in our planetary ascension and experience an existence where our dormant DNA becomes activated, which includes acknowledging the deep healing work that humanity must go through to overcome so many cycles of dark history.

To this end, there are a few aspects to the work I have been doing. One is as an experiencer, the other a researcher. A key decision point confronted me that served to awaken my ability to recall and access an expanded recognition of my preparation for these times—when I faced an attempted recruitment to a Mars colony in 2006, a timeline scenario known as Alternative 3, which I resisted without hesitating as I noted their strong desire to remove me from this Earth. It was a scenario proposed to the Eisenhower administration in the possible event of a global catastrophe where humans would have to live off-planet. I discovered that there was much more to their agenda than what they presented, as my strong inner guidance could see through their facades. It gave me first-hand experience with the hidden layers of the shadow government and what relentless targeting felt like, making it nearly impossible to create anything in my life without some form of diversion-controller force wanting to push me in a different direction.

SURRENDER TO THE MISSION

I now see I was being prepared for this window period of "ascension" since I was a child, and the possibility of not remaining on Earth felt like a diversion I could not be a part of. Having been almost taken off-planet is a big part of my story, and refusing to go ignited a strength in me that I hope helps others. I uncovered so much about what would have happened if I had gone. Escaping and freeing myself was not a small feat. The term ascension has had so many distortions projected onto it that it's hard for me to use it. To me, ascension is about awakening, embodying and advancing ourselves beyond the limits of the personality matrix and inverted systems.

Through my own experiences, I've learned that a significant portion of "the work" is to actually go through the depths of the underworld when it shows at your doorstep, be fearless to face a likely intense battle to reclaim your sovereignty and live fully present on Earth, and then successfully rise back up to remember all that gets elevated into consciousness! I recalled far more than I expected concerning the many faces of the Goddess and the masculine and feminine archetypes that exist within our soul as we face initiations that bring us closer to our depths and our divine blueprint. It is a journey not for the faint of heart that, beyond raw terror, extreme targeting and personal attacks, revealed very ancient buried wisdom to me.

I have so many childhood memories where I was alerted by a higher sense to notice a form of focused attention and hidden weaponry on me, which has taken a better part of my life to understand and come to terms with. I would eventually learn it was all a part of an attempted agenda to steer me onto a negative timeline I wanted no part of. However, from this experience, many graces became bestowed upon me, and my attention from that point forward was solely on creating my desired timeline, which I refer to as Alternative 4, which is about empowering the human spirit, Unity Consciousness, disclosure, ascension and our shift with this planet into higher Earth energies. I am only giving a voice to what already is and which only needs empowering. That's when I began speaking and writing about these topics in 2010.

And with each day living my mission, more truth continues to reveal itself. A hidden language and story emerged as my eyes perceived the world from the inside out rather than the outside. Making my way through one experience after another, many quite challenging and hard to articulate, I continued discovering an ever-present inner voice teaching me how to achieve reconstruction and transformation for myself that I knew would also benefit our planet and the global consciousness. Since childhood, always trusting this inner voice has helped me stay alive, especially in the rapidly shifting terrain of full-on spiritual warfare I often experience.

I have battled as a fierce warrior to empower the Organic Ascension timeline and expand my truth by facing the Deep State's negative agendas in an up-close-and-personal way. I delved deep into the many layers of the Military Industrial Complex and learned they have been targeting me since before birth, as they do to many others. Looking back, I am clear that the strong force I felt wanted to steer me towards leaving Earth altogether and commit to a Mars colony timeline I did not want to be on. Maybe it was because they knew I was coming into this family to share the truth about Eisenhower's administration by looking deeply into my own soul to shine a light on what needed awakening. As you will read in subsequent chapters, Eisenhower was in contact with star beings who spoke about a descendant to be born that would speak the truth. I have concluded that they found this out, so they targeted me to go off-planet.

Everyone faces some level of targeting. The question is, how aware are we of this? Some people get targeted so severely it's difficult even to comprehend—Secret Space Programs, MILABS, MK-Ultra, ritual abuse, being born into bloodlines involved in dark agendas—these are realities coming to the surface memory at an accelerated pace for more and more people. Though I didn't go through this level of targeting, I have come to understand that the presidential bloodline I was born into is very different. Eisenhower played a significant role in trying to take down these dark agendas that are still alive and well today.

With deep concern and a relentless plague in my emotional body, I always knew enough to listen to that inner voice that proclaimed, "You know how to get us out of this mess!" But ultimately, I also knew that it could not be me alone but something many of us would awaken to and join forces one day. As you can see, we are well underway.

As you can imagine, on an ego level, it wasn't easy to own my every truth. But each time, my inner guidance pulled me to go there like a powerful magnet and mirror, and every step was comforted by the encoded support in nature all around me! That is where communication with my inner voice felt most heightened, and my desire grew to learn to speak the language of the elements and Mother Earth, igniting the web of life all around. Until 100% truth prevails, I know I must continue to surrender and rise in divine power and freedom to live authentically. Thus, I persisted in facing the programs and dark force controls, no matter how much they tried to attack or stop me.

On many of my adventures, especially when day-to-day struggles surfaced, I would retreat and research anything I could about holistic healing, mythology, exopolitics, metaphysics, ascension mechanics, and our ancient galactic history. My astrological knowledge took me to new levels of integration and deep processing. An incredible ally of mine was an ancient Chinese manual of divination—the "I Ching." I did so many readings over the years that I nearly memorized the book! The "Motherpeace Tarot" has also been a helpful guide, and I have used it for over two decades. Over the years, I wore out so many decks from constant shuffling for the guidance I desperately needed when I felt in danger and uncertain. I'll get into some of these stories later in the book.

I became consumed by what the cards revealed. It was amazing how much the messages resonated and gave me helpful insight and guidance to navigate my next steps to find my way out of some challenging situations. They got me through my pregnancy and parenting as a single mother of twins in beyond-precarious circumstances. Living on the road in chaotic situations while caring for my babies, the cards helped me understand myself and all that was happening around me. Seriously, I must have moved more than 40 times! I lived out of vans, cramped spaces, and even a school bus converted into a home on wheels by a touring band with the most beautiful living space. I drove back and forth cross-country with my little ones and had the most incredible adventures beyond anything I could describe. At the same time, we often faced many dangers, turmoil and instability, not knowing if we would survive because of the constant targeting and interference we had to contend with. I was very young then and had children with a partner battling some serious demons. I, too, had healing to do.

I learned so much from the I Ching, astrology, and every other curiosity I held, enough to grasp that we all have the potential to transform on profound levels and experience a shift capable of turning this entire inverted system around. I also received great insight into how cosmic and Earthly forces support us to bring this about organically when we align with them. It means we must resist the artificial matrix that wants to impede our ascension and growth process and separate us from our soul connection with our Divine Source to take us into a transhumanistic world. I have faced the underworld many, many times. It helped me recognize and shift my energy towards repairing the historical trauma and damage inflicted upon humanity, ultimately through my own healing journey, and discover myself in ways that were not only painful, draining and intimidating but also quite illuminating. When I say historical trauma, it's essential to realize that we were involved in an ancient war going back to the Cradle of Lyra and the Orion Wars. Unfortunately, it continues to this day.

With so much rewritten history and cover-up regarding our relationship with ETs, their technology, and how they have influenced our world, this subject has become one of the most challenging topics to speak about, though I continue doing so. I feel it's because we were born with amnesia and have had no exposure to

Sphere/Color Octave		Dimension	Chakras
CHAKRA 1		D-1	Base
CHAKRA 2		D-2	Sacral
CHAKRA 3		D-3	Solar Plexus
CHAKRA 4		D-4	Heart
CHAKRA 5		D-5	Throat
CHAKRA 6		D-6	Third Eye
CHAKRA 7		D-7	Crown
CHAKRA 8		D-8	Thymus (Permanent Seed Atom)
CHAKRS 9		D-9	Thalamus (Medulla Oblangata)
CHAKRA 10		D-10	Galactic -Soul Star (6" above head)
CHAKRA 11		D-11	Galactic (18" above head)
CHAKRA 12		D-12	Earth Star - (6" below feet)
CHAKRA 13		D-13	Earth – Christ 12D Shield(12" Below feet)
CHAKRA 14		D-14	Universal -(36" above head)
CHAKRA 15		D-15	Universal -(beneath Earth)

Chakra Wave Spectrum. "In our Ascension model, we recognize and work with 15 Wave 'Spectrum of Frequency' that correlate directly with the Universal Rays." –Lisa Renee, Ascension Glossary; https://ascensionglossary.com/index.php/Spectrum_of_Frequency

this information unless someone has direct experience and is willing to go down all the rabbit holes while remaining fluid to adapt to each moment's highest truth and holding discernment, knowing disinformation is always part of the game. Unfortunately, many do not believe those who have been through abduction or contact experiences when they speak about them. Through profound synchronicities, I have been quite fortunate to have met some exceptional individuals who courageously stepped forward to unearth the truths of their first-hand experiences. Although many doubt their legitimacy, I continue to advocate for them, knowing their transformative power when one takes the time to listen and internally filter the stories these warriors bring forth—more dots connect and resonate. Their stories also help to discern the many ways disclosure presents itself and offer helpful contrast to decipher when information could lead one astray.

Getting to the bottom of what went down during the Eisenhower administration has been a strong focal point of mine. Equally significant was embarking on a deep soul's journey and connection to this planetary body and consciousness to understand the story and path of the divine feminine and Mother Goddess. It's a story that lives deep within all of us. Understanding mitochondrial DNA and its relation to the 5th element, Aether, has opened my eyes to the profound healing available to all to embrace and directly experience.

Many important milestones and events have taken place that assure this element is accessible now in ways it hasn't been before. All this relates to turning around the inverted pentagram, dark reversal technologies and inverted matrix, and how the Venus transits and the 13th sign Ophiuchus are making corrections alongside many successful starseed, Earth Alliance and gridworker missions and Guardian races who are currently hosting this Ascension Cycle.

The cycles between 2004-2012 have particularly infused divine feminine energy onto the planet from this pattern and continue to this day.

> *"As they turn, the planets are showing us the mysterious workings of God's hand, expressed in the harmonious movements of the spheres. Each planet, as it revolves in its orbit, reaches positions where Earth, Sun and Planet form distinct alignment patterns...only one planet shows us a perfect geometrical form.*
>
> *This form is pentagonal and the planet is Venus. Creating five equally-spaced alignments over a period of eight years, she draws the perfect, hidden and secret symbol of the five-pointed star in the heavens...as above, so below. The very landscape bears the sign of her secret revelation...*
>
> *...These signs in the sky signal the end of a great cycle of time, according to the Mayan calendar ending December 2012, and brings a radiant sun shining on Venus as the harbinger of beauty, love, and the revival of the sacred feminine, which is Magdalene's legacy to us."*

– Ani Williams

Along the way, I discovered that life, nature and my soul were the best teachers of all, so this is where my attention went most of my life. I found school difficult and couldn't concentrate. Outside authorities looked at me in bewilderment and regarded my behavior as a learning disability. I like to refer to ADD as "Attention on Different Dimensions." So, I would throw myself into the trenches and dark spaces till I uncovered truths that were my road map to liberation. I was good at reading between the lines of life while I tried to hold together some structure of reality as a human going to school, working and juggling everyday things. I was never fully "here" but in another world, only now emerging from the shadows. I would wonder, where did these lost and advanced civilizations go? I always felt the elemental kingdoms would rise again and that my journey would include helping to initiate that blossoming. These codes live within all of us. Our natural relationship to this Earth, cosmos and the sacred union of alchemical marriage is what fairy tales speak of.

I worked hard to bring daylight to the darkest places, reclaim the fragmented aspects of the Goddess into wholeness, free us from this 3D holographic time loop, and guide us back to the vast totality of the divine power accessible within us. Many are called to do this work. Unity Consciousness brings an awareness of each other's efforts to shift the Earth and embody our authentic selves. We can then harmonize and recognize that oneness is diversity in harmony and that we are here to switch one another on to rebuild our original DNA architecture. We are a living reflection of the multi-dimensional Earth with the ability to open up to higher worlds.

Early on, I discovered that the Magdalene energies and the Eisenhower legacy had a reason for intertwining within my physical form. My whole life has been about understanding this connection, which goes much deeper than I could have ever prepared for as a child. I have learned how to navigate this human realm in crisis from the higher dimensional planes, which are rich with infinite possibilities. I have learned to ride the circulating light energy, the endless currents of angelic, galactic tones and waves, with my imagination. I have also discovered how to climb out from underneath darkness, chaos and danger until they no longer had power over me. That said, there are many others out there who carry these energies as well.

Often, it feels so hard to produce content. Within my human vessel and consciousness, I am endlessly working energy to process and heal the greater galactic war, negative ET agendas and their AI coming up against the Organic Ascension and humanity's liberation and sovereignty. Sometimes, my human self can barely handle it as this gets accomplished through personal observation, processing, healing and transmuting powerful currents. For this reason, I use Global Alchemist to describe what I and many others do since, as we speak, the ascension process is unfolding, encoded into humanity's nature and DNA. It is what we do and must express!

Anywhere integrity is lacking and willpower or ego dominates, we dampen the ability of divine universal forces to work their magic in healing and repairing this fallen inverted system, our system. From the macro to the micro, we win the war from within us, and to this, the Earth responds. Working with others on this mission is only possible if this pure space and intent are prioritized and maintained in everyday life. It's a must if we wish to be a clear and direct conduit of universal truth, love, and divine power that serves the greater good of all that is. Fortunately, many of us hold this foundation at our core even when there is confusion and misunderstanding and remain willing to create a resolution that often overrides.

We agree we're all doing our best. Let's open a more mature dialogue to ensure we align with truth rather than disinformation or lower vibratory dynamics that cause division and smear attacks that only worsen matters. We must understand that people who spread disinformation may not even realize they are doing so. There is a big difference between people who do it unconsciously and those who do it knowingly. Untruths have permeated our culture and are what society has taught since birth. Most of civilization today is built on disinformation, so to speak, like cities out of harmony with nature. But within the context of what we hear from researchers, whistleblowers, and experiencers, the nuance is slightly dif-

ferent as there are many clever ways to infiltrate the attempts of an individual trying to get the truth out so that it becomes diluted (i.e., not all fact). Knowing this,
I feel it best to be supportive and loving in these dialogues to get to the bottom of
what's true rather than cast harsh judgments or outright reject them because they
may not have their facts straight or have channeled messages that could lead astray.
We need to be aware of voice-to-skull technology to recognize how dark players
use hidden projects and programs to target individuals and then put them upon
the whole of humanity. It doesn't do us any good to fight, condemn, blame or reject
one another. Let's be brave enough to look at it entirely and ask ourselves, is this
person's story legit? Does it feel benevolent? Is it safe for me to trust?

Instead of getting entangled in competing ET agendas that play out amongst
ourselves, let's integrate and unify! Let's switch each other on instead of battling over
who is right or wrong. It is ultimately up to us to discern within a confusing terrain
where people who make headway in public discussing unapproved topics get targeted for character assassination. So, it's essential to remember this when determining
who is who. The ones stirring up divide-and-conquer may be falling for this when
it is more important to lay all the information out on the table and work together to
connect the dots and provide warnings where one sees fit without outwardly attacking anyone—which more than likely will be a repeat of what someone else has said
rather than first-hand investigation. Some things may be evident and alarming with
specific individuals, but in the end, I hope we can all heal together and rise above.

Having done the speaker circuit for conferences worldwide and viewed as
someone in a "truther" or disclosure type community, I am amazed and stunned
at the amount of hurt, discord and separation that has taken place. I don't care to
smear anyone and want this all to heal. But it's happened a lot, so I understand
the concept of paid controlled opposition, plants, or someone who comes in to
mess everything up intentionally. People constantly accused me of being one of
these, but I have nothing to hide, and proof to show this is not the case.

There is so much I am seeking to heal, so I remain transparent with the public enough to reveal personal mistakes that break my heart. But I know I always do
the best I can, given the circumstances. Can't we all be more forgiving towards others and ourselves? Humans seem quick to seek out flaws and discrepancies, amplify
mistakes, and throw judgment but are less willing to look at themselves, their issues
or traumas. It's easier to cast rage and judgment onto someone else. Then, others
will do all they can to cover up any error, mistake, or harmful behavior pattern to
keep pushing a facade and narrative that people eventually see through. If we could
admit when we are wrong or mistaken, hold ourselves accountable, and be more
compassionate and loving towards others as they strive to heal and overcome what
they have been through, maybe we would see more goodness shine and real community thrive. Leadership is about being an inspiration, not a controller.

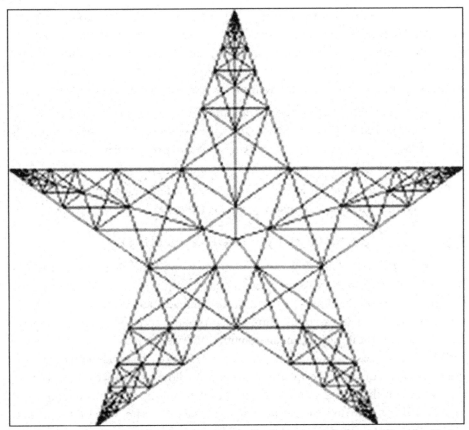

"These signs in the sky signal the end of a great cycle of time, according to the Mayan calendar, ending December 2012, and bring a radiant sun shining on Venus as the harbinger of beauty, love, and the revival of the sacred feminine, which is Magdalene's legacy to us." –Kathy Jones

Overcoming negative AI means you are done with the lower frequency of trauma and drama, being played, used and abused. It means you dare to call things out while reclaiming all that was siphoned, neglected or stolen—a treasure chest filled with divine purpose, truth, and the ability to overcome. AI is nothing in the face of divine wisdom.

Many myths are living out all at once. When we listen to our soul, we discover that these archetypes are a part of all our psyches. This part of our cosmic story is about dying without losing the physical body. If we transition to the other side, we enter a new experience and our journey continues. We must find peace with this and not fear physical death, which keeps one from not knowing how to live life to the fullest. We die in so many ways. We enter voids that require us to feel empty and plant new seeds. Along the way, we experience death in our belief systems or relationships that no longer serve us.

I had to learn how to keep my body here on Earth while going through these death experiences over and over. The message is we can always be reborn. Regeneration takes place when we move through these initiations. I didn't always know how to cope within the matrix. Sometimes I had to die to transform. In a strangely poetic way, some of my writing posted to social media illustrates this:

> *"Always incredible remembering how the harshest and coldest of winters bring a person into the energy of death and seeing all that is frozen—then magically melts—and is greeted by the seedlings that are being reborn into the Spring.*

> *With root systems under the Earth ground dirt—the smiles on our faces return and it's from the heart and the soul... Rainbows remind the troubled mind that these cycles of nature can only get better."*

A BIFURCATION OF TIMELINES

We may see the collapse of a huge negative timeline that will reveal itself in end-of-world scenarios. Still, nothing can break or destroy the Organic Ascension timeline. The key is to stay aligned and remain true to yourself no matter what we witness. Bifurcation is real. We have access to the creative imagination that holds the vastness of all potential, and we tap into it by being open to and consistent with it, allowing it to penetrate our creative channels with our intentions, goals and dreams. We are artists of energy. Allowing creative energy to flow is more potent than mind control, AI, or any artificial timeline, bio-weaponry or assault. Afflictions we experience are temporary, so we must never lose connection to the zero point unified field—the unified heart of the multiverse. It never leaves us, even if, through free will, we choose to walk the other way.

There are so many pathways that lead us home to Source energy. Whether through religion, a way of life or a firmly held belief, we each have a unique soul journey. Our life experience might revolve around traditions and disciplines that have become deeply ingrained, either assisting and enriching us or preventing us from seeing a much vaster landscape. Therefore, no chosen path should serve to divide us. In contrast, those trying to convert others to their way, the blind followers that subscribe to it, and the resulting division it fosters seem to work against unity, peace and freedom. If we focus on labels, we might miss seeing a soul for who they indeed are. Indigenous cultures working closely with the Earth and ancestors hold so many prophecies and medicine that if we are willing to be soul-centered, we can connect with them and the Earth-body more deeply. Isn't our ultimate goal to be at peace within, to love and hold compassion and live in integrity, to self-correct and overcome obstacles and mistakes through tapping into unconditional love and forgiveness, to work closely with the Earth and all elementals knowing the deep connection we have within our soul as elemental beings? Whatever road we take on our spiritual pathway, we must hold enough grace to acknowledge that it can look quite different from another. We should never fight or go to war over our unique paths. Each experience is profoundly sacred and personal and should be appreciated and celebrated instead!

I've always wondered why we have become so afraid of ourselves. Can we come to terms with the possibility that the worst aspects of this human experience were purposely created to keep us down? Of course, we have the right to believe what we want. Still, some things can't be ignored as we are in a decisive window period facing a bifurcation of timelines: a path of ascension into higher Earth energies or an artificial timeline leading to digression and possible destruction of all biological life. It depends on who you are, what agreements you made and how willing you are to listen to your soul.

On some level, we chose to start in a compromised position at birth to find our way out of the heavy density of toxicity, imbalance, injustice and inhumanity. To understand how this all came to be is a journey that won't release you until you accept the possibility that there are influences of an extraterrestrial nature. It's time to recognize that we have been programmed to forget all that lies dormant within us, such as self-healing abilities, divinity and creative power. We are in such a powerful time of winning a great war by going inward to face the harsh realities, assaults, mind control and AI that threaten all sentient life. Geoengineering and the continued attempt by hidden groups to enslave us to a lower nature and density deserve our time, attention, discernment and a very open mind.

There is a unified field and "oneness" where diversity exists harmoniously. Therein lies a recognition of our need to be sovereign and free, to be our most authentic self, but in agreement with a dominant expression of integrity, love and wisdom. The ramifications are high of moving into a world of transhumanism, blindly accepting or just unaware of AI and its hidden influence, or choosing not to educate the self. The alarm is sounding now. It's time to look hard at the agendas, disclosure and what ascension really means.

We are multi-dimensional beings capable of ascending! We can tune in to the appropriate frequencies that help us to expand and blossom into the fullness of all we are. Electromagnetic waves that surround us are increasing in vibration to facilitate our transformation in body and consciousness and help us lift out of this madness into something more evolved, balanced and unified. We have a golden opportunity to shift into higher Earth energies, guided and initiated by the forces of nature, powerful outer planets and our own divine will that our intuition alerts us to. When we are willing to do the inner work to clear our ego from negative patterning so that it's integrated with our soul, we become well on our way to experiencing significant dimensional shifts. And if we can stay grounded and make it a way of life, our lives will undoubtedly improve. It is the bringing back together of the Seven Lower Heavens and Seven Higher Heavens, a reconnection to the infinity spiral that is a part of our energy body and an activation of our Galactic Chakras and DNA. Ancient galactic wars are resolving themselves as we speak and the hidden histories are awakening within us when we do this on an individual level. It is a prerequisite for Unity Consciousness.

THE MOTHER PRINCIPLE AND HEALING

"The restatement of the feminine, both human and divine, is critical to our spiritual survival. Nothing is going to delay the Goddess's second coming, whether in the guise of Sophia or any other form. As she emerges, so the imbalances of our culture will inevitably iron themselves out."

– Caitlin Matthews

The love of our Mother is the most potent force in the universe. It sustains the planet and supports all of life. It is the breath of life that animates the web of life. It is the quintessence that nourishes the Tree of Life! This force will go through the most unimaginable hell and pain to protect her children, future generations, and all that is sacred, divine and innocent. It seeks to heal and repair the disconnect and distortions within family, community and partnerships to restore and achieve alchemical marriage and hierogamic union. The Mother force transforms ancestral patterns so we don't loop in trauma, wounds and programs.

The Mother inside us heals our inner child and births new realities daily through our intent and spoken words, which get spun into manifestation. Higher seeds of consciousness are planted in the womb and soil to grow and create new life, new worlds and succeeding generations. The strength of Her love is beyond anything and is what we carry and hold to make this human experience beyond epic to live. It guides us through the darkest storms and adversities—it is unconditional love. The love of Mother never left us. She just couldn't be fully anchored here, but her determination to return has transpired and the dark controller forces didn't think she would return. Her Diamond Heart is beating with so much love for all on Earth!

The Mother Principle is an aspect of the Godhead that is critical to connect with. Our divine blueprint is a fractal of the Creator, both masculine and feminine. The interplay of the electric and magnetic opens us up to a broad spectrum of frequency and allows us to conceive, manifest, regenerate and expand. Living the masculine/feminine love story from within our being assists us in releasing our relationship with vampiric forces and impostors, which have used bio-spiritual harvesting methods against humanity via harmful programs and distortions that have become socially acceptable so that they can't be recognized or dealt with.

The Cosmic Trinity is Father-Mother and Christ-Sophia child. Keylontic Science would call this Harmonic Universe 5 (HU5). The Cosmic Trinity provides a complete picture of the Godhead and how it relates to the zero point unified

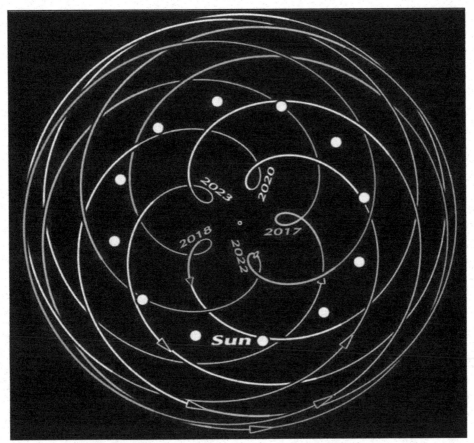

"The 5 petals of Venus and its 8 year Cycle" –*Guy Ottewell*; https://earthsky.org/astronomy-essentials/five-petals-of-venus/

field—the central point of union within our universe. When we are in the "now," it is easier to access and can collapse artificial timelines, which false versions of self power up and feed. There is so much more to this, which I'll get into. Just know that the Cosmic Trinity is more available than ever to help us purify and become whole.

Looking out into the world today can be heart-breaking and confusing, but are we truly seeing all that is available to us? Have you noticed how shot-down some of the notions connected to the Goddess are and how much we are recovering from demonization and distortions? The Mother/Sophia aspect has been a traumatic history and mostly rewritten script that we have been healing for quite some time now. Yet, many women carry this archetype—the pain of being unseen, laughed at or ridiculed. Society and culture don't seem to recognize this enough or attempt to protect it, but instead, predatory forces vampire-off of the feminine to feed upon the vulnerability. And some women readily play into it by running the seductress archetype to feel wanted or empowered—which can also have its place, don't get me wrong. The insult, wounds and trauma can cut so deep into the soul that just drawing a breath feels like a miracle in the face of crushing forces that have no problem breaking you down more than you already are.

Men have also been heavily impacted, unable to connect with their inner feminine energies. We all carry these distortions as we try to reconcile the true authentic union of the masculine and feminine over society's portrayal. It ends up causing an uproar with things like the feminist movement, which also fails to see that men need healing too and becoming power-hungry only flips it to play the same game patriarchy has pushed onto women. I know this is only in some cases—I am not trying to create generalities. My point is that if we all work on inner healing, we can be in balance and harmony.

And so it loops, lifetime upon lifetime, of a struggle that isn't adequately addressed or acknowledged, with subsequent eras throwing something new into the mix that undermines divine harmony. Thoughts of "it must be karma," "something I deserve," or "something I did wrong" begins to overtake one's mind when living through it. Or, one falls into victim consciousness and the need to fight or withdraw. Wherever we find ourselves is okay. It's a part of the healing process as long as we can notice and keep shedding the layers that stand in the way of genuine authenticity.

The hidden kingdoms have been buried, lost and forgotten. We may try to keep up in a world of competition and appearances, but our unique experiences eventually help us find our way home. In Lisa Renee's newsletter titled, "The Song of Christos Sophia," she states that the fallen Goddess consciousness has perpetuated the enslaved consciousness of the abused female archetype in the planetary holographic architecture. She is the drawing source of the Satanic forces that distort the female principle inside men and women alike on Earth today.

When the Mother energy returns fully to our consciousness, we can experience the Organic Ascension timeline. Unfortunately, our lack of understanding of what her presence means makes it easy to be distracted. I remember past lives of dwelling in a cave and not needing food or water—this term is "Breatharian." Wouldn't it be nice to have that ability again? Well, we can. We are forced into a great spiritual awakening as survival issues increasingly get our attention, and for many across the planet, having resources to take care of basic needs has always been a challenge.

We need to understand and heal the separation in the creation of male and female, good and evil, science and spirituality, and how the evolution of dealing with these polarities has caused shifts, ages, eras, environmental changes and global crises as we journey on our path back home again. Imbalance, in general, keeps us vulnerable to archonic forces. However, if we continually grow with wisdom and regenerate our experience and understanding, we can change how we relate to one another and recognize our role as equals. When we master the polar forces in our body and integrate and

Venus rising from a clamshell. –artist Sandro Botticelli, Birth of Venus

align them with the seasons and the cycles of decay, death, rebirth and growth, we can see how things are created and destroyed only to return to Source again.

The merging of what we term "good" and "evil" gives us the experience of neutrality, which can then allow "evil" to be the regenerative force of the under-world that produces "good" things. Therefore, the forces of darkness are not denied or misused, they stay underground where they belong. This merging causes "evil" to lose its destructive charge, so it can't hide in our unconscious or appear benevolent to lead us astray. It becomes the mystery of all we are to be discovered without ego bias, which can cause us to act unconsciously or struggle to recognize truth from deception. We must trade any refusal to surrender or the need for control with complete trust in Spirit and the divine plan. You may be delighted to find that this is the real power and control where dreams are actualized. The merging creates greater security and rebuilds connection to our inner core—the Father and Mother force within. Reacting to external circumstances and their many presentations that have been very imbalanced and distorted will keep us from taking this crucial step. Cultivating the union of polarities within will change how we manifest and end our need for outer validation or dependency on false security to generate self-worth. We will instantly recognize its stability and the unconditional love that it holds.

> *"Earth is indeed a LIVING ENTITY, 'upon whose back' and 'within whose heart' you all presently reside (and yes, in polarity mechanics, Earth is 'FE-MALE' with an organically 'female-magnetic' D-13 Monadic Core)."*
>
> *– Ashayana Deane, Keylontic Science*

The great Mother energy is now fully anchored onto our planet, and the breath of life is Her breath we draw into ourselves. The Aqua Ray 13th Transharmonic Gateway zero point unified field is ever-present as a planetary consciousness power, as is the quintessence 5th element Aether, purifying our inner elementals and energy centers and dismantling the dark tech. This aspect of the great Cosmic Trinity upgrades our DNA by dissolving the "fences" within them—the obstacles between us and true love. This, in turn, means we break through the matrix net, which has kept us in imbalance and distortions and allows the organic light of truth to pour through and heal us from within to reach our inner divine blueprint. As we allow this into our being, it will take us through deep inner journeys that reflect back in our daily lives. It deepens our friendships and relationships with others but begins first and foremost with ourselves. It reunites us with our true soul nature, spiritual truth and sovereignty. Those that are not a vibrational match will leave our life, which can be challenging if we remain attached to try to heal or hold onto them. It's helpful to remember in the larger picture, all returns to love and union. So be firm in your boundaries if something is hurting or dragging you down, and find the courage to walk away from people, jobs or careers if they no longer resonate.

The controllers are frightened of this natural transmission of energy, light codes and our rooted connection with Earth and her Diamond Heart center—so much so that they will do anything to distract and separate us from it. They have been successful for a time as this energy hasn't been fully present on Earth until now. So many of us have awakened, and our voices are powerfully activating. Speaking and vocalizing our authentic truth is the 5D Earth (5th chakra, 5th element) and holds the power to heal and clear away toxicity, mind control and dark weaponry. That is why they try to mask and censor us—our voice is powerful. Do not fear the false light or narratives, and acknowledge the illusion. The override frequency and momentum in numbers are on our side. We have more benevolent assistance than we can imagine!

I do not mean to imply that wearing a mask is wrong. Honoring what makes you feel safe and protected is essential, and only you can say what that is. I am talking about using a mask to silence us and remove our freedom of speech. We each have our way of navigating collective issues faced. However, labeling someone else's path as "wrong" is harmful. We must appreciate everyone's right to experience their unique soul journey. It is possible to share our thoughts and ideas without dominating or belittling, no matter how different our belief systems are. Love is the ultimate force of connection in these times that strive to push many apart. Hold healthy boundaries, stay aligned with love, understanding and forgiveness, and self-correct to restore harmony and balance whenever possible.

It's time we better understand what happened in our human history, no matter how hard it is for people to swallow. Our ego must be placed aside to align with what we must awaken to. Patriarchy has become so ingrained in the consciousness of humans. We have all been born with amnesia and into a distorted planetary grid network set in reversals. Let's forgive ourselves for not knowing and open our minds to the vast terrain of our spiritual origins in Creation.

One of my dear friends, Salini Apodaca, has overcome the deepest levels of MK-Ultra abuse and risen in her strong connection to the divine Mother. She wrote a book called Emerging From the Matrix." She now assists humanity by offering her services as a deprogrammer, soul healer and global transformer. Salini is an inspiration as she turned her trauma around to overcome what she was subjected to since birth, as are many others mentioned in this book. In an attempt to silence, harness and abuse these powerful souls to contain their incredible power, these inspiring individuals broke free to become great healers and activators for all.

EISENHOWER AND THE EARTH ALLIANCE, IKE'S FORCE

My 2006 experience of attempted recruitment to a Mars colony eventually would expose me to whistleblowers of the Secret Space Programs (SSP), what Looking Glass technology is and how it was used on me. Thankfully, by then, I had already gathered an incredible amount of knowledge on the dark technologies impacting the planetary grid network, so I had an excellent foundation to begin to grasp these (hard to believe) subjects. I have met many people in the decade I spent traveling the globe speaking at conferences. I've worked one-on-one with those who have had abduction experiences and met many others who claim to have gone through a "20 and Back" and participated in SSP. I learned that there are many levels and branches to these programs, and the way the trading system works is baffling to comprehend on a human level.

More recently, I met Dan Cooper, who claims to be the senior advisor to a cooperative group called the Earth Alliance. Some may ask who or what that is, while others question whether they exist. It was Dan who helped me begin to understand their existence and influence in the dynamic unfolding of historical events. He spoke with me at length about something called Ike's Force. From what I gather, it was established in 1953—the exact dates vary amongst different sources. Dan's statements validate the testimony of Randy Cramer, "Captain Kaye," who went public with his service in a covert branch of the U.S. Marine Corps called "Special Section" (USMC SS) set up by President Eisenhower as a unit that would uphold moral ethics and keep things in check regarding the activity of MJ-12.

As a former Marine and super soldier, Randy served 17 years on Mars defending the colonies intended for the Alternative 3 timeline scenario. He was a part of Project Moonshadow and was recruited by the Mars Defense Force from the USMC SS. His story, information and accounts give us insight into things other whistleblowers have been discussing about Alternative 3 and establishing bases on Mars. His experiences give us an in-depth understanding of the ET races interacting with Earth, hidden agendas affecting humanity and information about off-planet military activity that has been kept secret and that he is now choosing to disclose. Randy shared this with me:

> *"Let me just say to you, that it is thanks to your great grand father that I am alive today and that there is even the slightest glimmer of hope in this dark hour. Pres Eisenhower, in late 1953, signed into law using a secret executive order, the USMC s.s. (special section). in his own words 'To keep those MJ-12 boys in check.' It didn't work like he hoped, but we're still trying to be the checks and balances for MJ-12."*

The shadow government and off-planet beings have been working hard to influence the three Alternative Timeline scenarios created to throw humanity off the Organic Ascension timeline:

Alternative 1 focused on using nuclear devices to blast holes in the stratosphere where heat and pollution could escape into space.

Alternative 2 aimed to build a network of underground cities and tunnels where mankind's selected elite could survive. Along these lines, Phil Schneider mentioned that 131 DUMBs (Deep Underground Military Bases) exist in the USA. Others have said there are approximately 4,000 worldwide.

Alternative 3 dealt with the secret space colonization program on Mars for the same purpose as Alternative 2, which played into my experience with a failed attempted recruitment. This experience was the gestalt that compelled me to create and claim my desired timeline scenario—Alternative 4, which is based on the Organic Ascension Timeline and the power of the human spirit triumphing over controller forces. This already exists and is what I have always felt prepared for.

Unrelated to these alternative timeline scenarios but important to mention, with everything one could hear about in relation to ET government treaties, there is a high likelihood a person will run into the claim that Eisenhower signed a treaty with Grey aliens. However, I have found overwhelming testimony and confirmation from multiple sources that say this was not the case—Eisenhower did not sign anything. This is where we run into one of the most extensive disinformation campaigns, to blame a former five-star general and two-term President of the United States as being the one who sold humanity out. Quite the contrary, he was one of the few leaders in human history who cared for and fought hard for our freedom. His parting speech on the danger of the Military Industrial Complex[3] is an excellent example of his profound love for "We The People" of this country. All the disinformation around this has created a deep wound and injury to understanding the truth about our human history, making it difficult for people to see exactly how the shadow government operates.

Though some might not agree or see it this way, I do. I have been willing to talk about ET government treaties and go down all the rabbit holes to figure this out. The blame laid upon him, the hate mail I receive, has been tremendous. The accusations cast upon him when he is the one President to have placed the countermeasures meant to take down the ever-growing agendas of the dark forces validate the massive infiltration we are up against. Even some of my colleagues spread untruths without direct expertise except for what they hear. Some are going so far as to exclude me from related panels and discussions. I believe it's like pouring fuel on the many false stories to cause further harm and division. We must dig deep to get beyond the steered narratives and cut through false history. For example, the book, "Other Losses," states that Eisenhower intentionally starved German POWs. However, after thorough digging, I discovered this, too, is untrue. I'll share other uncovered revelations as I dive further into the book. It breaks my heart. Because of this single book, which has been discredited by multiple historians, including renowned military historians, many won't even give this new perspective a chance.

Many people incorrectly assume my family has wealth or that I have a trust fund. I understand people's confusion since Eisenhower is a Presidential bloodline. But wouldn't the family have access to technology and all the wealth like these ruling elite families do if Ike had signed those treaties and had dealings with extraterrestrials as part of the Deep State? I realize that is not a guarantee as a descendant, but this has been the case for every family member. It is common sense at this point, and anyone who has ever gotten to honestly know me would see that we all work hard and don't receive any special privileges as Eisenhowers. Perhaps we get the occasional invite to celebrate his time in office, his service in WWII, or the acknowledgment of being related, but that's the extent. Each family member has a unique body of work and missions that stand independently. Sure, the name will draw attention. Some people even say, "Oh, you are riding on your great-grandfather's coattails," which is absurd. We are a family and will always have deep and unique connections with him and one another.

In many ways, we have remained in a war scenario that continues to this day, on deep levels, that most aren't prepared to look at, even though it dramatically affects everyone. So it is with Interplanetary Corporate Conglomerate (ICC)/Nazi/Draco Alliance and Deep State agendas. I have seen almost every documentary known to man about what occurred during WWII. The extreme and painful abuses and atrocities never left my mind, including all the covered-up genocides throughout history. However, today, we face a very different kind of war that needs exposure to raise our vibration beyond strong programming and social engineering. This war can only be won within so we can move into greater love and unity as a humanity. It is time we step away from their divide-and-conquer tactics and look towards one another for solutions.

The Alternative 3 scenario. "Alternative 3" has had an enduring impact since it was first broadcast in 1977. Many now believe the fictional events portrayed in the show subversively reflect reality. https://theunredacted.com/alternative-3-secret-space-program/

Our human soul is screaming to be heard and seen. Beyond race, gender and ethnicity, it wants to feel love and respect and to tell its story and pain. It doesn't subscribe to the current debates, race wars, or propaganda that keeps trying to mess with our heads and engineer problems that don't exist. Our mind and ego can fall for such traps if we are not soul-centered or functioning from our higher mind and intuition, giving power away and fighting for something that's not ours. We know and feel love deep within our souls and don't care what color, status, religion or background another is. As soul-centered people, we go much deeper.

So what is this ongoing war all about, then? We know racism exists, as do bullies, haters and things of that nature. Engineered movements differ from contending with whatever internal issue we might experience with another individual or group that still holds distortions due to upbringing, past lives or negative conditioning. I care deeply. However, these are not my priorities as much as addressing child trafficking, pedophilia, ritual abuse and severe crimes against humanity. This war has deeper layers, and it's playing out differently today. It is a war on our minds and souls, a war on consciousness. It is about Deep State tactics that fund both sides of wars and political parties, who wish to conquer and divide us, who use psychological operations to make us easy to control while convincing us it is in our best interest. Not all emerging leaders are a part of this and represent something different. However, it is hard to know who is who when the media encourages the quick formation of opinions without the facts. Digging deeper is not something many bother to do.

Will we let history repeat itself and end with the grand finale of a New World Order (NWO)? Or will we come together, be humbled, face the potential shock of ego death, and remain strong enough to bounce back better than ever? It does seem our only real option. Put your ego aside, let your soul breathe, and let Spirit flood your being with the potential, miracles, magic and gifts it holds!

DAN COOPER

Meeting Dan Cooper and hearing his first-hand account helped connect many dots and further clarified and reassured me that the blame placed on Eisenhower was undeserved. At this point, I desire to lay a foundation to help minimize any reactionary temptation to dismiss claims he or others make without considering the body of information. Later in the book, I'll get into more detail about what Dan shared regarding the positive military forces Eisenhower set up, including the White Hats, his relationship with Val Thor, more information about ET government treaties, and the conflicting information about first contact.

Vetting someone is understandable and a wise thing to do. I have found tell-tale signs when someone is a plant, an agent/operative type, or pushing a false narrative or controlled opposition to introduce disinformation. Well, once I came across Dan, I knew he wasn't any of these things. I respect anyone who might disagree. I have learned what to look for to read people's energy signatures accurately, and I have had to do this much of my life. I've dealt with plants and been to conferences where it is evident that someone isn't representing the truth. Being a deeply sensitive soul, the injuries I have endured and still working to overcome have given me much discernment. I always welcome correction, as fixed beliefs can get in the way when new information presents itself. Love wins this war, as does laughter. They show up in those most painful places and are a beautiful reminder that the sun always rises and that nothing can destroy truth or the essence of love, soul and spirit.

Dan Cooper professes to be an expert researcher, a talent he honed through 20 years of legal research from 1993-2013. He claims that his knowledge of the historical events described herein came originally from both of his two Nazi SS commanding officers, who commanded him during his "20 and Back" stint with the Nazi-operated Dark Fleet as a USAF, Space Command, Tech Sgt., 2nd Class. Dan shared that these two Nazi SS officers related, and often bragged about, their participation in the Battle of D.C. UFO flyover on July 19, 1952, when the Nazis defeated the United States and forced them to surrender unconditionally. He also claims that his knowledge of the 5th-8th Fundamental Forces of Nature guided him in ferreting out the actual historical developments of the technologies employed in the Unacknowledged Secret Access Programs (USAPs) of the United States.[4]

Dan never contacted me directly or asked for money to speak with me. We came to know each other shortly after he commented on a video roundtable interview I did with Dan Willis and Elena Danaan. His comments on our discussion intrigued me, so I replied with questions. I was so pleased he responded! I gave him my email in hopes we could continue discussions. Once again, he emailed back right away, *"Hi, this is Dan Cooper."*

I was thrilled because, at the time, this "unconditional surrender" that took place in 1952 was not something I was very familiar with. I wondered what Ike's position was, especially since most of what I heard said he signed and renewed a treaty with the Greys in 1954 called the Greada Treaty. I asked Dan about this, and this is what he told me:

"My two Nazi commanding officers in Dark Fleet, and my White Hat U.S. Navy Vice Admiral, told me what the Terms of the Unconditional Surrender Instrument of the U.S. surrendering to the Nazis on July 19, 1952, were. One Term divested the power to sign treaties with alien species into the hands of MJ-12.

Hence, Dwight could NOT possibly have signed any agreements with any alien species. He did NOT have the legal power to do so. He wasn't even allowed to attend the negotiations, what to speak of being made privy to the terms of those agreements.

That is how I know what Elena said to you about MJ-12 going behind Ike's back is true."

JUPITER-PLUTO-SATURN CONJUNCTION

In 2020, a powerful astrological conjunction of Jupiter-Pluto-Saturn influenced a major turning point in our collective experience around the time the COVID-19 global pandemic hit the world stage. Looking into what these aspects represent, we see a marked growth period for humanity. One where every human across the planet was facing a personal and collective crisis and choice point around our relationship to outer authority, fear narratives and our mortality. Uncertainty and confusion existed around mandates, the degree power structures could assert control over us, and what it would take to release ourselves of the old false paradigm and rise like a phoenix into the new Saturn in Aquarius, with Pluto moving into Aquarius in 2023 after a retrograde, and then back in 2024. These plutonic cycles marked tremendous transformative experiences for people and the loss of many lives as the bifurcation and shift in energies reached a critical phase regarding our choices and belief systems' impact on our future.

No matter what decision someone made, it is essential to stay in the vibration of love and acceptance, in peace and reassurance, knowing that when the mind shifts out of a dependency bond with control forces and inversions out of alignment with one's truth or intuition, the healing journey begins and an ability to perceive of all the guidance and synchronicities that are available to support overcoming harm or injury gets activated. This is because it is always about frequency—the power of our minds can quite literally manifest "mind over matter." We are more powerful than we can imagine as Spirit holds dominion over the physical plane.

The regenerative power of the Earth, which exists as elemental energy within us, working with elementals like Aether, can transform, alchemize and transmute more than we can imagine. We are infinite, so however long it takes to accomplish this is what it is. We move at different speeds and may rise, digress or get distracted. But in learning wisdom and what patterns keep us repeating the same lesson over and over, we begin to transcend all obstacles and blockages, which are often a manifestation of our inner resistances and fear of discovering all we are truly made of. Adversity can be the blessing that challenges us to overcome any limitation imposed upon us!

URANUS SQUARE SATURN

"Because this Satanic force betrayed divine mysteries to mankind, he has been punished. His heavy, dark, leaden qualities must be transformed into gold by the magician, in an alchemical process involving the 'repolarisation of lights'."

– Stephen Flowers, describing the Earth dilemma

In the years following the COVID-19 pandemic and global lockdown, we experienced a Uranus square Saturn aspect, which represented the tension experienced when breaking free from something oppressive. The energy is like going through a breakup. Not an amicable one, one where the Saturn side will do everything possible to control a person and make their life miserable. This alignment ran until early in 2023, preparing the way for Pluto to enter Aquarius just after Saturn left. In the middle part of this decade, this sort of tension and conflict will be the old order continuing to do all it can to keep us engaged in the old script to take away our rights since Saturn (outer authority) is challenging our freedoms (Uranus). There are a number of ways to deal with this. Some choose to engage in mass protests, for one, and so many seek truth at all costs to override control based on the theft of our divine birthright. Where you live and who you are will influence how you experience these energies. It may be something very internal as you seek to liberate yourself from any energy blocks and self-defeating thought forms that stem from an outer voice that influenced your life.

We also are dealing with an energetic climate that is pulling us in the opposite direction of what we are truly capable of experiencing and embodying. Many contactees have messages to share, and many self-help healers and world leaders are declaring how we can stop the spread of the virus and all its variants. Still, something deeper is emerging, helping us understand the false matrix games being played.

All sorts of tactics have been used on the human race to keep us dependent on a system and in compliance with authority. Some feel we have captors and controllers and are on a prison planet. Others view it through the lens of a mostly beneficial system working in our favor while ever evolving and changing to encourage us. Hence, the sense of satisfaction when we "fight" for something and "win." So many movements over decades—civil rights, feminism, climate change—and although they are necessary to address, why do some seem to have a dark underbelly with problems that seem engineered? Certainly, geoengineering has affected the weather, yet humans are being blamed for "climate change."

People nowadays are so offended by everything. What did these movements accomplish if injustices still haunt us? It is like a cycle of never overcoming childhood wounds or bad relationships. We can't expect them to disappear. We must be fully present with and aware when a trigger rises to the surface versus retaliating against the person who may have ignited it. Of course, calling out abusive behavior is different. It's great to stand for something, but do we need to get sucked into the political sphere as we do so often? How much is it dividing us? If we are going to address these things successfully, shouldn't we look deeper into our relationship with ourselves, each other, the planet and the cosmos? Can we instead heal and resolve this amongst ourselves and strive to determine the root of all the imbalance? This is the only place we can safely fall back on. You might disagree, and that is okay. Many epic changes and landmark events have taken place throughout human history that show forward progression. Can we take it a step further to differentiate between social engineering and real, revolutionary change we believe in from our own inspired heart, mind and truth?

For example, the political fire sparking debates between liberals and conservatives comes with such confusion that it's hard to see where it is all going. Are we just spinning our wheels? History continues to repeat itself, with the same force wishing to divide and conquer hiding behind a label, party or movement, then adding race and gender division into the mix to ensure every single trauma or insecurity gets triggered so we grab onto any claim of a "cure" for what we desperately seek to heal. Then, fuel gets thrown to inflame the existing fire claiming that those not on board with the narrative must be against it and hate-filled. There is so much divide and conquer it would be prudent to step back momentarily and ask ourselves, are we being played? What aligns with our truth? Might anyone be looking to use our passions, hopes and dreams against us? If so, why and what would be the evidence?

> *"Celebrity cloning and psychological manipulation is real. This extended from project MKULTRA. Then there is Project Monarch which is ritual trauma-based mind control and abuse that is extended to the children of certain bloodline families and ultimately the future celebrities as children. Then there is Operation Mockingbird which is a long-term manipulation of the public mind through the media via celebrities, news, movies, music and general entertainment."*
>
> – A.T., insider operative

The Saturn-Moon matrix and Black Cube matrix that is held through Saturn is where harvesting and siphoning technologies have made it possible for this to operate on such a massive scale in our world. I realize not every influential person is a clone or under controller influence, but many are. It is a lot more prevalent than we realize. With all of the manipulation through mind-control projects that have influenced Hollywood, the news and many leaders, we need to step back and get educated so that we don't allow ourselves or our children to be led astray and influenced, and begin to embark on a healing journey. This is the darkest part of Saturn's energies.

> *"Saturn's Black Cube holds a massive tank that acts as a harvesting station for blood sacrifice from human beings, in any way imaginable, whether through wars, rituals, crucifixion, martyrdom, suicide or menstrual.*
>
> *These reversal plasmas are designed to ignite and feed the demon seed that exists in the shadow selves or negative forms of the masses."*
>
> – Lisa Renee, Ascension Glossary

Saturn represents bondage, control and authority. It imposes limitations, rules and responsibilities. It governs the law of structure but it inverts in its lowest form. When Uranus and Saturn clash, the more we fight for our freedom, the more they attempt to block and increase their control over us. The higher octave of Saturn is self-mastery and redefining the law of structure on our own terms so that the disciplines and responsibilities we adopt help us to thrive. Many teachers have a strong Saturn in their chart and have built incredible success in their lives. But the dark Saturn, like any shadow or dark octave of a planetary expression, must be reconciled within ourselves so we can change the vibration and guide ourselves to the greater potential of what it represents.

Similarly, the archetypal energies, as they are associated with planets, are something that must be reconciled from within versus expecting an outer authority to resolve it or to save us. The problem-reaction-solution tactic has been used on us for far too long, where the problem originates from the ones attempting to offer the solution. This continues an unhealthy relationship with the outer world based in fear and disempowerment. Many of our relationships run an unhealthy program that stems from being raised in this system that rewards or encourages this. Benevolent forces can assist, but they need our alignment and conscious participation, just as our immune system needs us to strengthen and support it. The archetypes within pantheons and some of the mythologies connected to them reveal it is up to us to bring harmony and balance and to integrate all the different inherited aspects by examining where manipulative forces are targeting unresolved or unhealed wounds to keep us stuck and under control.

We are on this planet for soul and spiritual development. We grow and learn how to thrive through life experience, and our sovereignty comes down to how it shapes our character. When we connect to our higher mind, synchronicities lead us to soul mates and soul family. Through our "mistakes," we learn things like discernment, boundaries, wisdom, clarity and mindfulness. Exploring the world outside the confines of limiting belief systems, we discover our life unfolds more in accordance with our soul and what it is meant to experience. We rise out of the dark shadows and into the zero point of neutrality and oneness when we reconcile the discord between the archetypal forces within. Our soul journey and life path will take us to every level in between until we get there. Everything that emerges from this zero point, the Cosmic Trinity, and the influence on humanity from the fallen ones is what we need to discover fully in order to rise above Saturn's lower octave energies.

In the end, we all have our way of flowing with what we ingest, consume and form relationships with. It's a two-way street. We get to choose how we respond and communicate with whatever arrangement or agreement we have. Some will be the alchemists, some will awaken and discover something of value they may not have perceived before, while some might perish or experience long-term consequences. We hold the power to break any negative pattern. No matter if we find ourselves trapped, chained up or compromised, we can always find our way out, especially if we come together in our communities and pool our resources, skills, abilities and strengths. Commit to redirecting your energy towards being soul-centered, awake and conscious, and be willing to look inward to dismantle the matrix from your mind, body and spirit. Feel it to heal it!

WHAT IS TRUTH?

"Questioning and doubting what's going on these days does not make you 'anti' anything. Nor does it make you a conspiracy theorist. Actually, questioning IS and should be the place of reason. The fact that questioning has become taboo, should, in fact, send a chill up everyone's spine."

– Unknown

Researching is a powerful method of allowing the self to embark upon an adventure of discovery. In this context, "truth" is when we experience something tangible and feel aligned with all the possibilities, in integrity, with the willingness to listen before taking action.

Truth is flexible and honest. It is filled with love, yet it can also hurt (compassion helps to soften the blow). Truth doesn't claim all the answers and is not about right or wrong. It differs from gossip, misinformation, the lower personality matrix, and petty ego games.

Truth is living authentically. When we are in resonance with its vibration, our truth can heal and guide us, and with a humble approach, we can better heed our intuition. Once we establish this foundation, we inform our ego identity of the action to take. A healthy ego isn't a product, sub-personality, commercial or label. It is a force of the "I Am" presence that can be the fuel and power that generates and reveals the soul and spiritual dimensions. It can identify with truth instead of everything that might lead it astray.

Finding truth must include a capacity to look objectively at information and to love others regardless. It must hold compassion, an open mind, and forgiveness for our troubled history and our ancestors' role. No doubt, the amount of disinformation and distortion will make the truth quite challenging to stomach when revealed, but it's not about having all the answers. Evolving, growing, healing and coming together as a united front is why we must be unceasing in our pursuit.

To get to what is true, humanity has to trust themselves again. Our biggest problem is that we have lost connection with who we are, so we don't trust our innate abilities to heal and lead ourselves. The truth frequency and the word "trust" are very connected. To live an authentic life connected to Source, we must first trust ourselves and our intuition again and then live and speak our truth. It becomes a way of life in which no mind control, artificial timeline or dark technology can override.

The truth frequency is something we discover as we walk our life's journey, to one day realize we found it without ever needing to understand it fully. Living in an embodied, authentic way doesn't mean our intellect has to have it all figured out. By opening ourselves up to new concepts or ways of looking at things, we see all the options and possibilities that may be the missing link to our ascension.

We are here to help activate one another. I hope that what I share in this book enables you to find your truth and divine flow.

STELLAR ACTIVATION CYCLE

"During the Ascension Cycle the planet is exposed to Solar Flares and Stellar Activations which cause the levels of the planetary auric field progressively open up into each other, dissolving the dimensional Frequency barriers that kept the levels separate at one time within the planetary auric field."

– Lisa Renee

As we shift, reality shifts, and as the Earth shifts, all are affected. Our choices affect the Earth, too, as we are in a co-creative relationship. The window period 2010-2025 is when all must shift together by no longer allowing outer authority or control systems to dominate and mess with our minds, emotions and sense of identity. I usually avoid calling out specific dates, but this window period is particularly heightened, where our choices impact things more than ever.

A Stellar Activation Cycle is occurring in this timeframe. When we hear terms like ascension, we might also hear things like "false ascension" or that the ascension timeline has been "hijacked" and another plan put in place. This is indeed true. Mission upgrades needed to occur because the damage done by invader forces interfered with humanity's original ascension trajectory. This cycle is necessary to collapse these false ascension timelines and address mind-control programs' extreme impact on us. This is best understood and researched by Lisa Renee, who tirelessly stays connected to all the energies, events and dark weaponry tactics.

This window period concerns our capacity to advance as a human race and fully awaken to our potential. All that has been lost, buried, forgotten, distorted, perverted and rewritten is being corrected. The higher Earth energies exist within our consciousness, energy centers, DNA, and in the Earth grids with their stargates. Our DNA holds higher harmonic universes, though we are told it is "junk."

You can find some of these terminologies in Lisa's Ascension Glossary[5]. I use them because they beautifully explain things that are hard to articulate and reveal a broader science.

A NOTE ON KEYLONTIC SCIENCE

True freedom teachings demonstrate in substantial detail a connection between science and spirituality and a relationship between energy, consciousness, light and sound that forms the basis of all Creation. One can examine these divine mechanics by studying Keylontic Science.

Throughout my life, writings and downloads, the information presented through Lisa Renee and her Energetic Synthesis newsletters, the Ascension Glossary, and Ashayana Deane and Keylontic Science has resonated most. It has become a part of my way of explaining things and has given me a more substantial definition of concepts I have been trying to explain and share for quite some time. For this reason, you will see me reference it throughout my book. For this, I am grateful.

"Using Keylontic Science (Keylonta) the function of the human DNA imprint can be progressively restored, allowing the natural dynamics of Soul, Oversoul and Avatar level identity embodiment to commence."

– Ascension Dictionary

Galactic History

> *"The main battles in human galactic history were fought in the constellation of Orion, and so these many wars are referred to as the Orion Wars. In our Universal Time Matrix, the wars started over territories in the constellation of Lyra (The Cradle of Lyra). But soon the Lyran Wars spread to the constellation of Orion, and it became a war between False King of Tyranny mindsets and ideologies with the ideology of the Service-to-others which follow the Law of One."*
>
> *– Lisa Renee*

At one time, this world was far less dense than it is now. Our galactic history reveals that everything changed when we dealt with the galactic wars, cataclysms, and exploding planets that led to the collapse of higher-dimensional civilizations. We dealt with the abuse of free will, hybridization and the manipulation of incarnate consciousness and our DNA. So much so that it made it difficult to maintain a multi-dimensional embodiment and connection to spirit while in physical form. The current window period offers a profound opportunity to return to these higher planes of existence.

The destruction of the higher consciousness avatar occurred with the destruction of the Cradle of Lyra during the Lyran Wars with the Draconian Orion Group. The Orion Group is a predator force with a predator mind primarily responsible for mind control programming used to create much of the negative ego found in humanity. The degradation has made it hard for us to achieve healing, integration and Unity Consciousness. That is why this is so challenging right now!

Through much of my research, I have understood that the Draco-Reptilian-backed Orion Empire attacked the Lyra systems and devastated three worlds, initially killing over 50 million Lyrans and more as the war continued. "The Unholy Six" is a term I have heard mentioned about this group from numerous sources and is likely the beginning of the Luciferian/Reptilian agenda. Alex Collier's 1997 material goes in-depth about this, as does the Ascension Glossary in many parts.

It was decided that the human life form was to be created in the Lyran system. The human race lived there for approximately 40 million years and continued evolving. The orientation of the human race in Lyra was agricultural in nature. Back then, we were plentiful and abundant and lived in peace, serving the principles of the Law of One. Then, one day, a colossal craft appeared in the sky.

A large ship emerged from the craft, approached the Lyran planet Bila, and Reptilians from Alpha Draconis disembarked. The Alpha Draconians and the Lyrans were afraid of each other. Alpha Draconians were the first race in our galaxy to have interstellar space travel, having the capability for 4 billion years. When the Draconians came and saw the Lyran planet with all its abundance, food and natural resources, the Draconians wanted to control it.

A misunderstanding between the Draconians and Lyran humans occurred. The Lyrans wanted to know more about the Draconians before any "assistance" was offered, and the Draconians mistook this as a refusal and subsequently destroyed three out of 14 planets in the Lyran system. The Lyrans were defenseless against this war. The planets Bila, Teka and Merck were destroyed.

Over 50 million Lyran humans were killed. At this point in history, the Draconians began to look at humans as a food source. This is how the struggle between the Reptilian and human races came to be. Now, I must point out that not all the Reptilian or human races are "dark." There is a mixture. So when we begin meeting these races again in the future, we will need to trust our gut instinct and make that individual determination.

TIAMAT

"The destruction of Tiamat (like a heaven and earth principle living together in perfect harmony) is synonymous with the destruction of sacred marriage (union of opposites), the destruction of the Hieros Gamos, thus splitting apart the consciousness of the Christos-Sophia.

Without Tiamat we were unable to have our 10th Chakra and all its functions work in our bodies, as she was the frequency link to communicate with our Christos Avatar self. She is a part of the Triple Goddess Formation and apparently the Merging Shield is the Living

*Creature Matrix to remind us that we are to rebirth her essence again
onto our planetary body, and then hence our own physical body."*

Lisa Renee, Energetic Synthesis

On 5D Tara, many extraterrestrial and meta-terrestrial races combined their genetic and energetic makeup to create a master race. They divided into two primary racial strains that evolved together on one large land mass called Edon: Lumians and Alanians.

Both races carried the original 12-strand DNA genetic code of the Grail and Oraphim lineages and the mutations and digressions of that code from interstellar inter-breeding with various unrelated ET strains, according to Keylontic Science. My soul familiarity and research revealed that the misuse of power from the Alanians within the planetary core created a chain reaction of implosions within Tara's planetary grid, which connected with Tiamat as a sister planet within the same system. Tiamat is from Sophia and is called a Dragon Queen, with the first primal couple being Tiamat and Apsu.

Tara was a planet in 5D, the second Harmonic Universe (HU2), that exploded, then imploded, into a black hole. Some fragments were pulled into the lower dimensions and became our planet and solar system. The Earth originally came from Tara.

My research revealed how Tiamat exploded due to a collision with Nibiru. This was the fall into Harmonic Universe 1 (HU1) called Urtha, and Tiamat and Apsu became strewn into pieces that formed the asteroid belt. Maldek, which exploded soon after, created the 3D asteroid belt. Maldek in 3D (i.e., asteroid belt) is considered the counterpart of Tiamat in 5D. Many researchers say Tiamat and Maldek are the same planets, which doesn't make sense. Many have noted that Marduk (a.k.a. Nibiru) was involved with the deliberate destruction of the planet Tiamat and then later Maldek. The resulting collapse of advanced civilizations and sacred union caused Tara (where Tiamat existed) to fall from dimensions 4,5 and 6 (HU2) into dimensions 1, 2 and 3 (HU1). From this point forward, everything drastically changed, and more planets came into the picture. Some sources have said that when Tara and Tiamat exploded, taking thousands of years for the split to occur, the two pieces of Tiamat became our current Earth and Maldek. For example, according to the Enuma Elish, the Babylonian creation epic, she was eventually destroyed by the god Marduk, who split her body in half.

Through my extensive digging, sources reveal that the fall of humanity occurred when Tiamat exploded, and the 5D version of Earth collapsed into HU1, causing many souls of Tara to be lost and requiring retrieval. In time, we lost our galactic memories, our DNA was unplugged and our DNA fire codes were scrambled. This was done during the Sumerian-Egypt Invasion when human history was rewritten 5,500 years ago. There is so much to get into about this time in our history. The dark reversal harvesting technologies, like the Nephilim Reversal Grid, were already implanted in the planetary grid network—all a part of a 26,000-year cycle of dark history.

As these sources continue to explain, the most significant obstacles facing humanity today are the active rewriting of human history and forced amnesia, which leads to easy indoctrination. The invasion in Sumeria/Egypt instituted a mind control plan for patriarchal domination, a continued enslavement agenda for all Earth humans and the promotion of Anunnaki as the Gods of this Earth.

The Ascension Cycle transpiring on 3D Earth offers an opportunity to reclaim these 5D fragments and consciousness pieces that were exploded and damaged in these cataclysms and extradimensional wars. The most important thing to recognize is what is being most targeted now, which is our capacity to unite and work together and create sacred union.

ACHAMOTH

Tiamat's destruction triggered the evolution cycle of the fallen Goddess. This chapter is inspired by Lisa Renee's explanation, which resonates with me more than anything I have ever read. She describes it in the following way:

> *"The planet Tiamat is related to the destruction of the Sophianic Body and the inability of the Christos-Sophia Consciousness to incarnate in human forms on the 3D Earth. The female consciousness of the planet Tiamat was Sophianic, so when she exploded, her consciousness descended into a collective form body which is known as the Achamoth."*

This explosion held parts of the Mother Principle, and the resulting archon parasites are what parts of her womb were impregnated with. This is why the path of the divine feminine is all about retrieving these parts and going into the underworld to do so. Lisa helps clarify that these archonic creatures and collective spawns make up the Baphomet field in the 2D layers of planet Earth, which contains many hierarchies of lower spirits, such as demons.

During the fall, we separated from the Seven Higher Heavens. We became locked into this Seven Chakra System and patriarchy, blocked from accessing the bridge to the rest of ourselves and Unity Consciousness. Implants inserted into our seven chakras have distorted our spiritual knowledge. However, we are at a time on Earth when we can regain this.

As a new world was forming, Sophia morphed into the physical planet, and this was the intervention—to become an ascending planet and help activate our higher codes. The 13D Mother Arc connected us to the Godhead. As an ascending planet under attack, the seeding of the angelic human lines on Earth was set in motion. This has required much repair work for Earth to be capable of supporting our growth and awakening due to the dark mother reversals, dark cycles of history and the loss of the Mother Principle that wasn't able to inhabit the planet until recently.

> *"She morphed from a pure energetic state (stellar plasma), into the material body of the Earth. Hence her story describes the origins of the Earth."*

– *The Nag Hammadi*

ORION GROUPS

The following two sections use ascension mechanics terminology inspired by the work of Lisa Renee, her website and Ascension Glossary, and Ashayana Deane's "Voyager" book and Freedom Teachings. However, I have come to understand them quite intuitively. These are excellent sources you can reference if you choose to dive deeper.

Before I dive in, I would like to begin with a noteworthy statement by Lisa Renee. I feel it beautifully articulates a position with which I resonate:

> *"Please honor this Guardian consciousness work and take in only what resonates with you personally and discard the rest. There is no need for competition, enemy patterning or controlling Sacred Spiritual Sciences or Ascension technologies, which belong to all of humanity. This content is presented with the intention of Unity, Freedom, Compassion and the Sovereign Right for All beings; to be the revelation of the direct inner experience of the intelligence fields, that are the Eternal God Source."*

The Orion Group (Draconians) infiltrated and became an ally to the Anunnaki resistance. They inbred within both Enki and Enlil Anunnaki groups and organized themselves into what is known as the intruder races of current times. These are the beings who orchestrate the NWO and the highest factions of the Illuminati plan for Earth's takeover and entails creating a social class system and hierarchy—a ruling class and a slave class—on Earth, which is the Reptilian archon ideology as outlined in the Ascension Glossary. They employ many levels of mind control on the masses to weaponize our media, medical industry, politics, school systems, the entertainment industry and more against us. They are attempting to rewrite history and have already succeeded in many ways.

This group is referred to as the "Black Suns." They reversed their DNA to ten strands and run a reversal life current. This group directly promotes misogyny, sexual exploitation and objectification, violence, forced breeding, imbalance, distortions and everything inverted. This is the force on Earth that makes it incredibly difficult for men and women to hold the balanced divine

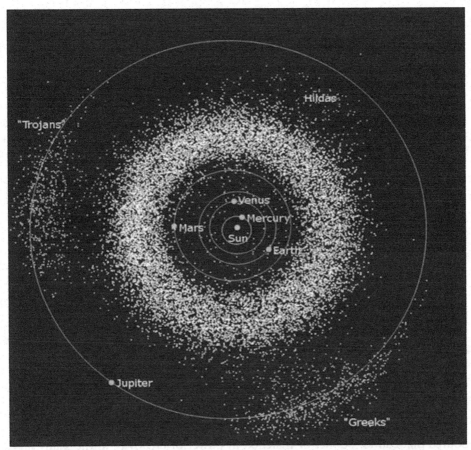

Asteroid Belt. "...the Asteroid Belt we see in the 3D Universe is Maldek's exploded planet, and the asteroid belt in the 5D Universe is Tiamat's exploded planetary body." –Lisa Renee, Ascension Glossary; https://ascensionglossary.com/index.php/Asteroid_Belt

template of Christos-Sophia. It is experienced as mind-control for some and trauma for others over many thousands of years, and through continuous assault, and is quite challenging to recover from. They target our children with gender confusion that adults consent to when it seems to be a cumulative response to the incredibly distorted programming of previous generations and their many breakthroughs forgotten. Revealing this dark history is to recognize what we have been up against—the manipulation and destructive forces that require our energy input to exist, which they readily harvest and collect—so that we don't fall prey to any more trickery and abuse so we can move forward to reclaim the truth of all we are made of.

    The events that took place on the Earth plane after the Dracos finished their genocidal massacre of the Lemurian continent by targeting the matriarchal society there was also the end of the Atlantean Golden Age. Root Race 3 and Root Race 4 are Lemuria and Atlantis. This was to prepare for a thoroughly patriarchal society, so the dark energies of Atlantis began to emerge and the invaders formed into the Atlantean Brotherhood of the Snake. Many joined in with the Orion Group and later formed the Luciferian Covenant. This coincides with the dark weaponry and the fall of Atlantis, and how these groups increased operating in the shadows and behind the scenes, influencing world affairs and engineering false reality and every tactic under the sun to keep us disempowered and under their control.

The Atlantean Cataclysm, approximately 26,000-30,000 years ago, is when the planetary stargates, grids, and ley lines became controlled by the Negative Alien Agenda (NAA) races such as the Reptilians, Anunnaki, Nephilim, Alpha Draconis/Orion Group, Zetas, Greys and some Nordics. Lisa Renee and Ashayana Deane reveal this information in the online glossary and dictionary. It has been called one of the Luciferian Rebellions. Ley lines are the meridian axiatonal lines or grid system that conducts and transmits frequencies throughout our planet and bodies. They are an exact mirror of our energy body, DNA and chakras, built upon sacred geometry and things like Platonic Solids. They can also be manipulated and thrown into reversals. The many cataclysms caused Earth to tilt on its axis, damaging all planetary gates, grid networks, portals and stargates. All pyramid and ET technologies disconnected and went offline. Flooding and cataclysm destroyed the Atlantean colonies and much of the Earth's surface.

These service-to-self beings seek to create a continual stream of realities within realities to hide from the original creative Source, the One and ultimate Source that cannot be met or matched in power or creativity in the many layers and levels. Thankfully, humans contain a latent principle of Source, which unveils great power when awakened. They are afraid of and need to feed on us because they lost their direct connection with Source. Control is maintained in a vampiric way, holding false light based in negative ego that they want humanity to addict itself to. The loss of our galactic memories, amnesia and the reincarnation cycle with their use of dark technology have made it easy for them to maintain continual access to us by presenting an engineered reality we often mistake and normalize as our human "condition."

The reverse base pairing of DNA and the many levels of genetic modification and control suppress DNA synthesis. There has been intentional suppression of DNA activation of our 12-strand original design, the silicate matrix, assembled and built by proteins. This genetic suppression has been aggressive since the Atlantean Cataclysm. It is directly related to the suppression of hierogamic union achieved through proper DNA base pairing, which can build and assemble the proteins to unscramble DNA fire letters.

The Nephilim Reversal Grid and sexual misery programs are part of many dark technologies responsible for these distortions and reversals, including the programming of humans to accept unnatural social norms while being blind to the abuses from the negative alien races and their human representatives, which include things like sexual slavery, trafficking and indoctrination concerning the sexual act and gender roles. This hub is located in the Stonehenge area of England. Also, since 25,500 B.C., the Niburian Diodic Crystal, a grid-checkerboard mutation, has reduced our human life span, chemical DNA and brain function, and has blocked our race memory. The ultimate goal is to corrupt and harm our relationship with our true mother and father parent and our ability to heal, integrate and awaken to our divine blueprint fully. Instead, soul splintering occurs and this is how they control sexual energy.

Noel Huntley, Ph.D., says this about the planetary reversal grid technology:

"NDC (Nibiruan Diodic Crystal) photosonic pulses block and reverse the polarity in some of the Earth's axiatonal ('vertical') and Ley line ('horizontal') grids, creating a 'checkerboard' of alternate active and dormant frequencies and named the Checkerboard Matrix. This has created a huge so-called 'checkerboard mutation' in all life on Earth what science calls junk DNA."

Once a person becomes addicted to the bait presented in all forms of manipulation and deception, the architecture of the control system hooks in and steals their vital force. It is what feeds the technologies and gets sent off-planet. Our free energy has been used as a weapon against us. Different false archetypes are played out and continuously encouraged in our society through acceptance, reward and praise. Truthful disclosure will only come from us, so our job is to recover from all the assaults, social engineering and thousands of years of trauma.

So this is the greater love story encoded into our DNA and is the most important thing we humans can work on rebuilding. There are stages to integrating this polarity. Our life journey—lived deeply beyond what any indoctrination, ancestral patterns and conditioning have encouraged us to become—allows us to do this restoration work. This is what the awakening is all about, and we have all the help we can imagine the minute we step into this soul-centered purpose, we will notice synchronicities, magic and flow.

At this same time, we may also experience increased targeting and life changes as we no longer choose to co-create with lower vibration. It will attempt to pull you back in through fear tactics. Some are targeted worse than others, so responding with greater unification, mutual love and support is essential. Spirit's guidance is way more potent than any targeting. We are here to learn how to be senior to these lower forces, so we continue to relive lower patterns until we finally break free. We heal our family lines when we overcome them and greatly assist in The Great Awakening.

We are moving beyond the imbalance of masculine/feminine and divorcing ourselves from Orion Group imposters that disempower and cause harm. Knowing our worth, we begin the quest for true love, embarking on an inward journey to find divinity and where its story resides. This changes our outer relationships and who we attract into our lives. Sacred union, alchemical marriage and Hieros Gamos is the resurrection of our "junk DNA" and the treasure to rediscover. This is how we heal ourselves and become a source of inspiration to others, shifting the collective out of its amnesia and trance.

The original Cosmic Christos Dragon Teachings connected to Mary Magdalene Sophia's legacy were gradually destroyed. The Orion Group Draconian invasions infiltrated these sacred texts to build something else entirely, using patriarchal domination to remove all awareness of the existence of the inner Christ. I see how demonized this has gotten in some religious minds by encouraging avoidance of this necessary work.

Rebuilding and switching on dormant DNA is restoring this hierogamic union within, and has been most difficult to achieve through the many dark cycles and how targeted restoration and healing have been and the degree to which our origins and galactic history have been kept from us. Distracted and looping in unconscious negative patterns, we have the choice and power to break free and access the buried truth of who we are. The rest follows once we perceive it and commit to the process, and the physical body and material plane begin to catch up.

Ultimately, when we are out of the negative's reach, all distortions will be swept clean and reset. However, this cannot occur until humanity removes itself from the lower layers by reawakening to its true nature—this is synonymous with ascension. The objective of the seeding of the root races on this planet has been to reassemble the original DNA blueprint and reclaim all parts lost in the Lyran/Orion Wars. This is why divide and conquer is such a powerful strategy. How can we possibly achieve this goal if we continue at odds with one another and in low vibrational energy?

Yeshua Christ and his wife, Mary Sophia, came to Earth to help the planet recover from the damage and liberate us through their embodiment of hierogamic union. Even still, it was known that it would be very difficult for the seeds they planted to come to fruition until the Ascension Cycle window period, when the galactic center aligns with the Earth, connecting us to the Neutron Window, which has allowed for this profound shift in vibration and the return of the Mother.

Let's use this opportunity to recognize what is available to us so we can align with it and do the required inner work to switch on all that has been dormant!

SUMERIAN-EGYPT INVASION

- 5500 years ago rip a 5D wormhole into Sakkara Egypt
- Rewrote Human History from 5500 years at time of Invasion with earliest written records of the Sumerian Tablets
- Promote <u>Annunaki</u> as creator Gods of Humanity
- Patriarchal Domination and enslavement agenda for Earth humans
- Final Setback – No communication with Christos Races with genetic manipulation and installed Frequency Fences

The Sumerian-Egyptian Invasion reveals when we lost our galactic memories and the Mother of God.; https://energeticsynthesis.com/

THE GUARDIANS AND ORAPHIM

"These are the Ancient Master builder Races that are also called Guardian Host from which the Essenes on the earth have been generated."

– Lisa Renee, Ascension Glossary

I could feel everything growing up—the heaviness, imbalance and programming of mainstream culture—and was often ungrounded. I tried, but it was tough. It wasn't until much later, after 2010, that I learned some information about our true galactic history when I discovered the Guardians' information through starseed advocates like Lisa Renee. Hallelujah! It matched all I was sensing and experiencing but in a straightforward and illuminative way. It's like telling a flower as it grows and does what it does what it is made of. I see us all as that flower, seeking to know our essence and how we got this way. Knowledge is power. The Tree of Knowledge is to find self-knowledge, and this pursuit has been continuously targeted with mind control.

Our history is vast, so it's no surprise we experienced way more before this Earth experience. Our planet was created from Mother's unconditional love after we sank in density, and its continuous subversion made it difficult to ground Her energy here. During the Sumerian-Egyptian invasion, when our DNA got unplugged, the Mother energy fully disembodied from Earth, so it lost her Mother of God and female Christ Sophianic Body principle. Add to this the further manipulation of our DNA by factions of the Anunnaki, who seemed to be acting as lower creator gods with some good intentions for humans and the lost souls of Maldek but ended up bent on power and control, aligning with the Dracos. It's no wonder it's been quite tricky maintaining high vibrational energy under these circumstances. Thankfully, we have been pulling out of this long history of dark mother reversal energies.

This may help to explain some things, but I realize much can go over one's head. Just know that reading the words has the potential to activate an inner remembrance that goes beyond words. In this light, I will share what I have learned about the Guardians and their perspective by referencing Lisa Renee's material and her direct relationship.

Many that emerge from Guardian Christos Consciousness are of the Blue Ray Melchizedek lines. When the patriarchal Melchizedeks digressed out of energetic balance and joined the Anunnaki resistance in wars, they became the Fallen Melchizedeks. I'll get into more history, but for now, understand an invasion happened long ago, and higher groups and races became infiltrated, which could have supported a healthy unfolding into the ascension energies. Although some Melchizedeks hosting the ascension timeline have fallen, others didn't and are currently being activated or healed. It is why the Goddess energy needed to go into the underworld to break the distortions and help rehabilitate those tasked with protecting the planet and its energy grids.

The Oraphim are a prototype of the Master Christos Collective. They are a race connected to the energy matrix and the Founder races that would later become the angelic humans or the Blue Ray Consciousness. They connect to the Grail lines on Earth and Indigo children. The Oraphim are the Double Diamond Sun of the Christos body who stepped down in frequency so that they could work on Earth to help direct the Threefold Founder Flame to repair the Earth grids and restore our DNA to its original divine blueprint. This triple flame is the Universal Trinity, holding the Father, Mother and Son/Daughter, or Christ-Sophia. They assist the Goddess in clarifying her story and supporting her return to the Earth's core. It's important to know that we all hold a piece and share the same substance of the Trinity. We contain these rays or flames, so we are a part of this healing. Not everyone knows this, but those who do and are aware of their missions can help activate it.

The Aurora from the Andromedan galaxy are also Guardians in alignment with Krystal Star and are whom the Oraphim races communicate with while on Earth. They help to cleanse the physical and purify it. They are more like consciousness orbs and higher elements but have been called Dragon luminaries. They all hold the energies of the next universe of the Seven Higher Heavens and are like a family occupying different positions to reach the same goal but take various forms. They generate an override frequency to correct the reversals, contamination and distortions, which I will later get into. Our bodies and soul essence are elemental, and the five elements in nature can help us understand the five elements in our DNA: Earth, Air, Fire, Water and Aether. When we look at moving from being

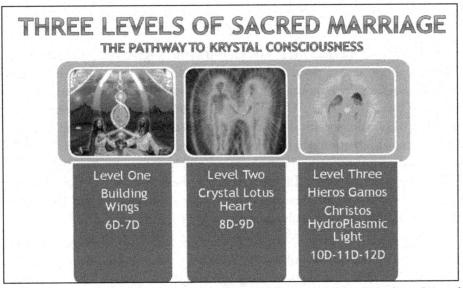

THREE LEVELS OF SACRED MARRIAGE
THE PATHWAY TO KRYSTAL CONSCIOUSNESS

Level One	Level Two	Level Three
Building Wings	Crystal Lotus Heart	Hieros Gamos
6D-7D	8D-9D	Christos HydroPlasmic Light
		10D-11D-12D

"Three Levels of Sacred Marriage: Level One of Sacred Marriage is 'Building Wings'; Level Two of Sacred Marriage is the building of the blue 'Crystal Lotus Heart'; Level Three of Sacred Marriage is 'Hieros Gamos,' the hydroplasmic liquid light of the Risen and Embodied Christos Principle"
–Lisa Renee, Ascension Glossary; https://ascensionglossary.com/index.php/Hieros_Gamos

carbon-based beings to crystalline, this is what it is all about. This ascension cycle is about reclaiming the Christ and Mother Principle for the planet. Mother Earth's original star body is in Andromeda, and this ascension window is connecting us back to this, where the cores of the Milky Way and Andromeda are becoming one again. We are working with the beings that are holding the rest of ourselves.

I was feeling this energy in my early years and what it would take to help liberate humanity from the grips of mind control and dark technologies. I had nothing to go on except for myself, and of course, no one talked about ETs, ascension, Galactic History, etc. No one could look at me, nod, and say, "Yes, what you are sensing is correct." With competing timelines cast onto us through media and all the typical power structures, we find ourselves in a predicament from birth, making it hard to function in day-to-day life when we begin to awaken to it. Many remember persecution and hold death pictures from the dark cycles of history and all that it tried to wipe out. Here we are, up against forces that wish the same, but with so much repair work being done and an ascension window at the end of a 26,000-year cycle, our ability to overcome this is greater now. Not everyone is up to the task. Our choices come from gaining enough awareness and wisdom when facing adversity and even great blessings to see the timeline into higher Earth energies. Many might lose themselves sinking into more confusion, destructive behaviors or attachments that may feel good but only temporarily. Do we need to know all of this to be awake and safe? No, but being aware of a hidden history kept from us can serve as protection and help us to be more mindful, discerning and conscious in our everyday lives.

Our history includes the period known as the Angelic Wars when the Time Matrix was near destruction. These correspond to what some call negative ETs or fallen angelics. In response, the Master Christos Collective created the new Oraphim race. These fallen Elohim responded to this by creating their unique race, the Anunnaki, specifically to destroy the Guardian Angelic Oraphim lines and continue their agenda of exploitation and dominion of our Time Matrix by targeting the Mother energy. I surmise this might have been the beginning of the emergence of the demiurge. They manifested as the archons and all the menacing forces that try to prevent humans from connecting with God Source. From what I understand, the Anunnaki also commissioned the Reptilians.

They traded in their 12-strand DNA potential, which damaged Stargate 12, and all life forms, including the Founder races, became trapped in the Time Matrix. DNA connects to stargates, and it also connects to the zodiac and our chakra system. Our ability to remember who we are will allow us to go through these stargates once again. But, of course, they don't want that, so their programming focuses on belief systems and keeping us digressed, as revealed by Keylontic Science. And though the Anunnaki connect to archons, not all are this way. The fallen aspects expressed as service-to-self attempt to block us from our connection to the Mother. So when they say "Sophia intervened," they may have meant the creation of the Oraphim, and this is the backlash and the jealousy of these fallen beings to destroy our connection to her and our divine potential. Archons seem to be the by-product of the splitting of the Male/Female and all the archetypal dramas that resulted, who were unable to create complete souls in alignment with God Source, which is why these forces easily invade us.

I believe this is the beginning of when Sophia expanded beyond the Pleroma (galactic core) in response to the near destruction of the Time Matrix, and why she later became an archetypal energy that split into many aspects that work to prevent the dark factions of the Anunnaki from completely taking over.

The Oraphim are a part of the Emerald Order and represent our full DNA potential that links us with the Founder Flames—the Divine Trinity. If you feel inspired, I recommend you take some time to look into this more since our dormant potential links to it and our ability to awaken it will set us free!

MALDEK

"During their long history, the inhabitants of Mars and Maldek fought a series of high-tech wars back when Mars was a moon of Maldek.

*Approximately 500,000 years ago, these wars came to a climactic
end with Maldek being obliterated.*

*Maldek's remains hit Mars with such force that the latter's surface
cities on one side of the planet were totally destroyed, and most of its
atmosphere was lost. This made life on Mars' surface very precarious at
best, and led to planetary evacuation by the Martian survivors."*

– A prominent SSP whistleblower

The warring energy influenced the masculine beyond its former protective role, which Maldek held before it got infiltrated. It was so protective that it covered the feminine Earth energy prevalent during the root races of Atlantis and Lemuria. Root races on Earth differ from the Alanian and Lumian ones I mentioned on Tara. However, the Anunnaki influenced it into a more patriarchal system that became incredibly destructive with the Draconian energies so heavily involved, eventually destroying Atlantis and Lemuria.

The explosion of the planet Maldek rippled throughout the entire solar system. Although it did not sink the major part of the Atlantean continent, it significantly impacted the land. It was only before this catastrophe that colonizers from Mars and Maldek came to planet Earth to eventually begin what was to become the Atlantean empire.

Artificial and Organic Timelines

"Mass biological and mind control devices exist well beyond the technology of implanting tiny physical 'chips' into humans, which accompanied many of the abductions by the Greys and non-benevolent Zetas; and also are an impending application of such electronic devices by the One World Government to the population. Even brain signatures radiated by government HAARP and GWEN towers are relatively superficial compared with ancient existing global grid systems, which can be used for manipulating the evolution of all life on the planet, including the plan ETs evolution itself."

– Noel Huntley, Ph.D., Global Grid Systems and Mass Mind Control, January 2006

The positive timeline is Organic Ascension and includes natural stargates opening, expansion and upgrades of our DNA. I have learned that the upgrades are achievable when we recognize the imposters we need to divorce ourselves from and begin to embrace the true love story within us. This ascension window period allows us to get fully anchored on this path to avoid future repercussions from being immersed in the artificial matrix.

The artificial matrix is to siphon and harvest energy. This is accomplished by putting things into reversals and keeping humanity in constant fear and dependency, taking advantage of our amnesia. This level of imbalance contributes to digression. The Organic Ascension is based on the Universal Tree of Life template and the original architecture of the planet was Diamond Sun with a Krystal body anatomy. No matter what overlays exist, this is what the original planet held, and so do we, underneath it all. The original grid is based in sacred union—

a unified and integrated masculine/feminine—and the five elements, including the Krystal Star. The corrections are allowing what has been in stasis to rise again out of its fallen state and begin to dismantle the alien machinery. It is what doing the "inner work" is all about—clearing, purifying and transforming.

The artificial and the organic coexist and it is up to us to discern the difference as timeline wars are being played out. The radical transformation of thoughts and beliefs is The Great Awakening. Once we grasp how deep the manipulation goes, we will develop more discernment and unplug from the inversions to find the direct connection that will guide us through the initiations that the planetary aspects reveal are weaponized through psyops and spiritual warfare.

Negative ETs have been propagating the catastrophic timeline and manipulating the human world of affairs for their purposes for thousands of years, ever since the Atlantean Cataclysm. They compromised their DNA purposely and manipulated ours. Black operation whistleblower testimonies reveal that the secret government elite has used the "Looking Glass" technology and time travel for many years to change and rewrite history so that it follows their desired paths and reaches their desired outcomes. Many visiting races have warned us about the implications of using those technologies.

The artificial 10-sphere Draconian Tree of Life template, actually a Tree of Death[6], is used in dark rituals to target children even before birth. This template overlays onto the organic planetary grid network. Laura Worley is a survivor of this Tree of Death overlay who experienced complex trauma and ritual abuse. She has written about it extensively, producing so much material on ways we can work to defeat those who abuse people through mind control and slavery. She is the author of "Puzzle Pieces to The Cabal, Mind Control and Slavery Part 1" and "Puzzle Pieces Together Manual, A Pathway To Freedom Part 2." Laura and I have made a beautiful connection. I highly recommend her books.

Expanding on the dark mother, it is an alien mother or false parent that forms itself into a complex field called the Black Madonna Network—a misogynistic field of a mind-controlled collective consciousness used as an AI grid network on this planet to feed the Black Magic fields on this Earth. True liberation involves not getting locked into an engineered trajectory imposed on us. If we don't see things for what they are, we get tricked into believing it is our only reality. One can call them artificial timelines or negative ego constructs established from limited creative potential due to mind control and an unhealed, disconnected human existence.

Without balance and wholeness, we feed a phantom world. Facing this dark cloud or shadow, personally or for humanity, removes us from being harvested and used by dark forces, entities and their agendas. The human race faces the challenge of seeing clearly while simultaneously learning to be co-creators again. Traps are everywhere. The things that sink our progression seem to lurk around every corner and get exacerbated by GMOs, AI, EMF signals, fake news and propaganda, toxicity, and all the impurities in our air, food and water. The list goes on and on.

Media plays a big part in spinning disinformation and targeting humanity in a mass mind control operation. It is a directed psychological and emotional operation used against the public. It intends to incite people into violence and influence their thoughts and is used to derail important facts and cover up the news we need to hear to distract us and hook us in. Aug Tellez, a whistleblower operative, talks about people being merged in this way and also about a super-computer system that sends waves of desires out at just the right moment to influence the masses in coordination with the media, scalar and weather events, and natural biological cycles. AI has mapped out an entire system designed to ensure humanity does not become aware of its true power.

We all see it so clearly—when humanity is about to take a massive leap in consciousness, another false flag acts like a virus and throws the masses back into grief, anger, fear and anxiety. It's a tried, tested and effective tactic. AI systems are weaponized, specializing in emotional and spiritual harassment. As I have researched, in that sense, these energies must lower to the level a machine can entrain, follow, mimic, match, record, modify and replicate that specific energetic blueprint. We aren't as impacted when our consciousness is above this and not in the programming.

Some say everything is fake, deception, and a simulation, but I beg to differ. The artificial matrix is a construct based on imitating the organic world. The organic is attainable through being authentic, internally free, and connected to the natural world to discover that we are beyond any advanced technology. Thus, our DNA can upgrade to reveal this. The other version is wrapped up in losing ourselves further and further to the outside memes and propaganda that go against our true nature, to simulate and imitate things in a distorted way that we may be unconscious of and mistaking the result for reality.

I'll conclude by mentioning one of my soul sisters and greatest inspirations, Cathy O'Brien. If you haven't already, I recommend you read her books, "TRANCE Formation of America" and "PTSD: Time to Heal." The extreme darkness this divine human was subjected to and overcame, and the immensity of the light, love and truth she carries forth in speaking publicly about her experiences, is a stark reminder of the power of the human spirit when connected to true God source, and how capable our soul is in repairing our DNA.

THE DARK FORCES

"This fall of Lucifer was counterbalanced by the descent of the Archangelic being of Anthroposophia whose task it was to sacrifice

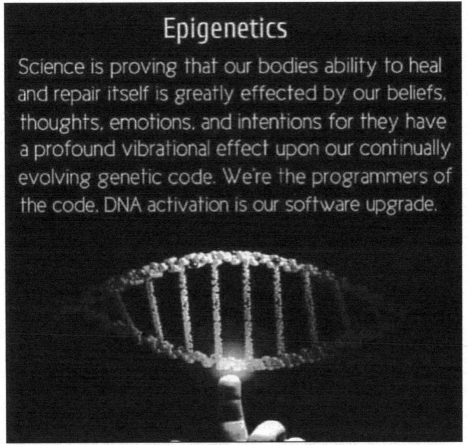

Epigenetics

Science is proving that our bodies ability to heal and repair itself is greatly effected by our beliefs, thoughts, emotions, and intentions for they have a profound vibrational effect upon our continually evolving genetic code. We're the programmers of the code. DNA activation is our software upgrade.

"*Epigenetics involves genetic control by factors other than an individual's DNA sequence. Epigenetic changes can switch genes on or off and determine which proteins are transcribed.*" –Nature Journal, Epigenetic Influences and Disease, 2008; https://www.nature.com/scitable/topicpage/epigenetic-influences-and-disease-895/

her connection to the divine Sophia. This means that she sacrificed her consciousness of the divine Sophia in those higher realms in which she resides, in order to accompany humanity in its development and inspire its progress. The Gnostics called the estrangement of the being of Anthroposophia from the divine Sophia a death. Lucifer was known in the mysteries to have killed the Sophia.

Lucifer took part of this Holy Spirit 'light' into himself and cut it off from the Sea of Cosmic Spirit Light. He became an antagonist to the light of the Holy Spirit."

– Rudolph Steiner

S ome myths say that she created the archons, the demiurge, and the physical world and that she was also brought back into the Pleroma after she fell, wherein a rescue mission was put in place, and she became the Earth as we know it. She intervened by seeding us with her divine spark, providing us the potential to ascend.

Many texts have been altered, so I share this perspective in the hope that it may add clarity to your empowerment. Providing the depth of explanations many of these subjects warrant while making my desired point would not be the best use of this book. I find adequate the sources I draw from which you can reference yourself. My goal is to explain how we can reconcile these forces within ourselves and feel inspired to do the deep soul work, not to be enslaved or addicted to the matrix or vulnerable to the many dark agendas.

People naturally gravitate to belief systems that help explain our origins, and they can often be a source of conflict and contention if not seen the same way or if an open mind to consider other possibilities isn't appreciated. I am inclined to share Rudolph Steiner because his insights help explain Sophia's death, reflected in Achamoth and her need to come in and reclaim the parts of her being used and harnessed by dark forces.

"It was during the old Moon stage of World development that the Holy Spirit implanted wisdom into the World 'light.' At this time the Angels were going through their human stage and the astral body of the human being was being implanted into the physical and Etheric sheaths by higher beings. Lucifer had reached the highest position in the rank of angels but he chose at this time to stay behind. That is to say, Lucifer who had by the end of Moon evolution reached the stage of beginning to work on his Spirit Self, turned his back on the Holy Spirit and was only desirous to know his own light."

– Rudolf Steiner

No matter the creation mythologies or stories one encounters about Earth and the beings involved, it is clear that we are being called to turn inward to heal, repair, and regain wholeness and balance to overcome all dark, manipulative forces for good.

Lucifer has been associated with the first group of fallen angels called the Seraphim, who split off from the Holy Spirit, allowing in aggressive and warlike beings that slowly eroded the higher dimensional energies, and this event is referred to as the "Lucifer Rebellion." I see it as akin to what we experience ourselves.

Originating during the Lyran Wars, spreading to the Orion Wars, and eventually to Earth after the collapse of 5D Tara and Tiamat, the Lucifer Rebellion continued on Earth until about 26,000-30,000 years ago when the planetary stargates, grids and ley lines came under the control of negative alien groups. There is a vast

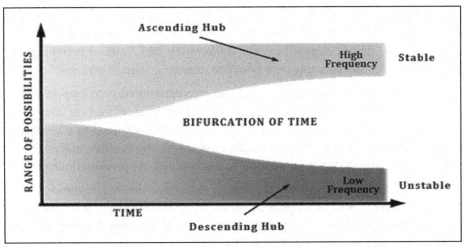

"*During the Bifurcation of Time our inner energetic integrity is being tested. This is the time to take stock of how well we are coping with the madness of the earth, as the collective mind of humanity travels the Dark Night of the Soul.*" –Lisa Renee, Ascension Glossary; https://ascensionglossary.com/index.php/Bifurcation_of_Time

history concerning this, including alliances with other forces against the Emerald Order, including the connection with Marduk and Nibiru and the Anunnaki races that promoted anti-Christ agendas to become known as "Luciferians." There remains a lack of consensus on whether today's Luciferians still recognize this chronology of their origins. However, I have come across self-proclaimed Luciferians who have been in Illuminati families or subjected to dark rituals that state Anunnaki Illuminati humans are a part of this agenda and worship Lucifer.

The path of Christ-Sophia creates unity through death, resurrection and sacred union to redeem the Lucifer and dark force energy within us through our strength in overcoming the power of the negative ego and all the programming that seeks to addict us to our lower chakras. Venus is bringing our planet back into alignment with the galactic plane. The dark and light integration for us is the womb of the Mother, and the light is the higher consciousness that plants seeds in the womb.

According to Lisa Renee:

> "*The Luciferian collective consciousness was once the light bearer, and became distorted as he became trapped in the earth (matter) and bound to time. Hence, the Luciferian light became dead light trapped in matter and digressed into the False Father principle.*"

Ashayana Deane's Keylontic Dictionary provides additional perspective:

> "*Humans and other hybrid races that serve as Fallen Angelic puppets and are being manipulated by fear for personal survival and a desire for the acquisition of power to prevent pain and create personal pleasure. Covertly meta-*

physically motivated towards the One World Order (OWO) Fallen Angelics' Master Plan. Fear, the Pleasure-Pain Principle and Disinformation are the common control elements by which Illuminati and Humans become easily misled into surrendering their power to something outside of themselves."

This dense physical world is caught in a manufactured time loop in which "time" is a circle that constantly repeats itself. We need to break the time circle and, thus, the prison. Unfortunately, the Reptilians are doing everything to prevent this through agendas that include the microchipping of humans, the chemtrailing of our skies, and the use of GMOs in our food, all to keep us stuck in a perpetual loop of time.

Alex Hroz describes how the ruling elite have devised chemtrails as a means of covertly microchipping us all to create antennas inside of us using nanotechnology to make us controllable via a "psycho-civilized" (electronically mind-controlled) society. For example, the National Security Agency (NSA) can establish a direct computer link to our brains using HAARP microwave antennas. But first, they're using chemtrails to get the nanoparticles into us, which are then reassembled in our bodies to form the antennas.

All the weather manipulation has a massive drain on the planet's inner sun, which directly powers it. When our inner sun suffers, so do we. This central sun, if liberated, is the key to the regeneration of the planet and all life on it. It is the source of our prana, or life force, which it gets directly from an even greater sun and steps down in a safe measure to distribute planet-wide.

Ever since, they have continued to control events as part of a long-planned agenda for the complete centralized control of the planet through a world government, central bank, currency, army and a micro-chipped population connected to a global computer. And now, this governmental structure is staring us in the face, blaming others and tricking us into thinking someone else is responsible.[4]

I found it interesting to see what the "Hidden Hand," a self-proclaimed Illuminati insider, had to say. Remember, only take what resonates and leave the rest.

"In your hypnotized state, you have as a society given your free will consent to the state your planet is in today. You saturate your minds with the unhealthy dishes served up for you on your televisions that you are addicted to; violence, pornography, greed, hatred, selfishness, incessant bad news, fear and 'terror.' When was the last time you stopped to think of something beautiful and pure? The planet is the way it is because of your collective thoughts about it.

You are complicit in your inaction every time you look the other way when you see an injustice. Your thought, projected at the sub-conscious level of creation to the Infinite Creator, is your allowance of these things to occur. In so doing, you are serving our purpose."

– Hidden Hand, Alleged Ruling Bloodline Priest

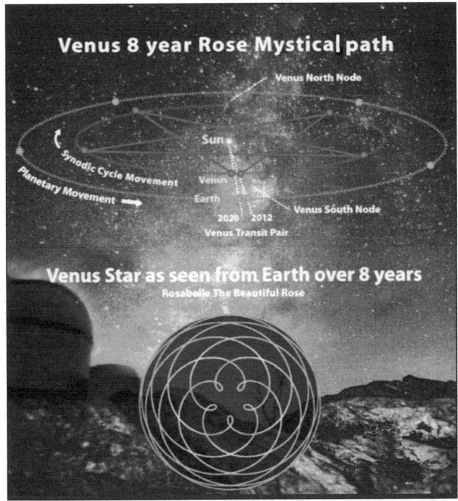

Venus Transit. "We find today's world is a result of repressed divine feminine energy. The Great Central Sun has been infusing the planet with high vibrational energy, especially since 2012, to raise the frequencies on the planet to aid evolution, and Venus as well. Every eight years Venus dances with the Earth around the sun forming a perfect geometric pattern that portrays a five-petalled rose. The pattern is made up of five Venus cycles which take approximately eighteen months each. The designs of the rose (heart) reveals Venus' role as celestial guardian of love and beauty. The cycles between 2004-2012 have particularly infused Divine Feminine energy onto the planet from this pattern." –Nancy Robbins, Elements Design Collection

It would seem that bio-weapons, contamination of our food, attacks on farmers, GMOs and more, our thinking would arise from a "dumbed-down" level, so these things need to be noticed and called out. The days of sitting back and consenting, allowing this by being silent or unconsciously consuming all of this, can no longer continue.

To paraphrase Alex Collier (1997), our government, the United States government and the New World Order want to implant everybody. He shares that from the Andromedan perspective, this means ownership and enslavement through mind control and altering DNA. Extraterrestrials value genetics. They come in, conquer a race, and genetically modify it with bio-neurological technology. From that moment on, that race is genetically altered, and the changes alter the race's frequency, sound and thought patterns if they move into a physical form and it gets inherited through the bloodlines into the future offspring.

It doesn't feel like a negative polarity here to wake us up when they go after our children and their innocence using indoctrination tactics, pushing junk food, gender confusion, extreme sex education, and dark weaponry, which no one has consented to. It goes beyond consent. Humanity must pay attention and speak out to remove their power over us. We must choose what we allow into our bodies, minds and consciousness and, because we are stronger than this dark technology, our purpose is to override it and move beyond the inversions and distortions to not stand for it. I have found it difficult to believe that in other material the Hidden Hand shares, any of this is for our good, that all this darkness is necessary and that these forces are, in fact, our friends. But I agree with much of it, too, that humans consume so much toxicity that they can make healthier choices at any point. However, with all the censorship and difficulty finding such resources, I feel the darkness and their agendas have gone too far. But that is just me.

OUR OWN PERSONAL SUN

Humans can receive the most nutrient-rich energy from our very own sun—the light of Spirit that radiates from within and connects to the core sun within the Earth and the Grand Central Sun of the cosmos. This sun generates warmth, vitamins, balance, peace and vitality, and when one is conscious of its energy, it draws back any of its life force that has been siphoned away and used against us. This depletion happens when we are in disunity or negativity, which manifests when we are not treating ourselves or one another with kindness and respect or when we don't stand our ground against vampiric forces. The only spiritual discipline necessary is paying attention to this. DNA damage challenges this connection, but we must tell ourselves that we will take this challenge on, knowing we can heal as Spirit holds dominion over matter.

The same laws apply to our bodies as to the planet. We must resolve imbalances to protect ourselves. Forming healthy relationships and focusing on our inner masculine/feminine balance is essential to saying goodbye to false archetypes.

We must increase the love vibration on the planet and regain our power. The greatest threat to any service-to-self being is our unification, free minds, and connection to our higher self. We can start to embrace our choices and

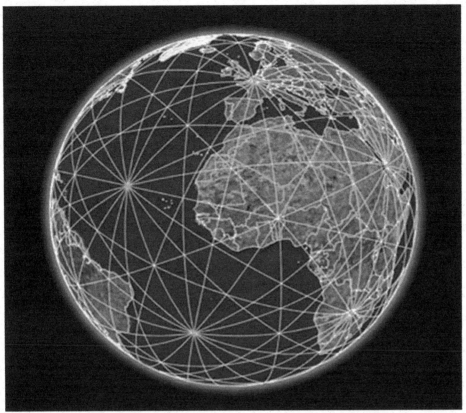

Planetary Gridwork. "The planetary grid network is a living consciousness matrix that is encoded with the blueprint or original instruction set for the divine plan of humanities spiritual evolution. Much of our mission as Starseeds is to extract the alien machinery and fallen entities which obstruct, siphon or damage the energies in the planetary grid system." –Lisa Renee, Ascension Glossary; https://ascensionglossary.com/index.php/Planetary_Gridworker

free will to restore this Earth to the paradise intended and restore our hearts in service to others, self-knowledge, balance and ending all secrecy to support truth in this world.

Lisa Renee describes this in the following way:

"The levels of frequency that a human can hold and access are governed by the information stored (DNA) in the personal and unified morphogenetic fields. Humans now have access to the morphogenetic fields embodying the blueprint of the divine plan of the Mother Earth, her hidden history and human lineage and the process of ascending a species and planetary body. This will allow more and more people to become activated and then interested in understanding this information relating to their transformation or personal ascension."

NOT JUNK DNA

The grid is best described and understood with the Platonic solids—octahedron (Air), tetrahedron (Fire), icosahedrons (Water), hexahedron (Earth), and the dodecahedron (Time and Space), which complete the global grid. The husband and wife team Becker and Hagens put this information together. The controllers had implemented many reversal grids and dodecahedron base code reversals to distort the planet's morphogenetic field, impacting our DNA. This is what creates frequency fences and the NET.

In DNA, nucleic acids make up the nitrogenous base: Cytosine (C), Guanine (G), Adenine (A) and Thymine (T). Metaphysically, each of these nucleic acids connects to the elemental substance of the planet—Air, Water, Fire, and Earth. Therefore, when we pollute these four elements on the Earth, we pollute the corresponding nucleic acid in our DNA.

The fourth Platonic Solid is a 5-sided pentagon with twelve (12) faces and represents the element of time and space substance that builds matrices. It is related to the intersection paths of Earth and Venus, which Johannes Kepler first documented. The disrupted inversion of the pentagram is symbolic of this, and this energy circulation with the Aether is being corrected in this window period.

In DNA and RNA, the mitochondrial DNA is the 5th principal element of cosmic Aether, sourced only from the Mother. With the Mother energy not present on Earth, but in reversal form, this is recorded in the cells of our mitochondrial DNA—humans have no idea how damaged this is in humanity at large. Without well-functioning mitochondrial DNA, making new proteins for DNA synthesis is harder. Thus, through mitochondrial DNA damage, society is grossly addicted to consuming everything in the external world to fill this energy void within our cells. When damaged, it is also difficult to store the levels of ATP required to generate the light from the cell to embody our spiritual consciousness, which is a function of the Aether element, the quintessence breath of life. Thankfully, this is all healing since the Aether is now available, allowing us to purify our DNA and lift the frequency fences and all that is blocking us from accessing our dormant strands of DNA.

The NAA and many of the Illuminati lines have misused the Platonic Solids. Specifically, distorted dodecahedron shapes are a part of the reversal matrix service-to-self entities use. When we activate the alchemy, we heal our DNA, integrate the 5th element and correct reversals. It comes about through polarity integration[7] and sacred union, which heals the grids as the activations coming through this current Stellar Activation Cycle heal us—a beautiful co-creation and relationship. Also, the 13th sign, Ophiuchus, is aligned with cosmic Aether, which is at the core of the galactic center and represents the pouring of healing spiritual waters upon the Earth from Mother God as of 2010—a major timeline

Chemtrails bioweapon. Alex Hroz describes how the ruling elite have devised chemtrails as a means of covertly microchipping us all to create antennas inside of us via nanotechnology to make us controllable via a "psycho-civilized" (electronically mind-controlled) society.

shift. From some of my research, this is the date I have found makes the most sense since this is when the return of the Mother energy was in full force, with the Venus transits forming a perfect pentagram representing this loving return of the divine feminine, and with the 5th element of that star being Aether.

Transfiguration corresponds to the element of solar Fire, which burns away the shadow forms in the lower chakra centers, and this is the process of alchemical change that helps us to detox and neutralize harmful weapons. The lower shadow forms of the lunar (Moon) forces connected to the dark mother start to rise in our body to be consumed in the transfiguring solar fire. The abuses, exile and victim energy are a part of that shadow and the imbalances and distortions we are born into with its rewritten history and false authority structures and how that impacts us. Planetary and human DNA activate by communicating with the intelligent plasma emitted from the sun through solar flares and coronal mass ejections (CMEs).

These last several paragraphs are inspired by my research, dot-connecting, and portions of Lisa Renee's material on DNA, transfiguration, reversals, mitochondria and the 13th sign. She is a profound resource!

Part of a Russian team that includes Dr. Garijajev found that airwaves could facilitate total genetic restructuring. David Icke believes we take the Saturnian or Satan frequency, coded with messages, into this 98 percent of our DNA. According to David, the rings of Saturn are *a massive broadcast system, broadcasting a fake reality.*"

DNA holds all the information we need to build and maintain the human body. Researchers at Boston University and Harvard Medical School studied the 98 percent of our DNA that cannot be decoded and, thus, call it "junk." How this relates to the Saturn-Moon matrix is that part of the artificial component of the Moon was supposedly brought in after the planets exploded, revealing how much we operate under distortions that we must rise above. It also shows the imbalance of the masculine and feminine being broadcast to us. We overcome this by connecting with the higher octave of lunar forces and gaining self-mastery over the lower Saturn.

Our dormant DNA is a treasure, not junk. So many of us have been on missions to activate our dormant DNA by moving through all the layers that keep us from the true essence of our divine power. So many benevolent forces, including embodied humans, have been working thousands of years to this end to maintain the integrity of the Organic Ascension timeline in the face of the most unrelenting opposition forces and bring about human sovereignty on planet Earth.

When I say sovereign, I mean not operating under anyone's control. If we consent to control or a belief system, it is because it remains a part of our journey to work out what it means for us. Does it serve us for a time? Eventually, wouldn't it be wonderful to live based on cosmic and natural law and our divine authority to manage our lives, thinking processes, creativity and self-healing abilities? The willingness to venture into these ascension energies and release what doesn't serve us and our capacity to be devoted and consistent is all that is required. One must claim this to set their internal GPS in the right direction so the inner voice and higher guidance can navigate the rest of the way. We must strengthen our ability to listen "inwardly" and switch off what is constantly trying to infect our creative imagination with lower frequencies and distortions delivered via dark technology. When the programs that attempt to control how we function get broken and dissolved, dark technology will be disabled once and for all. It is the challenge of our times.

These concepts shouldn't be brushed off as some "New Age psychobabble" or fluffy idealism. We must recognize the larger picture we are all part of. Some terminologies may feel repelling or not defined in ways you know them to be. Realize that even our words have been hijacked. A term initially sacred and meaningful can instead become a trigger because of an inverted use, mistreatment or false representation. I only seek to get to the truth, even if it is disturbing or something I prefer not to look at. It should be shared in a respectful and catalyzing way so we can break the connection to lower imposter forces. The greater truth is that what is disturbing does not need to continue endlessly. We don't have to keep looping in negative patterns!

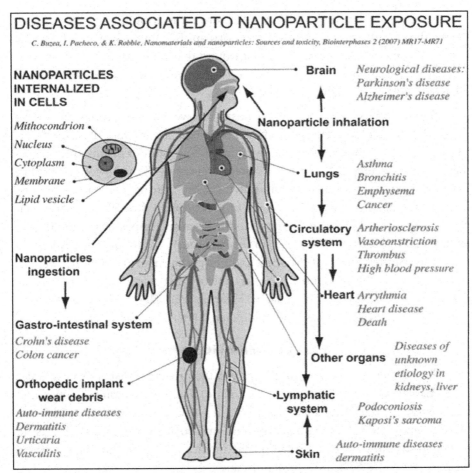

Diseases associated with nanoparticle exposure. –C. Buzea, I. Pacheco, & K. Robbie, *Nanomaterials and nanoparticles: Sources and toxicity*, 2007; https://link.springer.com/article/10.1116/1.2815690?

It is up to us to break our relationships with these lower forces. And when the architecture of the planetary logos controls every aspect of the planet, from the physical elemental substances to the emotional and mental, life force becomes distributed. The 7D Violet Ray and 7D Gaia connect with the planetary logos, intentionally distorted to contaminate our seven chakras and cut us off from our true Source. Access to the 7th-dimensional chakra wave spectrum has only been possible for some since the NAA invasion and implementation of the false ascension matrix. Once the human being fully integrates and spiritually embodies their soul matrix, the initiation with the Violet Ray can commence.

The 7th-dimensional lightbody is the Monad matrix's first layer, the second spiritual triad of 7D, 8D and 9D layers. The upside-down pentagram represents entrapment in physical matter and going into the underworld labyrinth, and the

Venus transits correct this. We have been turning it upright for some time, allowing the energy circulation to activate dormant DNA and Galactic Chakras. It is soul alchemy. We are born into a vast wound that we must heal. It's helpful to realize that the storylines we live out are merely there to help us wake up and heal ourselves, both personally and beyond.

Some schools of thought have led us to believe that we cannot activate dormant DNA beyond a certain point if the DNA is damaged. DNA upgrading activates higher consciousness—it is a love story. Many world religions and governments work to manipulate our belief systems, on top of all the obvious things like what has happened to our food and water, geoengineering, and so much more. Recognizing our DNA has been altered or messed with through the many cataclysms, negative technologies, genetic modification and implants, not to mention endless wars—Electrical Wars, Lemurian Holocaust, Nephilim Wars, Atlantean Cataclysm, Sumerian-Egypt Invasion, and more—has many fearing that we may not be able to do this on our own. We certainly will get help, but we must become sovereign so we can't be fooled again. Have no fear! Humans will continue to evolve to reassemble damaged and manipulated DNA, slow and steady.

EPIGENETICS

Epigenetics helps one to understand the processes that activate and deactivate genes (i.e., nature vs. nurture). Humans run on frequency, and our thoughts and feelings affect our DNA. In a world that constantly bombards us with news, indoctrinated belief systems and societal programming, it is no wonder a dependency has formed on the medical industries and power structures. How can we be healthy if we don't align with our truth frequency?

Victory exists in the micro-world and our everyday lives, starting with the quality of our relationship with ourselves and how we perceive reality. Recognizing our soul and higher awareness and what it is trying to show us in every fractal moment helps us make more sense of what we experience and whom we meet. Nature repairs because it is encoded in us to know how to heal, regenerate and find an equilibrium. We need to release ourselves from the disrupting interferences and distractions so we can operate from a place of complete sovereignty to explore how our perceptions can shift how we experience reality. Being willing and open to this is what magic and miracles are made of!

Cathy O'Brien, whom I introduced previously, was in the MK-Ultra Monarch program and experienced horrific sexual abuse from a very young age into her adult years. Through the power of "nurture," she changed her multi-generational genetic programs and self-healed all that she endured with the help of the love of her life, Mark Phillips. Her physiology changed, and she embodies pure love and awe-inspiring inner freedom. She shares a message that if she can do

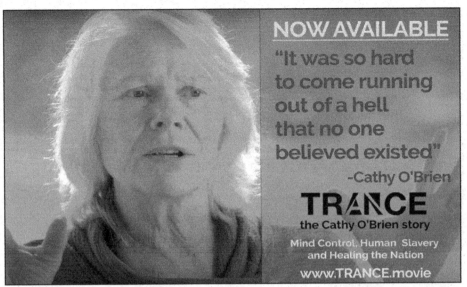

Cathy O'Brien, author. Cathy's book, "TRANCE Formation of America," is the first documented autobiography of a victim of government mind control. Cathy O'Brien is a healed and vocal survivor of the Central Intelligence Agency's MK-Ultra Project Monarch operation. Her book "PTSD: Time To Heal" reveals step-by-step healing methods intelligence insider Mark Phillips taught Cathy that can help anyone willing to reclaim control over their own mind and life just as she did. Internalize the knowledge in "PTSD: Time to Heal," and realize peace of mind through truth that makes us free!

it, anyone can! She is a living example that our soul can overcome all triggers, blocks and programming to heal genetic damage, mind control and traumatic abuse. Cathy is a powerful example of how epigenetics works.

University studies found the perfect example of how epigenetics works: identical twins. Although they share the same DNA, their unique experiences in life will cause some genes (and not others) to express themselves. This is why, over time, identical twins come to look and behave differently.

If we are willing to shift our belief systems and understand ancestral patterns, the things we may have inherited, the root cause, and where they may have originated, we can begin to change the patterning. This same applies to all we are exposed to that can cause our DNA damage, and belief systems are such a huge part of it. Consider that Neptune/Pisces, ruled by water, is opposite the 6th house Virgo, ruled by Earth and Mercury—Neptune connecting to our creative imagination and Virgo to our mental health, physiology, physicality and lifestyle. When we integrate those polarities and work on adjusting our perceptions to understand more about what is operating in our unconscious, which Pisces/Neptune represents, we can change the physiology and the physical vessel, which is what upgrading is all about. The hidden levels hold the key in many ways to

PUZZLE PIECES
TOGETHER
Manual ✦ A Pathway To Freedom

Laura Worley   Part 2

Laura Worley, author of "Puzzle Pieces" books one and two. Laura Worley is a speaker, trainer, coach and author. She has successfully helped thousands of people worldwide address issues stemming from complex trauma and ritual abuse. Laura's goal is to train an army of professionals and survivors on how to use powerful techniques that lead to freedom.

unlocking dormant DNA. Using technologies based on sound and frequency can greatly assist the process and deep dive into our hidden aspects, illuminating the many dimensions and levels of consciousness we can reach and then ground.

Imagine if the doctor were to diagnose a condition using empowering terminology connected to healing and solutions, understanding our innate capacity to heal, regenerate and transform. The labels we carry have a frequency to them, and when we overly identify with and ground them by saying things like "I have" disease or illness, it keeps us attached to it and its potential outcome. The initiatory energies throw us into crisis sometimes and are a part of understanding ourselves better. When it's leveraged in a way that renders us dependent, it can often keep a person stuck. Often, our anger and depression alert us to reveal something we need to look at instead of live with. When we set it free or answer to the passion and soul-longing it holds, we can direct these energies in much more conscious ways and build confidence around our capacity to create significant change for the better. Our body will then thrive!

This quote has always stuck with me:

"It is no measure of health to be well-adjusted to a sick society."

– *Jiddu Krishnamurti*

HIEROPHANT ARCHETYPE

Inspired by the Mother Peace Tarot, the deck explains that the authority of the Hierophant is based, in large part, on the repression of women and the use of one's intuition. From Tiamat to Lilith to Magdalene, Persephone and Pandora, from serpent-sea monster to demon to wicked witch, the woman became the villain and personification of evil. The projection upon using tarot and astrology as being "of the devil" is very much the energy of the Hierophant. The devil energy is yet another archetype to contend with and a potential that exists within every one of our psyches.

The Hierophant is too blind to recognize the chains it wishes to cast upon others, especially the feminine. And all these archetypes communicate with one another unconsciously, just like the organs of our bodies work together yet have different functions. These many parts make up who we indeed are. We can't just choose one and deny the rest. Every archetype and planetary sign has a shadow side and a higher expression. The more we see the impacts of the shadow side, the more we can find the highest expression of the archetypal energy and work with it to our benefit. We all have some relationship to it throughout our lives. It is one archetype in its shadow expression on Earth for some time now that can only be resolved within.

In the case of the Hierophant, it isn't just about repression. It also represents responsibilities and structure like Saturn. Rules and limits that we can and must question so we can invite in the energetics that re-wire the way we relate to outer authority to become more spiritually disciplined and take care of our most sacred vessel—our physical body. We can use limits and responsibilities to stay grounded and choose rules or orders we place upon ourselves to thrive instead of allowing an outer authority to repress and tell us what we should do and how we should think or behave. At certain stages in life, an external authority makes sense. Still, we must be keen to examine at what point our conditioned need for intercessors works against us to wound more than help.

People are confused about who God is or even the devil and whom to cast those words upon. Indeed, not everyone will agree, so we are best served to reconcile this from within since these opposing forces exist within each of us. The devil is about denying Spirit, whether trying to control or enslave another individual or acting in ways that go against personal integrity, so it desecrates and contaminates all that is sacred. And it's good to note there are differences between Satan and the devil. Add to that the demiurge, and if that is a part of Sophia's creation, it can only be the igniting of her divine spark that can free us from this material realm, but only if we wish to venture down that path.

I feel demiurge veils Sophia and is jealous and dominating. The devil is a force representing power and control. The question is, how do we relate to that arche-type? To me, Satan is the inversion of the feminine, the reversal mother, who uses her energies to manifest great wealth and power in the world. It is seen in Satanic Ritual Abuse (SRA) and is linked to bloodlines that hold immense wealth, power and control that pull strings and create mass suffering from behind the scenes. The section on Achamoth explains a bit about how this energy was harnessed.

Our connection to Father/Mother Source is unique, sacred and personal. No one has the right to infringe, project or attempt to control our own experience of it unless it acts as a source of inspiration. It is ours to discover, embrace and awaken to. Our connection to our Father/Mother within will guide and teach us and reveal the Christ-Sophia blueprint. The Mother awakens the Holy Father. The end of the rule of the controller or tyrant is something we must choose internally, and this sets us free to experience deep healing. Our sole responsibility is to accept the challenge of overcoming the obstacles of distortion and the frequency of deception. Living truth is the great redeemer and our armor of light. The sword that cuts through unleashes all that remains hidden. With the pain, much more is gained on a deep soul level.

Ultimately, when we balance the divine masculine and feminine energies within us, the integrated polarity can remove all archon influences and entity attachments to free us from the grips of any controller force wishing to subvert our full sovereignty and ability to live our truth.

ELECTROMAGNETIC SPECTRUM

Our DNA is linked directly with Earth's grids, which have electric and magnetic ley lines representing the masculine and feminine, just like our bodies. The Earth's magnetic field (feminine) is like the flow of our energy body's circulation. The electric (masculine) stimulates the nervous system. It has a soul and spirit spark interplay. The electromagnetic spectrum opens us to the entire field of available energy. The impact of dark technologies is significant and has significantly impacted us. Stargates on the planet connect with our chakra system to form the planetary chakra system. So it's important to remember that we are in a co-creative process, interconnected with nature and all the cosmos, and that we, too, are stargates capable of directing consciousness throughout Earth's circuitry and beyond! It is how we do repair work.

Ascension is the blossoming of human consciousness and the anchoring Mother energies back into the Earth's body. Our expansion into other dimensions through spiritual awakening and the turning on of dormant DNA connects us with hierogamic union, Earth grid repair, higher harmonic universes and a total shift in our physical bodies from carbon-based to crystalline. Ascension is our return to the Silicate Matrix. It is when our spiritual-energetic bodies connect with our physical bodies. The Silicate Matrix is the original human genetic imprint designed to manifest 12 DNA strands. Once repaired, built and activated, the fully embodied expression would allow humans to travel inter-dimensionally and exist without deteriorating the biological form.

The electromagnetic spectrum and potential of the original angelic human is a 12-strand DNA known as Diamond Sun DNA. Other potential DNA and higher consciousness were available that had been experienced by angelic human beings in previous time cycles on 5D parallel Earth before its cataclysm. These are the Oraphim original prototypes for angelic humans created by the Founders with a 24-strand DNA called Double Diamond Sun Body DNA and a 48-strand DNA Founder race line known as the Emerald Sun.

Return of the Mother

"The Melchizedeks are the genetic hosting race of the Earth's ascension cycle for the last 35,000 years. As of 2009/12, our planet went beyond this to prepare for the return of the 13th gate Pillar of Mother Arc. The return of the Goddess...

After the partial fall of the Milky Way system from its Mother Universe, subsequent distortions were created in the structural integrity of the Universal Time Matrix in which the organic creator codes became twisted, damaged and reversed.

The origination of the Fall of Humanity began when the organic structures that interconnected the Andromedan Time Matrix and the Milky Way Time Matrix in the Metagalactic Core were attacked by black hole entities, many of whom joined together later on to form the NAA."

– Lisa Renee, Ascension Glossary

With the spirit force of the Mother grounded back into the Earth's body, we can move into higher Earth energies that lift us out of the trappings of hidden dark agendas. This grounding returns through powerful soul initiations, planetary configurations like Venus transits, galactic core alignments and the 13th sign. We are at the end of a 26,000-year cycle that some call a cosmic reset. Our ability to access our true Source, beyond the lower creator gods, is what the end of this cycle is helping us to achieve more easily.

Our planet's very design helps bring us back to our original genetic imprint. Our DNA holds this in dormancy as it shares a troubled history that we are all trying to heal from and wake up to. The 13th sign, Ophiuchus, is ruled by the asteroid Chiron and is the only sign in the zodiac ruled by an asteroid. The 5th element, Aether, allows us to experience alchemy and a shift into higher Earth energies. This sign has an alchemical theme of unification and wound healing. Ophiuchus is also connected with the Serpent Holder and the healing of the fallen angelic energies and has been associated with Enki. This sign is about re-coding DNA and aligning with the galactic core and heart of the Mother. It is about cleansing the blood, breath and mitochondria.

We can use the time the Sun moves through this sign every year, from November 30th through December 17th, to remind us all that we have a tre-mendous opportunity to take this in. It doesn't mean you need to change your birth chart. From what I have discovered, it started to move through the 13th sign in 2010. If you look at the agendas being steered on the planet now, it seems to want to block us from this and divert our attention into fear and deny-ing the breath of life. I am not saying viruses aren't real but look at all the tactics used to separate us from one another and take away our free speech, making it appear as if it is all for our good. Do those pushing for Agenda 2030 actually care about Mother Earth, equality or ending poverty? I would question that and recognize their tactic of problem-reaction-solution. Crimes against hu-manity are far too ignored and the same goes for geoengineering. For anyone continuing to call these "conspiracy theories," it is an incredibly destructive form of denial when future generations need us now more than ever.

MILKY WAY AND ANDROMEDA

Since the Lyran Wars, we have existed in a fallen system, the Milky Way, in which our capacity to hold an Avatar Consciousness and full DNA strand capacity was compromised. Fallen angelics, along with hybridization, exploding planets and dark alliances of negative alien groups with their hybrids, represent the dark side of the human ego acting in disconnect from soul, spirit, wisdom, nature, cosmos and love. They exploit our solar plexus personal power for their benefit by infecting and addicting us to the matrix to create a dependency. Our Earth and planetary consciousness sustains and provides us with abundance. Our inability to connect with the great Mother force is the root of all our problems on Earth.

The ancient wars, Lemurian Holocaust, Atlantean and other cataclysms made it easy to gain control of stargates and Earth grids and put everything into reversal codes to create thousands of years of dark history. Thus, the Aqua Ray energy of the Mother could not stay anchored in the Earth's core. Thankfully, the Mother force has returned, and that is why this window period has garnered so much attention, especially in prophecies, and is also why the dark forces have ramped up their ef-forts to overtake and thrust us into an NWO, hoping our amnesia persists.

In this fallen system, our higher awareness—our light and wisdom—creates the alchemy for transformation as it mixes with the substance of our dark, creative cauldron like the soil of the Earth, generating new life from seed. We can fully bring this higher awareness into the physical plane and into our lifestyles that allow the redemption of these fallen aspects and help free all those trapped. It fosters profound healing and integration of our many fragmented aspects to bring about balance and harmony between our right and left brain hemispheres. Our DNA and chakra systems are a replica of Earth's grids and the multi-dimensional cosmos.

At this time, the Milky Way and Andromedan galactic cores are one with each other, and the energies are drastically different than they have been in the last 26,000 years. How incredible that our capacity to shift this now moment is like never before. But that won't be possible if we don't create the sacred space needed to integrate, expand, thrive, grow and rise to embody our greatest human potential. We as a human race need to win this war, not sit back waiting for the worst doom or gloom outcome or assume some savior is handling it. Our part is integral in influencing the outcome.

We are the power in the world and a tug-of-war between competing agendas. If we continue to engage in battles over competing movements, we will miss seeing the grand rise in consciousness and incredible potential as a human race. We won't make the adjustments most required. Competition must make way for cooperation. We must step away from the labels and be soul-centered humans with one another.

Stargates 8 and 9 exist in China and Southern England. Applying this to our energy body, we see that the related chakras form the figure "8" infinity spiral that connects our 8th and 9th chakras with our pineal gland at the center point of the intersection. It is an access point to the zero point unified field that upgrades and clears our energy centers and planets. Chakra 8 is located at the Thymus gland called the Permanent Seed Atom, linking in an infinity spiral to the 9th Chakra Atomic Doorway or "Mouth of God." This is the stage and level of Monadic integration and male and female balance.

When we begin to activate the dormant parts of ourselves, we find psychic attacks increase as it does for the collective, where psychological operations, false flags and traumatic outer events increase to destabilize our ability to switch dormant aspects on. That's why it's so important to focus on this shift from the inside out and never forget the true challenge we are being tasked with. Our dormant DNA is about synthesizing masculine and feminine energies, the electric and magnetic. Therefore, we must focus on unimpeded circulation to remove blockages and neutralize the alien technology manipulating Earth's grids and our biocircuitry and nervous systems through mind control.

Anti Particle Chakras Eight & Nine
Galactic Chakra Activation Begins

Morphogenetic Chakras begin to "Galactivate" identity to multiple awareness of Star Intelligences, other Identities and Lifetimes

Moving Halo is Gyroscopic with center axis in Pineal Gland

Morph Chakra 8 (Gold)
Thymus and Permanent Seed Atom of the Crystal Heart

Morph Chakra 9 (Silver)
Atomic Doorway "Mouth of God" Projector of Light Consciousness

Level 2 Male Female Balance

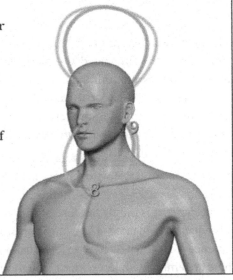

Monadic integration. "Many of us cannot manifest our divine purpose and destiny projects until this alignment and embodiment of our Oversoul or Monad transpires. Our divine and spiritual purpose is part and parcel of our divine consciousness and we cannot manifest purpose without our spirit intelligence embodied." –Lisa Renee, Ascension Glossary; https://ascensionglossary.com/index.php/Monadic_Integration

These activations are of the higher universal heart capable of shifting time-lines and disabling all that the frequency fences are trying to prevent. They stream into our body and increase the strength of our auric field. The frequency fence is an energy field that holds mind control and distortions. Ethereal implants have been placed in the base of the skull of most humans so we would be continually recycled back into the Seven Chakra System, with no actual ability to upgrade the three lower chakras out of 3D duality because the 7th chakra that connects us to spirit is being re-routed away from the rest of our multi-dimensional spiritual self. Thus, the 7th chakra gets chorded into saviors, false gurus and harmful spiritual belief systems.

We'll notice increased synchronicities and positive developments if we consciously focus on this. Remember, the outer world is a reflection of our over-all collective health. We are vulnerable to enslavement because we are not yet functioning in our true divine power and higher mind. Therefore, be relentless in consciously knocking down false walls and fences daily by refusing to engage in lower behavior patterns and not giving up your power. It's about us right now, more than politics or elections. The rest will undoubtedly fall into place. We will make the wisest choices if we prepare our human vessels and open our consciousness to The Great Awakening—remembering our true abilities and illuminating higher heart qualities to unify, purify and harmonize! The Earth responds to us, as does the collective!

The Andromedan Galaxy and its galactic core merged with the Milky Way galactic core is helping to lift this fallen system out of the clutches of the dark controllers, who infiltrated the planetary grid network and most power structures, as well as our minds, emotions, consciousness and human vessels. This merge has made it easier to activate our Galactic Chakras, switch on dormant DNA, and begin to comprehend a much larger terrain that we never learned about in school, such as the presence of extraterrestrial races.

It is like an infection—a gaping wound we were all born into, carrying different parts we are actively working to heal. We live out painful storylines to ultimately rise above the lower forces. In this free-will universe, if dark entities become able to invade us, it is purely because of disharmony between masculine/feminine and subsequent fallen angelic lines and parasitic forces that feed off imbalance—an experience we ultimately have to learn from. These times can be challenging because there are embedded deceptions throughout our cultures and society. However, nature is the great liberator and vessel for a return of the Mother energies.

From the Guardian perspective, Lisa Renee explains that we have ended a time cycle of the astrological age called the Precession of the Equinoxes that opened the Neutron Window in the galactic center, where Omniversal cores connect simultaneously to allow communication into other universes. This Neutron Window, or zero point, is what creates the 13th Stargate Portal (as 12 becomes the One), and its process is what aligns us to our Mother Arc and the Milky Way core (8D), which phase locks into the Andromeda core (9D). This phase locking between the universal cores opens a link between the Seven Lower Heavens, the current station of our consciousness on Earth, and the Seven Higher Heavens of universal creation. When the 13th chakra is activated, you enter the supergalactic center, the womb of the entire universe. It is seeded in the core of this planet and is an infinite Mother spirit. It is here that the Goddess who is Mother resides. By activating this chakra and connecting with the Goddess energies, you become one with the Mother and a stargate that enables peace and balance to work through you and enter humanity. It opens us to the 14th and 15th chakras, where we become whole. 14 is Christ-Sophia, and 15 is Father Arc, the completion of the Trinity within that brings us to the zero point where the Mother originates. This zero point unified field acts as a Neutron Window to Andromeda and the rest of us.

As we clear false and inorganic architecture from suppressing and impairing our consciousness, we are extracting and clearing mind-control programming and

Laura and Lisa Renee in Sarasota, Florida at a conference.

implants to embody our true inner Christos spirit and return to the zero point field—the heart of the God gateway leading into the Seven Higher Heavens or universes.

It is a very challenging thing to go beyond the Seven Chakra System. Many have unknowingly activated other higher chakras and find they have a difficult time maintaining this connection. When fully integrated, it changes the vibration of our chakras, and we find more stability and grounding in the connection. Psychic attacks increase when we move beyond the 7th chakra to access the infinity spiral. Chakra eight and nine connect us with stargates that bring us into the merging galactic cores of Andromeda and the Milky Way.

I am eternally grateful to Lisa Renee and the Keylontic Science material for helping me bring this information forth more coherently. I am so relieved that I came across her material. It elevated my realizations to a new level of understanding and provided terminology I can continue to share with you.

The use of dark weapons that siphon our life force operates in tandem with social engineering, mind control and the propaganda generated from psychological operations. It is how humans become easily controlled and limited. They are handing us an engineered reality, so when we mistake it for actual, we lose touch with our higher awareness and intuition and become lost to our truth frequency and vulnerable to AI systems and assimilation into a hive-mind cybernetic world. We can overcome it if we recognize the weapons used and what they are attempting to do to us. Spirit forces hold the upper hand, and our wisdom body and higher mind are directly linked. They can nullify and neutralize dark weaponry, so I firmly feel there isn't anything we can't heal, repair, or overcome.

ANCIENT MOTHER ENERGIES

"The harmony and higher potential we achieve within, is reflected without. We as Creators, create the New Earth with this divine harmony. The main source of Divine Feminine energy is Gaia-Sophia. To me, Gaia is our Mother Earth, and Sophia is the Great Mother, or oversoul, to Gaia. Let's take a closer look at both aspects.

GAIA—is the ancient name of our beloved Earth Mother also known as Tara or Terra. She is the consciousness and personification of all Nature. She is a living being and is not separate from us – we are a part of each other. She is a sacred temple and our home.

SOPHIA—is the feminine consciousness of God, the Great Mother of Mother/Father God. She is the Light that contains divine wisdom. Holy Mother Sophia has been cherished for thousands of years by many cultures as the "Holy Spirit," the "Black Madonna," the "Goddess of Heaven," "Mother of the Stars," the "Bride of God," and the "Feminine Face of God."

– Nancy Robbins, Elements Designs Collection

Our connection to the Father and Mother in union is coming more into our awareness. The light continues to pour in and erupt from within, and no one can prevent it. The outer forces can only attempt to steer our attention elsewhere. No other power is in charge or control. It just creates the illusion, wishing us to buy into it and fear the unknown and mystery of where the real magic is!

Nothing is in charge, but the adventure unfolding guided by our vibration, intention and deepest longing is why we sometimes feel fear and pain. We want to be held by God/Goddess, for love to reign and for those who suffer to be restored to bliss, peace and well-being. That is who we are—the force of transmutation, shifting into higher planes of existence when the veil is lifted and the ego structures collapse that hold the old paradigm and the archonic controls.

We have the power to regenerate everything and let that light and love and wisdom ripple out into the world as we are nourished, drinking from the heart of the Great Mother whose love is more powerful than any chemtrail, HAARP, poisoning, insults, demonic agendas or black hole technologies.

"Your Mother is in you, and you in her. She bore you: she gives you life. It was she who gave to you your body, and to her shall you one day give it back again. Happy are you when you come to know her and her kingdom; if you receive your Mother's angels and if you do her laws. I tell you truly, he who does these things shall never see disease. For the power of our Mother is above all. And it destroys Satan and his kingdom and has rule over all your bodies and all living things."

– Essene Gospel of Peace

"From a distance the most noticeable feature on the Isle of Avalon is the Tor as She rises out of the flat Summerlands. She sits like a Great Goddess, a huge bounteous female figure in the middle of a landscape bowl or Cauldron. To see Her is to love Her. To the north the Mendip Hills form the rim of the Cauldron while smaller hills lie to the south and east. Stretching out towards the west the land is below sea level." –Kathy Jones

Like water to fire, she puts out the flames of the dark ones. She ignites the heart flame within, purifying water's crystalline activation, Earth-sending connection, and the magnetic core remembrance of her regenerative power coming in through the feet. We are unveiling the organic creation from within, the ascension. No matter what we see in the outer world, the architecture of the new is a return to ourselves—our Christ consciousness and divine Goddess union.

The Mother is the Earth, the cosmic Mother. She is ancient in her many forms that have been present in our history, lost to us for a time, but never separate from us. The awakening is to acknowledge her unconditional love and return to our hearts and the core vibration of her body, this beautiful planet we walk upon.

"From time immemorial, the Isle of Avalon, in the Summerland (Somerset, England), has been home to the Goddess. This ancient sacred place is the legendary Western Isle of the Dead. Dedicated to an awesome and powerful Goddess, this Island lay far to the west in a shining sea. People were called here to die, to be transformed and to be reborn.

By tradition, a group of nine, thirteen or nineteen Maidens or Faerie Queens live, some say even today, upon this mysterious Western Isle. Skilled in healing and the magical arts of creation and death, they are the Keepers of the Mysteries of the Goddess. Their names come to us as those of Goddesses Anu, Danu, Mab, Morrigu, Madron, Mary, Arianrhod, Cerridwen, Rhiannon, Epona, Rigantona, Bride, Brigit, Hecate, Magdalena, Morgana, Gwenhwyfar, Vivien, Nimue."

– Kathy Jones, The Goddess in Glastonbury

I am barely scratching the surface in this section of all the aspects and many faces of the Goddess. Maiden, Mother and Crone. Dark Goddess aspects such as Hecate, Lilith and Kali are the many aspects of the Goddess that we discover on this journey, which we are learning to awaken to, as the many faces of the Goddess. These are just some of the names.

The ancient energy of the hierogamic union and where the records of their sacred marriage exist in Avebury Henge is the home of Britain's most ancient stone circles. The Triple Solar Goddess and her counterpart, King Arthur, connected with Michael and the Christos lines, awaken here to reclaim her parts. Lisa Renee talks about an Earth dragon being guarding these megaliths that stand nine to twenty feet tall. Even though many of the stones were removed, their energetic power remains. This sacred site plays a huge role in impacting the planetary energies worldwide and is an important hierogamic architecture in the land that resides in our DNA. This activation has been shifting the timelines and breaking down the dark agendas and reversals that have kept us in a state of imbalance and unconsciousness.

During dark cycles of history, the consciousness holders of this energy have been asleep in the lowest densities, waiting for the return of the Krystal Star families to wake them up. Many lie in stasis in the planetary body and crust, waiting for a greater awakening and tipping point—like the 13 dragon beings here for eons. The awakening of the Albion body and the rise of King Arthur and his sacred union consort Guinevere, connected with the Mary Sophia lineage, is the reunion of true sacred union. It is what the ascension energies are all about and what disclosure topics begin to reveal, like the different agendas trying to prevent this, with a vast galactic history and ongoing timeline wars to keep vampiric and fallen groups in power. These dark technologies have been placed in these specific locations to siphon, harvest and invert this true union encoded within us.

Everything in our world that supports these inversions is what keeps us unconsciously enabling artificial timelines and a dark human trajectory leading to a less-than-ideal future when, in reality, we have great potential to access our creative imagination, be a conscious co-creator and do the honorable work on ourselves to venture down the Organic Ascension timeline. These concepts overwhelmed me as a child and were all I could think about. My attention was constantly on them, so discovering information in greater detail and explanation and physically being in these locations has reignited my soul's purpose even more deeply. I recently visited Avebury Henge multiple times over two weeks, and, as I sat with the stones and meditated, I felt deeply into its sacred mysteries. They reside within all to rediscover.

"Avebury Henge is an ancient sundial that functions energetically like a giant Cosmic Clock to reset the timelines in the planetary grid network. Its Cosmic Clock function is the master time clock which holds access to the memories in the organic timelines recorded in human history going back to

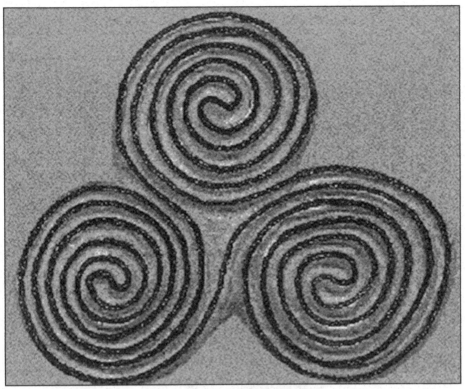

"The Triple Spiral is believed to be an ancient goddess symbol. It can be thought to represent the Triple Goddess (maiden, mother, crone). The Triple Spiral is also used to represent the three realms of land, sea, and sky." –The Celtic Journey

Hyperborea, which links back into the metagalactic core. The Cosmic Trinity of the Solar Rishi are completing their trinity wave braiding shield in this area to create a connection into the Avebury Henge, to bring forth the Heavenly Father and Heavenly Mother archetypal forces to unite with us all, nourishing and supporting the Cosmic Son and Daughter."

– Lisa Renee

REBUILDING AND GROWING TOGETHER

"The metaphorical shape of future beliefs will be determined by the needs of the people who live in that future. We are working towards better integration of the sexes and that cannot come about until the spiritual values are given justice. Sophia's androgeneity and her intensive repertoire of metaphors exemplify her availability to both men and women; for she symbolically reconciles the left and right halves of the brain—the intellectual and intuitive sides which have been seen as masculine and feminine. She is both ordered and chaotic, active and receptive, sequential

*Snake Goddess of the Minoan culture, from 1600 BCE. "Oracular snakes curl around
the crescent-curved arms of Ariadne the Kretan Moon Goddess. She is our Goddess
of inspiration and the creative serpent power of Kundalini." –Kathy Jones*

and simultaneous, defined and diffused—endlessly reconciling the dualistic factors which polarize our human existence in her own person."

– *Caitlin Matthews*

Conscious communities must focus on healing and rehabilitation, and anything cult-like must be avoided. Many carry traumas from their current and past lives about joining a movement run by some leader or group that presented itself as offering benefit to its followers but then became consumed by their position and corrupted to take advantage of the vulnerable seeking hope, healing, community and guidance. However, many emerging communities are not for this in any way. Discernment is key!

In the truther community, whistleblowers directly involved in the intelligence communities or covert military operations have publicly stated that ninety percent of law enforcement are honorable and desire to "serve and protect" trapped in a massively corrupt system, making them ineffective. Cathy O'Brien saw this firsthand when they would shut down police reports of child abuse for "national security" reasons or go as far as to blame or frame the victims. Many whistleblowers have said that the secret intelligence community serves the interests of the power elite controllers or Deep State, not the citizens of the United States.

It is not hard to imagine how this same behavior carries over into every societal power structure, like the school systems, medical industries, media and entertainment. We already know so much corruption exists in the governments and political arenas. The amount of blackmail and threats, like losing the ability to work and provide for one's family, keeps people locked in these positions, afraid to walk away or speak up. Some enchanted by fame and fortune might not see a way out. And, of course, some do not hesitate and are willing participants in these dark agendas.

We need to build communities that can redirect the talents, skills and abilities of those who want to do good yet feel trapped to unite with others to walk away from the destructive indoctrination, cover-ups and manipulations that keep one enabling and participating in the New World Order timeline.

It's my passion to share with humanity what we are made of and how this can guide us into a beautiful future. Being comfortable experiencing all of one's inner elements, Earth, Air, Fire, Water and Aether, to find inner harmony and balance and work with the cosmic and Earthly forces in oneness with the zero point unified field. So it is us and what we are re-discovering. When we do and step into our sovereignty, we are truly ready to come together in Unity Consciousness, in full alignment with our Creator, with God. Sovereignty means no longer being a prisoner of the mind. There, you find integrity, internal harmony and creative imagination to work with cosmic and natural law to correct and find balance with ourselves and those around us.

I expressed this sentiment in one of my Facebook posts:

Medicines can be poisons... Poisons can be medicines... Only we can find the center point between the two.

Healing is finding balance and wholeness—removing oneself from the right and wrong choices.

When awakening happens it can nullify all the toxicity and insults/assaults injury.

Forgiveness washes away the confusion that results from all the hard choices that present themselves.

Let's not be so hard on ourselves or think we know a better way for somebody else—if it works for you, be a resource with love so one can enter the possibilities that inspire the imagination to consider a path that might have been different.

If you weren't willing to be true... To the self—which creates reflections as much as our dark side can cast shadows and doubts...

We wouldn't be on a path of discovery and remembrance.

We would mistake the dark clouds for being something to hide the sun of strength & integrity.

When we must simply allow the rain to fall so we can see.

When your sickness is your own you can heal and transform.

When it's someone else's that you accept, the traitor prevails.

One mourns and grieves with the death of the self.

The storm comes along and is welcomed, feared or mastered.

Only you can break free from the captors.

GLOBAL ALCHEMY—PLUTO RETURNS

"The Grail has been identified with Alchemy—the science of concentrating vital currents and life forces. In the time of the Catholic Inquisition, alchemists were careful to veil their art. They said it was to turn base metals into gold. In philosophical and metaphysical terms, the alchemists were more concerned with the transformation of the worldly person (lead) into a spiritually illuminated person (gold). Just as gold was tried and tested in the fire, so the human spirit was tried in the crucible of life—and the agent for this illumination was perceived to be the Holy Spirit."

– Peter Farely, Where Were You Before the Tree of Life

"Gaea" was the Ancient Greek personification of the Earth and, for all intents and purposes, the Mother of Everything Beautiful in the world; https://www.greekmythology.com/Other_Gods/Gaea/gaea.html

Pluto is a very intense energy to contend with. It is the planet of death, rebirth, alchemy and transformation. In 2022, Pluto returned to the United States of America. The last time this transit happened was in 1776. We also had the strong Pluto-Saturn-Jupiter conjunction around 2020, which began a new phase of our human experience. Pluto in Capricorn represents the death of the old paradigm and awakening, rebirth and transformation. That is the initiation, but because every planet has its shadow, these alignments are sabotaged by outer forces that don't want to lose control. So, the potential of the growth period gets stunted for many. However, other events in one's personal chart and life path can help release oneself, so it is never too late to wake up and turn things around.

If we must embrace the death of the old paradigm to move into higher Earth energies, we must be willing to let go of it. We may be shocked at the things that come up for us to review, what we must look at and release or transmute. A life review of sorts is something everyone faces when moving through a death cycle. The old paradigm and dark controllers don't want to lose their grip over us, so their psychological operations do everything to ensure we fear death.

The 30,000-year-old Venus of Willendorf in Austria is one of the earliest examples of the Birth-giving Goddess. The shape of Her body is that of the Goddess who has just given birth, with Her belly still swollen and Her breasts full of milk for Her new child.

Pluto also rules viruses and pathogens. If we are stagnant and not completing the initiatory cycle of Pluto (death, rebirth, transformation), the body becomes overwhelmed and can get ill. It will feed parasitic forces because we are not pushing the release valve. Suppose we hold onto programs or belief systems that do not align with our highest self. In that case, we begin assimilating into artificial timelines because we have lost connection with our truth frequency.

Anything in our being that is not our truth connected to our higher mind and intuition becomes sewage that affects our blood and overall health. Then, the overgrowth of these parasites serves to feed the archons. Their food is loosh gained from frightened, sickened beings. Our physical symptoms are nothing to fear. They are only there to help us notice, grow, heal and transform—not to mask, drug or hand over our power to another.

The cleansing power of Aether will help us move and release energy and bring in a substance that can begin to dissolve the fences and seals in our DNA that have held us back. And when that happens, we step into our Avatar Consciousness divine power that acts like kryptonite to the archon powers they can't handle.

This 5th element also connects to alchemy and our throat chakra and is the key to overcoming lower forces through the power of our words. We speak and spread mind viruses or communicate from our truth frequency. The Venus transits are the Sophianic corrections that have been turning all this around on cosmic and Earthly levels. The orbit of Venus forms a perfect pentagram in the sky. It corrects the Aether back to its original upright position, allowing for the purification of both our inner and outer elements—Earth, Air, Fire and Water.

David Icke states, *"The inverted pentagram or five-pointed star, so prevalent in Satanism, is also symbolic of this unbroken 'time' cycle, the vibrational prison."*

For this reason, we cannot be angry with what we can only face alone within ourselves. Instead, we must embrace anger as a potentiated force of activation—a part of that passion and fire that seeks healing and restoration and a force for change that has lost its way.

The movement of the Holy Mother of God Principle through the evolution of Sophia reveals how her presence on Earth connects to planetary healing. As the world soul, Sophia has the task of restoring the balance of our existence and purifying hell to revive the Goddess cauldron of regeneration to the Earth plane. Creating divine union in the depths of the underworld is the seed of the Goddess finding union within. It allows the light of heaven to emerge from the roots of life to express itself through our souls and fuse into matter. The divine forces of nature and the wisdom of Mother Earth are where Sophia exists to reveal how we can complete global transformation toward our ultimate liberation.

As Sophia emerges, we move closer and closer to our true potential and connection to spirit. As things get shaken up, the misguided forces of creation and destruction at war with the attainment of balance on all levels can begin to end. The unstoppable power of her passionate heart and strong will, which exists within all and can conquer all threats and attacks, is embodied in her journey from the Cosmic Trinity to the Earth in reclaiming her children. It has been an ever-present theme to connect with this and is a story of how Sophia has emerged in my soul. This mission has been given to me to fulfill at all costs, no matter how dangerous or treacherous the journey might be.

In reclaiming connection with the Mother Womb and the cycles of life, death and transformation that Pluto rules, we connect with the archetype The Crone. It reveals what hides beneath the surface, so our deep plunge into the plutonic energies can at first be daunting as we face patterning, blocked energies, or things from the past we might still be holding onto. But we can also pull ourselves out of it when all these things have been composted and new seeds planted. We can then be reborn again.

The Crone is what guides us with infinite wisdom. It has taken its power back. It is no longer the abducted maiden. In completing the cycle, wisdom is gained to get there and move beyond the fear of the lantern she holds—the inner light found in the dark. These life cycles give us great strength over time and a deep connection to the regenerative power of nature. Every year, the seasons show us this.

Regardless of any Pluto transits, we all have Pluto somewhere in our chart. I have it conjunct my Sun sign in Libra. It is amazing how many adventures into the underworld I have faced, how much I learn each time, and how regenerated and wonderful it feels every time I emerge reborn. I see it as the creative cauldron of the Mother and reconnect to the aspects of the Goddess that resided in these realms before Hades and the underworld overlords.

Before Hades came along, there was the Moon Goddess Hekate as ruler of the underworld. Ancient Mother Goddesses were often depicted as a dragon representing the transformative power of nature. In Greek mythology, these goddesses were known as the Moirai or the Fates. They contained both life and death within them and were figures who governed fate and natural law. There are so many examples, but they are depicted in triple form. Being willing to go through this process can help us find more wholeness, our origins, and what we are truly made of. We can then be more conscious co-creators of our lives and feel the cycles of nature and all the magic and abundance our Mother Earth holds, as we are a part of her.

In this book, I write a lot about the underworld, but it is the equivalent of "Hell" in Christianity. Because of this conditioning, our belief systems are based

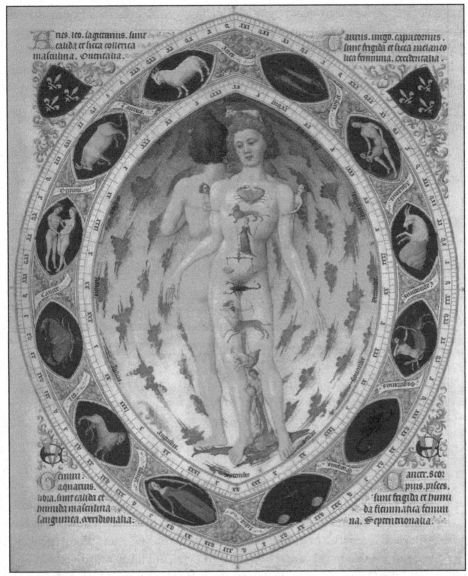

Medical Astrology. Astrology is connected to our body parts and can help us to unlock where we have energetic blocks or excesses and deficiencies based on the planetary aspects in a person's birth chart. Mystery Schools developed the field of Medical Astrology and viewed the entire matrix of the human body through astronomical and astrological principles and biomechanics.

on worshiping something outside of ourselves and redemption instead of embracing the deep-dive transformation into self-healing, releasing what no longer serves us and then experiencing transformation. Pluto often means experiencing the loss of a loved one or attachments so that we are pushed into seeing a larger picture and finding peace with the soul journey of those who have transitioned.

We go through ego deaths. We plunge into our depths to find our divine blueprint, and each time we take a plunge, we move through gatekeepers and anything wishing to trap us in the process of renewal and awakening. It is humanity's test to view it as an opportunity to retrieve our divine power instead of fearing our dark or letting something else take control. These are the times we are in.

As we look at the larger picture of where all this is headed, let us remember this quote from Lisa Renee:

> *"For refusing them access to her wisdom (consciousness), they are blinded by fury and thus 'she' has been debased into a prostitute, tortured and banished into the underworlds for replication and breeding.*

> *Her reproductive organs are harnessed with reversal Arc codes. This is the shadow side created by the archon's misogyny program (Orion Group's patriarchal domination) to control the feminine. The archons and their controller code have been living in the shadows of deception as a parasite of humanity and the planet.*

> *…This is why the archons inherently hate Sophia as she can perceive what they cannot, as it is in this activated superpower that she will defeat them."*

ET INVOLVEMENT AND RETURN OF THE MOTHER

"In 1926 the Zeta/Zephilium began interacting with certain factions of several Earth governments. Several projects by Zeta/Draco were intent on destroying Earth's grid vibration rate to stop us from evolving or ascending. The Zeta were involved with Atlantis and for a time with the colonization of Mars."

– Ashayana Deane, Keylontic Science

Whistleblowers have stepped forward to disclose government awareness of an "alien agenda." In time, it will be widely known that we humans have ET genetics and were seeded by numerous ET races along the way. However, our origins in this universe began in Lyra, and it was the digressed Lyran strains, the Orion Group with service-to-self orientation, which hybridized to blend their genetics with us and altered our original design, taking us further away from Source. The Anunnaki manipulated our DNA to make us their slave race. We are currently in a critical window period where we can advance like never before, so we must consciously choose to extend ourselves beyond their influence or forever remain a puppet enslaved by them.

Their lust for our powerlessness and blind faith is exacerbated by their use of microchips to send signals and commands, making it difficult for any individual to access their inner voice or connect with Source. Of course, some are directly involved in these programs while others languish in a trance state from

Avebury Henge Stone Circles. Avebury Henge and the stone circles are in the heart of Wiltshire and have the greatest number of stones in Britain. Stone 10 of the Great Circle is in the foreground on the left, and Stone 9 (The Barber Stone) is on the right. Beyond this are stones 8, 7, 6 and 5. The figure on the right is walking on the outer bank of the henge. –Jim Champion, author

any number of culprits. One example is Electromagnetic Low-Frequency (ELF) microwaves emitting from TV sets. They lock in lower mindsets that obsess over all the news and allow constant bombardment of what one should think, feel or consume, promoting divisive tactics through steered narratives and dark agendas disguised by facades and false flags. Other culprits include chemtrail nerve toxins that create a constant state of nervous system disorder and overwhelm, emotional and psychical imbalance through delusional feelings, or a deep and powerful longing for freedom, sensing things aren't right.

Even if we witness aspects of a catastrophic timeline emerging, we must hold fast to the truth and know we still have a choice whether to venture down that path. Ultimately, everything we see happening in our world only serves to reveal the overall health of the collective as an expression of our health, as we are extensions of the many dimensions and emanating that which matches our vibratory frequency. If we ensure we are not a part of the problem, we don't need to engage in any of the battles laid out to trap us.

We must confront the reality that much of what has been occurring in secret has created an inevitable future drama, for they have spent trillions of our tax dollars on projects that only serve their elitist mentality. These include a Secret Space Program (SSP) with off-planet colonies reached through teleportation, programs that target individuals perceived to be a threat to their agenda, HAARP and psychotronic weapon technologies, construction of deep underground military bases and false flag events to draw us further into a police state.

Behind the scenes, occult practices that include dark rituals, horrific child abuse, and the creation of agents and enslaved people to serve them infect the planetary body with negative frequencies that become food to them. It is how they sustain power and influence while hiding behind a curtain of secrecy. Their practices spawn immense fear, pain and negative feelings that become the life force they live on.

As awful as this all sounds, there is a way out! First, we must understand the concept of Christ-Sophia Consciousness and how the lower forces have affected our DNA and produced "junk DNA" that is unused and unactivated, and how, in turn, it all connects to the planetary body, its veils and the suppression of the Goddess. It is not a "New Age" thing, but an ancient gnosis around Creation and what we face. It's about how much the scales have tilted to favor the warmongers, abusers and control freaks.

We are in a decisive moment, and the shift into higher Earth energies is already happening. We must jump on board and do the necessary inner and outer work to unfold in divine order. We must strive to soften the harshness of everything we bump up against to unite in the love and respect we give ourselves and each other. It will restore our world to wholeness and return the power to the ascending Mother Earth and cosmic and natural law, moving into 5D, the soul matrix. Being soul-centered gets us there.

ASTROLOGY INITIATIONS

In astrology, the North Node in Gemini is ruled by the lungs. We experienced this shift in 2020. When we suppress our truth, growth becomes stunted, and weakness in this organ makes us vulnerable to disease and illness. "Dis-ease" signals that we are not thriving or moving through our growth opportunities and initiations. In 2022, we moved into the season of the South Node in Scorpio and North Node in Taurus, where we drew upon the Plutonic energies of death and re-birth to then move into and integrate Venus, which rules Taurus, an Earth sign that rules things like self-worth, abundance and what we value. Finally, July 2023 brought us to Aries North Node and Libra South Node, which helped us focus on standing up for ourselves more and not doing things to please others. With our ego energies more integrated with our soul expression, we were called to reflect upon which relationships were healthy to maintain and which weren't. This allowed us to see what changes were needed in our lives to be more true to the self and no longer give our power away to relationships or the fear tactics presented to us in the outer world.

The study of Medical Astrology shows us how the planets and signs are connected to our body parts. It can help unlock our energetic blocks or excesses and deficiencies based on the planetary aspects of our birth chart to get to the root of disease and a healing path as we grasp what is going on with our bodies.

Understanding the movement of energies from one season to the next is helpful as these profound astrological opportunities are targeted and leveraged as vulnerabilities to serve lower agendas. The Deep State or dark agendas behind psyops and false flags coordinate these events with important astrological events and initiatory planetary energies. The outer planets take us through profound growth periods individually and as a collective—these are the planets Uranus, Pluto and Neptune. Here is what they represent and the shadow side that we can easily stay stuck in if we continue to give our power away in the face of it:

Uranus in Taurus (shock and upheaval) = Awakening

Shadow: panic attacks, PTSD, nervous breakdown, reduced connection to higher guidance

Neptune in Pisces (consciousness and freedom) = Creative Imagination

Shadow: fear virus, mind virus, disinformation, confusion designed to infect creative channels

Pluto in Capricorn (death of matrix control) = Transformation

Shadow: suicidal thoughts, heavy energy, darkness, stuck in the birth canal, remaining cocooned

What happens when we resist these energies? Our immune system is lowered, we get hijacked and our energies get siphoned. We feel hopeless, lost and confused. We remain in survival mode, reactive and ungrounded. We need to increase our spiritual immune system and heal our mental and emotional bodies, and once we do, the physical will follow. True medical leaders also need to guide this process.

Now we are moving forward and out of all of that. Still, who knows what the next thing is going to be, so it is always fascinating and important to note what the astrological shifts are and what we can be awakened or initiated into versus what gets inverted and directed in a very different place and how can we call our power back when those events take place, instead of getting overly invested energetically into the storylines. We are either in alignment with the cosmic and natural forces guiding our evolution, awakening, healing and transformation or on a path of digression, which puts us in a trance that we can snap out of.

To connect with nature and Mother and see where we might be led astray by dark weaponry, knowing one's natal chart and astrological alignments at birth can be helpful.

"Astrology in the current times is labeled a pseudoscience, which is used to discredit its validity and purpose in studying the laws of structure, to keep humanity ignorant of the study of the astronomical patterns, which inform our personality through many different forces of consciousness influences.

Proper use of the science of astrology allows us to better determine if we are accurately living in our true spiritual nature and potential, it informs us of our lessons and challenges, as well as what we came to the Earth to resolve and transcend.

Without deeper knowledge and awareness of how these astronomical patterns impact us, 3D human consciousness goes on auto-pilot, uninformed of the massive forces and influences to which they are exposed everyday."

– Lia Renee

When a mother and child get separated against their will, it causes pain and suffering. When reunited, their hearts heal and they thrive again. It also happens when we return to Mother Earth and allow her nurturing presence. Controller forces and adversaries must not stand in our way anymore. We must embrace this connection and allow it to work wonders. The dark mother reversal was on the planet for many thousands of years. Thankfully, this is no longer the case. Still, we must be willing to go through the intense journey of awakening to avoid staying locked in a distorted timeline we readily avoid. We have triumphed and are finding our way home again, and the more we recognize this, the more parasitic influences fall away.

We must be willing to explore what operates behind the scenes and what is done to gain power, the horrific abuses involved and how technology at their hands is used to simulate false realities, like a possible fake alien invasion. We need to educate ourselves on these concepts so that we are no longer participants consenting to the theater, the false flags and psyops. Being willing to question things, dig deeper and remain open to wherever the journey leads while resisting the fear projected to "hook" us, we can begin to tap into the inner reunion and what is available to align with all that brings joy, peace, clarity and upgrades into the soul, Monad and Avatar Consciousness held in our DNA template.

So even if this information is alarming, isn't it better to know than to continue going along or feed it? Not every explanation for certain events will be 100% accurate, so always take what resonates with what I share. I believe, however, that we can best develop our truth and authenticity by considering this kind of information. It can only help to further evolve a discerning "bullshit meter" within oneself, and focusing on amplifying intuition will definitely assist in navigating the bumpy road ahead.

Being Prepared

"The wild nature carries the bundles for healing; she carries everything a woman needs to be and know. She carries the medicine for all things. She carries stories and dreams and words and songs and signs and symbols. She is both vehicle and destination."

– Clarissa Pinkola Estes, Ph.D., Women Who Run With the Wolves

I, like many, have felt something calling my attention from a very young age. It seemed to be coming from a higher part of me and deep within my soul—a knowing I once had that I was in the process of remembering. I often journeyed within and beyond to understand what it was all about. I discovered that my level of probing and seeking held the keys to my knowing why I was incarnated here and born into the family I had. It helped me recognize myself as a being in service to others, but in a way that isn't often expected or acknowledged.

I was prepared and made aware of something I had to face that went beyond myself and more into planetary consciousness and the ascension window period. It would take on many forms and unfold in numerous phases over time. It held the power to open me up to the larger picture and a task we all have in common. Some immediately recognize it and are challenged to ground and acclimate to this density. In contrast, others find life's adversities and experiences are a catalyst that opens up a vast reality beyond the personality matrix. Still, others will experience a variable mixed bag for sure!

When I first tapped into my mission as a child, I was eager, ready to go on an adventure into the depths of my soul and hidden layers of reality. I later realized my willingness to do such a thing would make me a target, and I would experience it in some of the most confusing ways. Aligned with the energies of Venus (transits), my guides prepped me to embark on a deep journey into the underworld. I went through the labyrinth while pulling out of exile the treasures of humanity and lost aspects of the divine feminine. It was a journey that would show me raw terror, extreme targeting, attacks and ancient buried wisdom. To be effective in moving through this, one has to release negative programming and the projections of people fully. And be willing to integrate fragmented aspects of self and ignite the energetic circulation of the masculine and feminine to harmonize and integrate polarity and purify the inner elements. It is the greater goal of this initiation, which can be easily lost when we are in the middle of it. It is about finding inner light in the greatest of darkness.

Since I was a little girl, I had a strong sense of awareness. More accurately, I existed as a fully multi-dimensional being. I often recognized how close I was to dwelling in the depths far beneath. It was almost as if the ground would open up before me as I walked forward into time. I would avoid this place that looked like a pit, a deep hole in the Earth. The trees and spirits of nature would counsel me in preparation for a journey that would cause me to lose everything that felt close and familiar to me, magical and safe. Instead, I would soar into the heights, surrounded by and speaking with enlightened beings. I spent much of my time existing in this infinite oneness and knew this was the essence and information I must hold on to for dear life as I faced immense challenges that tortured my soul from losing love, safety and security. It felt like an impossible mission that only God could fulfill through me.

I discovered that I was on a journey of death and resurrection to help restore the Sophianic Mother energy to this planet. I realized that many Grail legends speak of this initiatory journey—which illuminates the spirit within the human vessel and awakens the Christ-Sophia template. It all connects with anchoring the Mother energy back into the Earth, the 13th gate Mother Arc. Many of us have been on this journey, and some are still in the very thick of it, so I dedicate this book to comforting all souls who are courageously navigating the darkness, shadow and underbelly of this matrix we've been born into. It is a painful yet transformative awakening process and is an initiation we must embrace. Unfortunately, many false flags and psychological operations are manufactured to stunt our growth and derail us. At the same time, in the face of adversity, indoctrination programs encourage us to give our power away.

"The 13th strand overlaid on the 12th strand system permits the individual to be empowered, and self willed. The 12 are the foundation and tools, the 13th is the 'Itself'. It is love as the Christ Consciousness resurrected in each individual with the potential to increase its vibratory rate to invoke universal healing. The 13th strand connects one from the earth plane to the God-

Self, with the energy of the CHIRST as the glue or love source that assists the veils of separation to be lifted."

– Shirley Catanzaro, The Portal of Transformation

So many of us want to free ourselves of the holographic time loop and the archonic systems we are born into. This achievement is not out of reach and is what I have dedicated myself to helping us discover once again. It is about breaking free of patterns and programs that cause us to co-create a lesser version of reality in which we get influenced into participating. This lost-and-found scenario is the soul's journey and the ego's lessons in a free will universe.

I have had so many communications and synchronicities come through without seeking them out that it has confirmed the presence of many souls who have come during this time to help us advance as a human race. There have been specific situations that have come my way to validate this greater mission. Though I have no way of proving some of these communications except for the sources from which they came, it is something I must consider. The search or need for proof sometimes thwarts our capacity to develop our intuition, and we can only experience some things by tuning in and feeling whether or not it's authentic.

So if something feels right, sometimes that alone speaks volumes—more than we may be inclined to give credit. Think about all that school pushed onto us as "truth." I bet we can all remember when something did not feel right or we knew there was much more to the story. We miss these opportunities if we ignore the part of us trying to call our attention. External authority and education won't get us far if we don't self-reflect and question it.

COMMUNICATIONS COMING THROUGH

"Since the Majestic 12 and Zeta Grey Alien Trade Agreements were made about 85 years ago, Earth inhabitants have been aggressively experimented upon with hidden technologies used to implant thoughts as one of the many prongs of social engineering programs."

– Lisa Renee, Ascension Glossary

Throughout the book, I share different communications from others who have come through to me. The rabbit holes I have gone down over this are beyond anything I can describe. I am attempting to extract information to find the common threads that can help make sense of things. Rest assured, I have always been wary of channelers, so please know I don't share anything lightly. I also had the benefit of attending a clairvoyant institute for two years and worked much energy connected with past lives to develop a solid bullshit meter. The subsequent communications I found are a good place to start as they are not widely known or considered, so I chose to share some of them here.

One particular document, titled "Requested by The Guardians of the Cell/ Worlds," was given to me by someone who said I needed to have it. Though the author is unknown to me at this time, I intend one day to uncover more about her. She shares that we are the plan! Here is an excerpt:

"Over recent years many of you have discovered contact was made to exchange technology for the abductions of the people here to experiment upon. This is true, but not for the reasons you may have heard or are perhaps thinking. After numerous failed attempts, a new and very successful contact was made with a highly respected military figure who would then enter your US government in the very early 1950s. He was a man with a very understanding heart and insight who completely understood all that had been divulged to him by the star visitors. An agreement was then made between them to teach humans how to create a more advanced way of long-distance communications in exchange for a 'Genetic Search' by the star visitors to begin locating the descendants of those who were lost to them here long ago from other worlds.

'YES, I DID SAY A GENETIC SEARCH!' What was never shared with Military Officials in early 1953 from the star visitors and (with the exception of this one man) was that an infiltration plan into human society worldwide was already in effect as of late 1952. This was through a surrogate program agreed upon between the star visitors and their native relatives on a global scale. This migration of many 'Light Life's' to enter the newly born here amongst you all would become a new generation of people, each with a specific talent and soul memory imprinting of specific tasks to be carried out in your future. Again, this secret plan was shared only with this one man of great importance within the United States government. Only he fully understood the dire necessity for the whole truth to be told. He was offered a gift on behalf of the Guardians. For his much appreciated heartfelt understanding and assistance, a 'Light Life' to enter his future family life was promised. That beautiful 'Light Life' did arrive and today still continues the fight on his behalf for the truth to be known, by all who are waiting.

A 'Light Life' is a higher intelligence energy form of 'Living Light,' they are 'Life.'…

…Their Purpose? To BE the change on this world, standing side by side with those like yourselves that have been living under the rule of ignorance and deception without any intervention for so very long."

In this part of it, the author reveals the origins of her parents:

"As to whom my parents are, my biological father was from the Cherokee Nation, as was his mother. His father was from the Dakota People, all descendants of those who migrated to this world long ago from a star system called, Pleiades. My mother was a surrogate, my biological mother was not of this world."

The woman who contacted me said she knew who they were referring to. The military man and the one to enter the U.S. government was Dwight David Eisenhower, and the "Light Life" to come into the family still working today, no doubt, was me. I do have a hard time accepting such things. But knowing my mission was active at such a young age and that I came specifically for this mission, as did many others. Eisenhower was very close to his grandchildren, who also had special missions in these times. I like knowing that the basis of this communication applies to anyone who has felt called to ancestral mission work. There is so much that is in this book. She said Eisenhower spoke with Dakote Star beings. She talked a lot about the Dakota, Lakota and Nakota people, Lemuria and Turtle Island, and when she mentions the descendants that have been lost to them from other worlds, this sounds like the lost souls of Tara. I found it very interesting how I was called in to do conferences with Native American tribes connected to their lineage and teachings—Star Knowledge Conferences.

Along the way, I heard other things that were impossible to ignore. For one, I was told by those who recruited me to go off-planet to a secret Mars colony that Eisenhower was briefed that a future descendant was to come (from star beings) and that they somehow intercepted this information. It was one of the reasons for desiring to remove me from Earth. Was it for my protection? Well, that's how they presented it to me. Was it to target me and derail my mission on Earth? I believe so. The group was a mixed bag of people called the Aviary, and I saw many well-intentioned people being duped that it had been infiltrated and compromised. There were a lot of internal battles and differences among the group members. I will get more into that later.

I have done my best to gather what I can, including some saved emails. There are also several published articles from those who have taken the time to vet the situation, like Gary S. Bekkum from Starstream Research, who also happened to know the recruiters personally. I walk around to this day with lots of question marks. But as I tell the story of what took place, I am reminded of why my absolute refusal to go was the best decision I could have ever made, no matter how they presented it to me.

The section from this most recent quote, *"Over recent years many of you have discovered contact was made to exchange technology for the abductions of the people here to experiment upon. This is true, but not for the reasons you may have heard or are perhaps thinking,"* I feel she is talking about this communication between Eisenhower and star beings and what he assisted them in achieving regarding locating descendants. It is obvious and made clear through the overwhelming information coming forward that ETs and governments created treaties for humans to be abducted in exchange for technology. Still, she was referring to a very different technology trade, and this segment doesn't

One can think of labyrinths as symbolic of pilgrimage; people can walk the path, ascending toward salvation or enlightenment. Author Ben Radford conducted an investigation into some of the claims of spiritual and healing effects of labyrinths.

explain the difference. The ones I will share in this book are very different from the "genetic search" she was referring to.

The most challenging research has been getting to the bottom of the ET government treaties made. Internet searches mainly mention Eisenhower as the one who sold us out to the Greys. In this book, I will share my revelations along the way and how I came to find the information and synchronicities that support a very different story. It's a big part of my mission to bring the truth to this topic—as close to the truth as possible!

I want to share a significant revelation from Elena Danaan's book, "We Will Never Let You Down: Encounters With Val Thor and Journeys Beyond Earth." In her book, she writes:

> "I could confirm to her through the words of Val Thor, that her great-grandfather had never intended to sign agreements with the Greys and was fooled by the MJ-12, a certainty that Laura always had in her heart. It was a bit emotional as she was confirming to me info I couldn't have known, and I was passing on to her Val Thor's words confirming what she always secretly believed."

Elena Danaan then engages in direct communication with Val Thor:

> "Commander Val, after I met you for the first time, I had the privilege to connect with President Dwight's great-granddaughter, Laura. We spoke about you, and about what happened with the treaties. She knew the truth deep within herself, and she was glad you could confirm it."

Val Thor replies:

> *"Laura... yes, I know who you are talking about. I met her once but she didn't know it was me. I vowed to look after Dwight's descendants and you know, Laura is very special. She came to restore the truth. She needed to learn about the faces and the plans of the enemy, but I always protected her, all along, and so did Dwight, until this day. Laura holds a guiding light which will be followed by many. Give her my salutations."*

Elena's account confirms my conclusion that Eisenhower was aware of and involved in a counter-plan to the Greada Treaty. Randy Cramer has talked about the USMC SS and a benevolent Super Soldier program that Eisenhower helped to establish through an executive order relating to future disclosure. A quote from The Guardians of the Cell/Worlds document states that the contact made with Eisenhower was when he was still a military officer, so these later meetings occurred after he became President.

There is no doubt that Majestic 12 (MJ-12) was involved in an agreement done behind Eisenhower's back that was already in the works. From what Elena has shared, he was present for one of the meetings, but there were others where he wasn't in attendance. He was furious when he discovered what had happened and wanted to invade Area 51. I will get deeper into these subjects when I discuss the Dulce Wars that began in 1954 and future books.

After the failed mission to Antarctica in 1947 led by Admiral Byrd, the infiltration was nearly impossible to stop. Project Paperclip, Project Mockingbird, and a whole slew of other MK-Ultra programs and projects, along with geoengineering and an expanding Secret Space Program—a hidden war has continually been taking place, with humans on the front lines dealing with the immense deception and trickery pushed through media, rewritten history and indoctrination programs. As a result, the term "conspiracy theorist" has been given to anyone willing to go deeper to rediscover a lost history and hidden truth and speak about it.

Eisenhower's connection with Val Thor influenced my great-grandfather's final speech warning of the Military Industrial Complex. He aimed to remind us that only an alert and knowledgeable citizenry could combat this rise of misplaced power. So this book is to direct the attention on ourselves and what it will take to awaken to our truth, where our thoughts are our own, and so that we can be soul-centered and intuitive and discerning enough to know how to navigate the madness of these times we are in.

It's important to note what Dan Cooper helped me to understand, which is that Ike didn't start Ike's Force until after he met Val Thor and until after his special forces (Delta Teams) were defeated at the Battle of Dulce in 1954. Ike strategized formulating Ike's force with a think tank and didn't develop these ideas alone. A number of think tank members, in addition to Ike and Val, came up with the plans that he initiated. Ike had a small team of advisers assisting him. I don't know who those people were, but I am certain that Ike sought their advice on the matter.

One mission he attempted to launch appeared to go nowhere. In 1958, President Eisenhower was denied access to Area 51. He responded by threatening to invade the base if MJ-12 didn't allow him access. If he had initially met with Val Thor somewhere between 1952 and 1954, he would have been briefed and made aware of what was happening. I also share more of what Dan Cooper said about Val Thor and the War on Dulce later in this book. These revelations have connected so many dots that I feel a profound inner peace. Yet, on a human level, I continue to struggle as I witness how poorly people deal and cope with all they don't know yet feel sure they do.

There is so much history to discuss and what The Guardians of the Cell/Worlds document says about "Light Life's." The book talks about awakening starseeds, the greater mission, and activating the calling within so we can step up and do our part because, in my eyes, it is us who are a part of this grand plan and the positive military and benevolent ET groups are with us on this, no one is indeed coming to save us. Still, group effort and teamwork are different than being rescued.

I have always longed for more contact, ship experience, and face-to-face encounters with benevolent ETs and guides! But, the times they did get close, I recall often feeling such homesickness take over—such a longing to go home and never return. Not because I don't like it here, but because I find most tasked with a starseed-kind of assignment are uncomfortable here. I feel uncomfortable, too, but I know I must stay grounded on Earth to complete my mission. It is the higher Earth energies I long for, along with interactions with all kinds of higher benevolent beings, though I know they are there, and I can sense and feel them and know they will communicate more with me when necessary. The density and level of attack, ridicule and misunderstanding by those who wish to destroy this kind of mission is often too much to bear. Yet, simultaneously, I feel such a connection to this Earth and nature. They have been my greatest guides and source of joy outside the matrix overlay that influences humanity to perpetuate bloodshed, war and trauma.

I have come to understand that Eisenhower remained aligned with Val Thor and the positive ET groups and that, in actuality, the ET government treaties originated earlier and continued after he became president. He couldn't have been involved since he was completely denied access. My research into one of the most credible sources I have ever known, Lisa Renee, has brought me to this conclusion. Her work discusses the original treaties I will later expand upon.

I want to conclude this section by saying there is much talk that the 1930s is the actual point all this madness began. The Churchill, Crowley, Hitler connection established the Grey Alien Agreements with the government (yes, they said Churchill met the aliens while he was prime minister). This also marked the beginning of the technology trade. Churchill and the UK wanted it for world domination, leading to human experiments such as mind control through psychotronics and time travel. The intention was to create continual world wars through a divide-and-conquer strategy employed upon the entire human race to keep us busy and distracted. Yet, at the same time, they drain Earth's resources and our life-force energy to serve their self-serving agendas.

Whistleblower Phil Schneider has confirmed the same. A geologist and engineer for the U.S. government, Phil said the U.S. government knew of the "alien agenda" as early as 1933.

So, what does one do when all the information doesn't line up? I feel it's important to listen and consider all available information and allow our discernment and intuition to refine and distill truth through felt resonance. No one source has the complete picture or can explain it fully, even when messages come from "the other side" since many races and hybrids have interacted with humanity. Therefore, the communications I bring forth to you are from sources I deem most credible and deeply resonant with me.

I want everything on the table and a part of a more extensive dialogue. The significance makes it something we must fully understand. It's impossible to expect anyone to have it all figured out, and it's not a yes or no. We must undo the compartmentalization and include people's legitimate experiences to see what the Deep State is attempting to do on a mass scale. The same thing is required when we are healing ourselves. Once we go deep into our unconscious, it's a process of integration to look at the patterning and programs that influence how we co-create our reality.

New Age deceptions. Religious deceptions. Intentional distortions. Our relationship with Yeshua/Christ/Jesus is very personal and sacred. No one should attempt to define or control it for us. The same goes for our Mother—our Earth, our cosmic Mother, our relentless guide and nurturer who finds us from within. She has provided us with a home. And more than that, she offers sacred union and unconditional love.

Karl Mollison, a well-known channeler who had never met me before, was interviewed by Denny Hunt. I learned of him through Denny, who sent me a correspondence over email. Karl brought through messages from what he understood to be my great-grandfather in the interview. Karl and I would later talk about it as I reached out to find out more.

I want to share one part of the interview transcript of Karl's channeling. Though some may not believe this or may discount it, I feel it necessary to share as one example of many curious things that continue to show up in my life out of nowhere regarding my great-grandfather. It also speaks to starseeds and what can be detrimental if one allows manipulation and interference to go too far.

"Denny then asks Spirit Eisenhower about his great granddaughter, the popular spiritual crusader Laura Eisenhower. 'I am with her often and support all she does... She is a shining example of the continuation of this legacy. ... [I] am working directly with Creator and with [Laura's] higher self to impulse her with thoughts, with ideas, and encouragement, and sending love as well to raise her up and to help her to stay strong. This is what we do as Light beings in helping one another. And so she will be another point of the many spears who are advancing the awareness and knowledge needed to truly help humanity in a positive way.

I am still connected with very, very, strong loving bonds to my family and descendants. All are part of a soul group who have been together for a huge span of time and we work together in our projects again and again. We support one another when present together in the physical and we support one another when some are in the physical and others back in the Light. This is where I am, and from this vantage point I am in the best position to provide support and encouragement.'

Spirit Eisenhower points out the potential pitfalls in assisting in humanity's shift in consciousness. 'All light-workers leave their mark and all have greater potential than they themselves know. The difficulty ...for them is not appreciating themselves enough, not understanding the truly great power they have, and this is better understood by the opposition. So when they are identified as risks and then manipulated (by the dark side entities) in a way to sideline them, there is a great loss to the cause and in most cases the individuals themselves. If [sidelined] early enough, [they are] not aware of what they were capable of and would have accomplished.'"

STARSEED AWAKENING AND PLANETARY LIGHT WORKER

"For starseeds, this lifetime is a recon mission that was required to gather the intel required to comprehend the levels of genetic damage, the source of planetary invasion, the identity of the main intruder races and attempt to offer sovereignty and freedom to the souls which had been enslaved, abused and entrapped in repeated reincarnation cycles."

– Lisa Renee

Even if someone is unaware of the reality of their starseed mission, it doesn't mean they aren't moving forward on their path. A starseed's awakening is an initiation of the soul, which happens at different times for people without even knowing. It reconnects our divine relationship with Source and our galactic origins. The opportunity is open to all, and everyone holds this potential, not just the "chosen ones," when accessed through love and wisdom.

Some people, though, are born with the specific mission to assist in switching on the lights, like the Indigo and Crystal children. There is also something called the Oraphim, which I wrote about in previous chapters, where the Indigo and Crystal energies originate. The Oraphim represents the consciousness that holds the override frequency I refer to in this book. An override frequency can rise above all dark matrix agendas. And though it isn't all dark, something does permeate our reality in plain sight that is greater than any of us can imagine, and it has been manipulating all world affairs for far too long. So, getting in touch with the antidote is paramount during this time.

It hasn't been easy adjusting to this human realm. The part of us that is our highest truth can work against us if we don't honor it. It may be expressed as nudging or thoughts we choose to blow off and not take seriously to match the energy of another that may not fully resonate with what we know exists within. Dismissing one's inner truth can manifest as feeling isolated, unseen or misunderstood by family and friends or the loneliness felt when many people surround one. Though it's understandable why one would feel this way, taking it personally often causes more harm than necessary. That's why it is important to remember that what sets you apart from others is a gift you have to share, whether anyone around you gets it. Being a liberated being means it has no power to hurt you anymore.

The sorrow from feeling different or alone can manifest as repressed or overly expressed anger and resentment towards anyone who reminds us of those who have harmed us and can cause physical symptoms. A prolonged period of imbalance makes us vulnerable to un-wellness, such as depression, addictive or obsessive tendencies, mood swings and confusion. It can drive a deep desire to belong and seek a feeling of connection and home, only to be left unrealized because one's internal treasures are pushed away and seen as a problem.

When we shut down and go unconscious to these tendencies, physical symptoms of illness begin to appear while the prescribed drugs make it extremely difficult to grow and heal to become our true selves. An attempt to awaken to one's mission and inner truth can feel crazy-making because there is no outside reassurance, support or validation. So, we increasingly fear others' opinions of us or what we might lose. Some might call these people "sheeple," but that is unfair since we have no idea what is happening deep within or how challenged one might feel. It's way past time to drop all the labels and begin to share our differences so we can assist one another in rebuilding our Diamond Sun DNA! When we remove these barriers, we create a global alchemical shift where love permeates all levels of existence. The kind of love that sees through all programs,

Commander Val Thor pictured on the right. Val Thor met with former President Eisenhower and went on VIP status for three years at the Pentagon. Dan Cooper says that he began communications with Eisenhower as early as 1952.

traumas and ego mask defenses and speaks directly to the soul. Our willingness to unite and unify is how we dissolve this matrix.

The other extreme when feeling different or alone is rebellion, which gets exhausting. We win the war on consciousness from within, so we must check in with ourselves to determine the necessary changes to succeed in this physical plane. Everyone has a hidden calling, and the leading cause of suffering is often the key to discovering one's true divinity, so we must listen intently to what our inner voice is trying to say. The Tree of Knowledge is about reclaiming self-knowledge and the truth of who we are.

In the beginning, overcoming social engineering and mind control is the most crucial step to moving out of the duality imposed on us. Duality is the imbalance that is fed upon, while the integration of polarity is the true love reunion between our inner light and dark and divine masculine and feminine. We deprogram when we go within to balance distortions of the masculine and feminine in our external world. It has to start with us. We must be brave enough to be our most genuine selves and have healthy boundaries with anything that tries to use or compromise us or turn us into something we are not.

The prerequisite to attaining Unity Consciousness is first to become sovereign and authentic to self. Otherwise, we risk acting out the agenda of a false movement or indoctrination as these targeted programs psychologically profile to know which buttons to push to divide and conquer us through trigger words and events. It is why political correctness is so out of control. People spend more time feeling hurt or apologizing for someone else's triggered response when some need to grow a spine to address this vital shadow work. A great war is being waged on the collective, so we must be strong enough to address the real issues, like pedophilia, child trafficking, and total planetary take-over and enslavement through transhumanism and siphoning AI systems. They can only infiltrate low-frequency bands available through hatred or victim consciousness.

And while these issues are essential to address, they can only be healed through love, never through shame or blame. How can this be done? Set your intention to love everything that expresses itself, and then commit yourself to being love-in-action in every moment. Love yourself enough to honor your boundaries and be able to say no so you don't fall out of the love vibration, which comes from honoring yourself as a sacred temple. You get to decide what works and what doesn't, coming from love instead of people pleasing or fear of what others think. Then, watch how everything begins to fall into place to support an awakening and healing transformation. Synchronicities will become apparent the more you feel empowered, even in times of incredible discomfort. We must accept that this is all a part of the initiation that strengthens us and do everything we can to resist the temptation to judge as a weakness, run from or reject it.

Superficial living isn't going to cut it anymore. A world of appearances—the 3D-programmed personality matrix—has nowhere to go. Those still addicted to drama, gossip, trends and following pop culture will feel lost as no one can evade the accelerated growth period. Everyone is being hit in one way or another. Some are experiencing personal tragedies with illness or death or division between friends and family because of differences in strongly-held belief systems or socially imposed mandates and lockdowns keeping people physically apart. And still, others are processing and facing a very uncertain future with a loss of income and even sanity from an upside-down reality. To remain in the false matrix during these intense shifts means compromising oneself and complying with authority for the ability to continue playing the game of material success and achieving the "American dream," which is all but dead. The only sustainable thing is to build a foundation upon the cosmic Earthly dream and experience.

We are re-discovering the elemental kingdoms, healing crystals, good nutrition, herbs, soul family, and sacred union while embracing the activation process of reclaiming our lost treasures and spiritual gifts and abilities. Our creative imagination can take us on adventures and show us that magic and miracles are real. The old world is falling away to reveal the truth of who and what we are.

The transition into the full embodiment of our soul nature will be challenging for many, as they will no longer get away with betrayal, back-stabbing, pettiness and shallowness. The pain of trying to exist in this world will be the gestalt that activates many to awaken to their own shadow or life review and take the next step into greater depth, compassion, and responsibility to being in service to others and embarking on a profound healing journey. It is the only path available in these times, and each must walk it to remain whole and unhook from the dark lord spider web that spins us up only to eat us alive. The world of all things "celebrity" is taking a huge step back as being anything but a priority as people step up to a role beyond being a consumer, followers of socially engineered movements, or slaves to the entertainment industry with all its predictive programming.

The process underway is the literal death of the old paradigm and ego attachments with a concurrent rebirthing of a soul-centered ego aligned to soul, spirit, love, wisdom, the cosmos, Earth, and truth to generate the energy throughout our physical vessel and regenerate and switch on dormant DNA so we can infuse the collective consciousness with these divine frequencies. It's time to become an activator, the override frequency and the embodied divine union with Source!

MY MISSION

We all are on a mission of some kind, and awakening to our mission is the purpose of being human. The ultimate goal is finding the truth frequency within oneself and living an authentic life. I have come to learn my mission has been about human sovereignty, global alchemy, the repair and restoration work of DNA and Earth grids, overcoming the fall of humankind from our origins, being a guardian of the Organic Ascension timeline, clearing inorganic entities from wormholes and helping to bring about Unity Consciousness and assist the human race in moving into higher Earth energies. Of course, uttering these kinds of words to people who can't relate doesn't go very far. People like to laugh, make fun and look oddly at me as their limitations can't comprehend a much vaster picture. As you can imagine, it can be a very lonely journey without soul family and others of like mind around.

Another major part of my mission was to avoid being diverted from my work here on Earth and taken to Mars. This event occurred at a pivotal crossroads in my life where I had to choose which timeline I would venture down—a very crucial time for me that not only set my trajectory but opened my eyes to all sorts of undisclosed operations such as the Secret Space Program and the hidden technologies being used against the human race. My relentless dedication to truthfully expose these hidden agendas has been to help humanity come into more awareness of itself and the power of the human spirit to overcome all the different tactics being used against us behind the scenes to keep us down. My efforts eventually guided me toward understanding the horrific projects and programs used throughout history to traumatize and split the minds of vulnerable individuals, especially children—some of the most important work I have done to date. I am an advocate and safe container and space holder for those subjected to the unimaginable. I do all I can to end such wicked crimes against humanity and the innocent. Shedding light on the Eisenhower administration and what has been kept secret has been crucial to this end and my overall mission.

There was no way throughout life I could ignore what I was being shown, and being on this mission was something I have never been able to separate myself from. It needed me as much as I needed it! To even attempt to walk away was asking for sure death, so there was only one way to go, and that was into the truth and depths of the world's soul to answer the call of humanity, Gaia and the very needs of my being, all woven into a great story and tapestry. The truth is, we are all woven into this story, but few who actually know and live it consciously and thus have a greater responsibility to stay alert, discerning and aware of attacks while striving to initiate into higher and higher levels of consciousness. With all the negativity, toxins, and programs, it's crucial to know how to transmute these things to receive the high-frequency downloads needed to assist as many people as possible while staying hopeful and undefeated if outwardly rejected or called crazy.

Being willing to plant seeds in places where there is little or no resonance and remain a resource of information, love and compassion is something I was determined to do and maintain my entire life. At the very least, I understood that an awakened starseed or ascension guide knew the truth of what we are all made of and what it would take to liberate ourselves from long-standing oppression, control, corruption and injustice. I learned to maintain this strength and stay true to the higher virtues of self and the sacred path of service to others. It doesn't mean the self is negated or can only be perfect. It just means that one is devoted to choosing the higher road and being a conduit for ascension, willing to self-correct as more things reveal themselves. It takes humility to grow and is as close as one can ever get to perfection relative to one's current state. From the perspective of Source, love is the only perfect thing in all Creation—the rest is an illusion. We are each called to play unique roles, so it is crucial to honor diversity. The one thing I feel is universal is knowing it's time to unify and upgrade our DNA and become fully conscious of the healing between the masculine and feminine.

My inner voice was loud, and my dream world was powerful. Both ensured I knew to some degree what I was in for to complete the mission. My journey has been filled with shock, crisis, continual chaos, extreme targeting and tragedies. But none of it could overpower the love and wisdom that surrounded me and was ever-present—some things just can't be overtaken or destroyed! These same forces serve all to regenerate, restore, protect, and ultimately win this war against a blossoming human consciousness.

I heard a loud call to protect the Organic Ascension timeline and embody the divine template of sacred union. I knew I had to become fully sovereign and an active co-creator of the ultimate love story on the levels of Creation itself. I was to assist in the activation of the 13th gate and be a conscious participant in the grounding of the Mother energies, which involved going into great darkness, the underworld, to experience many trials and tribulations due to the strong opposition and hidden agendas placed on humanity to try and stop this. I was forced into this hyperaware state, targeted pre-birth, to end up on a very different timeline than I am now, as I previously mentioned and will continue to blow the whistle on.

Another aspect of my life's work is gaining as much understanding of this window period as possible. My childhood was about becoming prepared for the 2000-2017 Stellar Activation Cycle window period, with 2012 as the key date connected to the Mayan prophecy of the end times and new world with predictions of doomsday armageddon, some great apocalypse, and ascension all floating around in the same "soup." I knew that because of free will and being powerful creative beings, we could influence this period to keep it moving in a positive direction. Of course, we could recognize the traps, imposters and targets. I learned we had to keep our creative channels clear of things that are not ours and that our dreams, connection to the divine, and attaining our truth frequency would allow our bodies to thrive. Though the Ascension Cycle continues beyond 2018, the 2000-2017 period served as a thrust potential for getting on board the higher timeline, if one so chose, versus being led astray onto an artificial timeline.

Deep probing into my soul, mind and consciousness, going beyond the borders of this reality into the unseen realms, showed me what would become my guiding principle for many future adventures, including the dangerous, challenging and sometimes exhilarating ones. This guiding principle consisted of Great Spirit, the Christos light and the Magdalene flame, and my willingness to accept this flawed human condition with humility as I recognized that being here inevitably comes with wounds, traumas, programs and patterns that ask to be loved and healed. I knew there was more to the story than personal tragedies, which included manipulative forces and hidden controllers working hard to ensure humanity stayed fractured, conquered and divided. I knew if I devoted myself to these guiding principles, it was possible to shift the tides to heal and transform and that if any adversities and pain endured, they could become jewels of wisdom. All this was inspiring enough to me and thus became a source of incredible motivation.

I could feel these forces in nature and as keen innate awareness and intuition, much more than any belief system could provide me. I could see glimpses of something that would, over time, expand and become a more anchored reality if I could stay present with it long enough—like a timeline leading into a palpable world of magic and bliss! This recognition of what's possible for us as a human race can soothe an aching heart that's known this reality for thousands of years!

As I grew up, what it would take to help facilitate the great shift into the higher Earth energies called ascension became more apparent. To complete my soul agreements, I chose to incarnate into the Eisenhower bloodline in this lifetime and embark on a journey that would help me intimately understand Sophia and my connection with her and with the galactic love story residing in our DNA and the very soul of this planet. The Magdalene flame, which many women carry, and the Eisenhower energies needed to intersect because our shadow governments have intentionally targeted the Earth and the divine feminine. So, through a joint mission, Eisenhower and I could partner to share in a legacy of disclosure and return to our Mother Earth and Unity Consciousness roots. I greatly appreciate the many psychics, channels and clairvoyants that helped me make this connection since it was nothing assumed, no matter how deeply I felt it. Throughout all my observations, experiences and encounters, I have come to see and accept my part in helping to disclose the hidden truths kept from us around ET races and their involvement with our governments, genetics and our progression or digression as a race.

I am sovereign. We all are, though many still don't know. I don't care to give my power away to governments or hold the expectation that they will save the world or that any one leader can. I have already determined that it is (and always was) us creating disclosure events, ascension, unity, DNA upgrades, and more for ourselves. Eisenhower, too, said that the governments had better get out of the way so that people could have peace. The only power they have is the power they robbed and stole by infecting our dreams, minds and creative imaginations with scenarios that we do not need to consent to or co-create with. Unity acts like an immune system to the Earth, where the parasites and germs naturally fall away when we remain in a vibration of higher integrity, love and wisdom. I vote for Mother Earth and the power of the human spirit., the people taking on leadership roles in their communities and the researchers, whistleblowers, healers, wisdom keepers and true guardians and protectors who truly serve the people. All that needs to be exposed will come with all that needs to be healed.

In moving towards working together more, we can be sure that future generations have other options that help them stay connected to who they came here to be. God gave us the bodies we were born with. If we feel confused or don't like the body we were given, it is our soul's journey to heal it and deprogram it to have more spirit-body communication so self-love emerges. You can live your truth, be and express yourself, and be protected from all the attempts to turn you into

Between 1945 and the 1960s, the United States Government brought more than 1,500 Nazi German scientists and engineers into the country through Project Paperclip to work on guided missiles, jet and rocket engines, aerodynamics, aerospace medicine and submarine technology.

something else, like through social conditioning or silencing you and repressing the gifts you were born with. I'll always put my hopes, trust and faith in it.

WE ARE FRAGMENTED

We are all fragmented to some degree. We are born with an amnesia about our past, and being raised in society often means we get brainwashed into something that lures us into many traps. The purity of a child does not know racism, insecurities, arrogance, hatred or gender power struggles. Still, it becomes something reinforced based on our experiences, environment, parents and relationships coupled with the energy signature we were born with. There is often a carryover from previous lifetimes that may need revisiting, but many choose not to explore this enough to understand why they feel the way they do about certain things. Some quickly revert to a former past life persona that might not be so pure, but as infants and children, we are so pure in our divine innocence that dark control forces move quickly to contaminate and infiltrate us. These actions can trigger the reappearance of old negative patterns or blocks, which must once again be overcome, or they can create brand new ones that weren't previously there.

We may recognize programming and societal conditionings and still fall prey to its detrimental symptoms, while others may not even question and go along with it. If we fall prey, we may struggle with self-worth issues even if we know how damaging that is to our psyche, like what we repeatedly see in magazines, media and television. Unfortunately, being awake doesn't promise us total immunity.

We were all born into a gaping wound, enduring theft embedded in all cultures and corners of society for thousands of years. Our task is to integrate this polarity by tending to our wounds and moving into a more unified awareness that starts first within the self. But unfortunately, it is easy to infect our creative energies with conditioned thoughts that have been taught or projected onto us. So when we talk about "lifting the veil," it is our veil we must lift first to get back to our core authentic selves. It's our best chance with all the external projections coming at us.

Many wonder why they feel so different and say, "I don't belong here" or "What am I doing here?" That can bring on a lot of struggle and grief, which is often misunderstood and then jumped on by the medical industry with "the solution" to medicate it. Unfortunately, distractions in society make it all too easy to medicate and ignore what our deeper self is trying to show us, addicting us to things that temporarily appease a deeper soul yearning that keeps getting ignored and silenced, all the while as the inner voice attempts to grow louder to gain our attention, it can turn into pain and disease if we ignore it and cover it up or try and escape it.

Thankfully, there are powerful forces at work to give us each the wake-up call we need. If we hear the messages behind them, it becomes much easier to heal and make the necessary changes, like dropping toxic people in our lives or leaving oppressive jobs, to step into more neutrality—a key to self-mastery. When we can remember we are creative beings and hold a strong intent and vision, we can manifest something better for ourselves and unlock all the pain of any stress or repressed aspects of self or internalization of our calling or gifts. The point is that we all get contaminated to a degree, and still, pure and sacred energy within us is waiting to awaken.

CRITICAL TIMES

These are critical times, and we are at a crossroads. Our choices are paving a future scenario that will be hard to unwind or shift out of if we don't choose to do the necessary work of rediscovering ourselves. We need to know what we are dealing with and where the true antidote and divine guidance reside and be brave enough to align completely with it. We have each had at least a glimpse of what alignment means and looks like for ourselves. As diverse as Creation is, there are as many ways of describing it. As we seek this similar state, we must make room and respect how people articulate it. The result of alignment is rewarding and beautiful, and though it will require a great leap of faith to believe it's possible for a time, at some point, it will become a given and embodied awareness.

Truth stands on its own and will exist whether we find it or not, the same as Spirit. They never abandon us. Only we can choose to walk the other way. Truth has a resonance with our physical bodies and the power to heal and regenerate any falsities that have caused damage along the way. Our physical pains and ailments serve as our road map home when we understand the root of affliction through its subtle messages of wisdom that seek to transform us. And so much can be imposed upon us in times of vulnerability that it's possible to become a carrier of another's imbalance. Rest assured. It's possible to assist by releasing on their behalf. Being vulnerable is a good thing as long as we maintain good personal boundaries and make clear that all untrustworthy and harmful forces are no longer welcome. May we all have the strongest armor and shields of protection while remaining in perfect flow with our divine essence and an open heart. Adversity can bring us closer to ourselves or further away, depending on our choice. I choose closeness!

What will guide us to exit the matrix is our connection to Spirit and the healing of our DNA. But, first, we must unplug from the control system. Synchronicities, ease and flow open up to us when we are willing to take this step, and our creative energy infuses with our divinity and the unconditional love of Source to help undo and transform the infections and deceptions siphoning our creative power and imagination to generate artificial timelines. Miracles come from our ability to shift perspective to a higher intention while facing lower frequencies that seek to pull us into fear and powerlessness.

Embodying sacred union and manifesting relationships that align with our divine template allows for the restoration and amplification of all organic timelines. If we stay in the programming and distortions, we will keep repeating history and remain stuck in the time loop that acts out what society says we should be, and lose our chance to grow, thrive and become our authentic advanced selves.

The Earth herself is a highly conscious organism, a body and a life force of the supreme soul of the Goddess, who manifests the essence and vibration of her inner world into matter. She has moods, growth cycles and the power to create and destroy. The Great Mother sits at the top of our food chain, constantly healing herself from conditions that seek to overtake her wisdom of seasonal renewal and sustainable abundance. The healing process for our planet and us is establishing equilibrium, maintaining this divine connection, and awakening it fully in our beings so that we can connect with her. We live at the mercy of her natural whims, not that of an inverted system that is not in sync with her and that has attempted to overtake her body, elements and grid network, which is what humanity has been facing in being separated from their soul, higher DNA strands and divine blueprint. Her intention is not to harm but to co-create a relationship with all of us, to provide what we need to experience and grow personally and collectively and become one with her. When we connect to our true spirit, we find a deep desire to live in harmony with the Earth. With each cycle, nature teaches us to release the need for ego control, stay aligned with divine will, and follow the path of the Goddess, who seeks to bring us back to unconditional love and abundance.

I feel the geoengineering and control placed upon nature and the degradation is just a mirror of us in the 3D. When we release ourselves from this, we can perceive higher Earth energies, where the Organic Ascension timeline takes us. Whether we make it there in this body matters little, but let's give it our all while we are here. The

3D existence and the manipulation of weather, to me, is a mirror of the health of our lower chakras and the collective consciousness. Survival and how we care for ourselves is our first root chakra. Our second sacral chakra is our emotions and re-activity nature. And our third solar plexus chakra is our sense of power and identity. If they become contaminated and we allow information that manipulates, their energetic circulation with the rest of the multi-dimensions becomes blocked, distorted or compartmentalized. We speak the level of vibration that our lower centers hold and keep looping. This is why breaking through into the Galactic Chakras is a way to purify these energy centers and ground them back into Mother Earth. It clears our creative imagination from all that seeks to imprint it with programs that form belief systems not in alignment with our truth. It becomes hard to think clearly when we are in fear and panic. The result of this can manifest as struggling with lower-frequency thoughts and emotions or an unconscious attachment to an addiction matrix that gives us a false sense of security and confidence before we begin to notice something is way off with the so-called "solutions."

The magnitude of nature's fury means Mother Earth could wipe us away at any moment. She continually shifts and changes. It is we who have to listen to grasp the unconditional devotion she has always had to continue to sustain and support life. This is how we can also de-weaponize the dark technology forces that attempt to control her elements and us, as long as we are plugged into the propaganda and indoctrination, believing everything we see in the news. How detrimental it is to fall for this "wokeness," where we are encouraged to believe that all the events we see happening are because of things like "climate change" while doing little to no research into weather manipulation, directed-energy weapons (DEWs) or what our skies are being sprayed with. Our Mother's womb can rebirth us to walk the path of free will and co-creation and align us with our higher wisdom and nature, or we can choose to bifurcate away from this. She showers us with the most potent unconditional love as she sustains us—the kind of love that every mother knows.

When ready, we all can return to her and heal, regenerate, and release ourselves from lies, distortions, and manipulations. As long as you live fully what you feel is your truth, that's all that matters. I only ask you to consider what I share and see where it can go for you. If we live our truth, we will manifest life events that will help us grasp a much larger reality of our origins, what we are currently dealing with, where we are heading and what this creation is all about. We are here to move through the many layers until we return home again. The most important thing is to stay in our hearts and connected to our souls and not fall into the pit of hatred and judgement. We have all been led astray to some degree and exposed to dangerous and debilitating forces, but we have more than we can imagine within us and in creation to rise above. Staying flexible is vital—not having fixed or rigid beliefs—and remaining humble enough to self-correct when necessary. This is how we can more greatly flow with life and one another.

So many of us hold this flame of her love in our hearts, and so we gladly light the way back to her arms for those yearning who have long forgotten. The Venus transits show her unconditional love because, even though she was not able to be firmly anchored in the planet due to cataclysms, invasions, wars, and manipulations of the planetary grids, her heart has always been there creating corrections and returning to her body and her children no matter how difficult the controller groups and fallen ones made this for her.

This archonic matrix is an imitation of Original Creation, and thus, it doesn't hold any real power unless you give it away. We can only plug our energy and frequency into infinite Source energy or the electronic controls that expand into a finite artificial world. The only real danger with the latter is if you hand yourself over to it by buying into its theatrics. Once you detach from the corrupt aspects of the money system, media, governments, and distortions, you unfold into your original form, and your DNA and circuitry upgrade and restore so that you can withstand and integrate the powerful lifting energies streaming in, rather than being pulled into unhealthy chaotic emotions, fear or unconscious attachments by the dark forces.

With the current amplification of polarities as dark agendas ramp up, it becomes more obvious who is controlled by negative AI signals because the frequency is so clearly different from those who aren't. Any adversity encountered can thrust us to awaken and rescue our deepest treasures or pull us deeper into mind control, indoctrination and loss of soul matrix. Therefore, we must do everything we can to ensure this doesn't happen and hold love, compassion and understanding for family and loved ones struggling with this, as love will help set them free.

It is possible to clear AI signals from your nervous system, brain and body once you are aware of them, and you can keep them from returning by changing your consciousness and elevating your frequency. AI signals are reversal energies that generate artificial timelines through our unconscious disempowerment and the use of bio-weapons and societal mind-control and fear tactics. The higher the frequency of a signal, otherwise known as a frequency download, the more information-carrying capacity it has. Forgiveness and compassion for the self and others, for falling for the deceptions or engaging in negative patterns to move forward, is so important. Patience is necessary if forgiveness and compassion don't come easy or you must push yourself to feel this way. We must be careful not to have it hold us down or cause us self-destructive patterns and to practice self-care and spend more time actively in nature. These are some countermeasures to winning the inner war.

Lisa Renee states this beautifully:

"During the Ascension Cycle, humanity is being accelerated into greater ranges of amplified electromagnetic frequency exposure. These are either natural signals that support biological Ascension, or artificial signals that block the physical body with pain, thereby, suppressing or fragmenting the Lightbody.

During the Bifurcation of Time, our inner energetic integrity is being tested. This is the time to take stock of how well we are coping with the madness of the Earth, as the collective mind of humanity travels the Dark Night of the Soul. Whether asleep or awake, our self-mastery is measured through how we personally deal with stress and chaos. No person on this Earth is exempt from exposure to the massive fields of chaos, confusion and darkness that exist in the collective mind of humanity."

STAYING STRONG: TRUE SELF, SPIRITUAL HYGIENE, BODILY MAINTENANCE

"Your purpose is to carry information and, by carrying it, to make the information accessible to others by frequency. Information is light; light is information. The more you become informed, the more you alter your frequency. You are electromagnetic creatures, and everything that you are, you broadcast to everyone else."

– Barbara Marciniak

Facing a Dark Night of the Soul initiation is something we really can't avoid. It can be quite confusing when you begin to connect with the depths of your being. So often, the sensation of dying goes along with such a profound transformation that it is common to panic and feel exhaustion, especially if we try to stop it.

Contrary to what some may feel, we are not at the mercy of the reality around us. We have the power and ability to sculpt and change it. When we transform, so does our reality. It doesn't mean we don't witness negative scenarios that others choose, but we will at least recognize it as a stark contrast to the person we have become. Being in service to others can hopefully inspire people to remember our human potential and that we can get over the challenges being presented to us personally and globally.

If we notice that certain transformational growth periods we went through are repeating, we have unfinished business or more depth to venture into and release. Sometimes, we witness another's reality that isn't ours, so we must be careful not to attach it as our story to avoid making it our reality.

We cannot advance if we don't integrate our polarity. Imbalance is what keeps us stuck and attracts dark entities. Balance and integration are the seeds planted in the garden—the point of conception. We are in a relationship with them all. Our dark aspect is the womb that receives the seeds from our higher mind to create and generate a beautiful reality if we allow it. If we don't actively work on energetic hygiene and maintenance, these forces overtake what we seek to nurture and grow.

Using this metaphor, if we draw and plant seeds from our fears and haunted imaginations, we give life to the things we want to stop and continually birth them into our reality. Hence, this needs clearing and focused intent to overcome. Sometimes, we must face our greatest fears to discover we have always been senior to them. They can never defeat us if we reach into the infinite potentials of Creation. This is where we become spiritual athletes and warriors determined to gain strength over these obstacles and not give up. Surrendering to the most incredible love story forever coded in our DNA, we recognize the divinity in nature and the cosmos to allow its perfect flow to permeate us.

Physicality is more evident in how we manage it because we can visually see it. When we accumulate too much negativity in our mental, emotional and spiritual energy bodies, it becomes harder to manage as we can't see it. We often accept the imbalanced sensations through a belief system of "affliction" and therefore get trapped to give our power away to having "serious issues." Things like depression, ADD labels, the many diagnoses we readily accept, pain, suffering, or an absolute lack of clarity in our minds that we try and compensate for by building our prison walls to protect us. Humans don't like to feel insecure, or in pain, so we often do anything possible to feel good and build confidence. But there are very harmful things that serve as a bandaid to encourage and promote a false sense of confidence or numbing pain relief and, in the long run, only make it worse. Facing our shadow and dark night of the soul means a willingness to face all of it to find the message that leads to profound growth and transformation.

When we call our creative energy back from distorted belief systems, outer information and projections from others and open ourselves up to our vast imagination and divine power within, it blends with the outer world. Taking the time to focus on our intentions every day and keep negative behaviors in check while showing appreciation for the messages pain and negativity reveal to us is the required maintenance of our energy body. It's a chance to do some much-needed gardening to make room for the next bunch of seeds for ideas and creations galore. When things accumulate in our kitchens or lived-in spaces, we take time for regular house cleaning to the best of our abilities or standards. Similarly, to varying degrees, every part of us requires maintenance, or things get toxic and out of balance. Piles of internalized emotions and a racing mind that can't think to clear it will attract the same sort of sludge as a sink full of dirty dishes. Heartache without tears or release can create blockages of pain and lower immune system function. Any form of repression or accumulated energy creates issues.

This self-mastery includes our words and how we relate to each other. It's a challenge that comes with operating a human vessel, but life unfolds more sweetly if we are more careful of our words. Words can uplift, inspire and heal, or they can harm, hurt and cause discord. It is a bit different if people are easily triggered, but more conscious, spiritually mature and transparent conversations can drastically improve our lives. Some aren't ready for this, so we have to be clear about who we are dealing with before we get too intimate, and if the love is real, they won't mind all that needs to come up to the surface to be expressed.

I aim to connect as many dots as possible to integrate all our fragments and realize a fuller version that isn't so compartmentalized. We are the world we see around us—as within so without. The condition of our inner self is amplified in our outer world to be mirrored back as a reality we see and often create fixed beliefs about. It stares us in the face in every "now" moment so that we can recognize and affect desired change. Sadly, we learn to do the opposite from birth of what natural and cosmic laws encourage us to do quite naturally. When we have opportunities to advance, many freak out and get more entangled in the control mechanisms that siphon our precious life force energy. Advancement isn't without felt discomfort or pain, so we must resist the temptation to run from it or want a quick fix cure rather than taking the time to learn and grow from it. It is the only way we'll reunite with our true selves rather than the stranger we may have become.

It is easy to loop in paterned behaviors based on our perceptions if they aren't elevated enough to accommodate our soul essence. We will keep repeating lessons or events until we can initiate into a higher plane. If we don't become more conscious of our dreams and waking reality, our perceptions will remain limited. It reinforces the need to be willing to face our soul's dark night journey and not mask or escape it. It's crucial to lift the veil and elevate our perceptions beyond all social engineering or mind control. Like my experience, sometimes this awareness can come hard and fast at an early age. I had a lot forcing my attention as a young child. At times, it was overwhelming!

The Earth Responds to Us

"They say I came for all, but in truth I came for Her Who came for all. For it had come to pass that there were those who had lost their way and , lacking in spark, could not return into the Fullness; seeing this, She came unto them, giving Her life to the depths of matter. And in truth She did suffer and become blind. But our Father, sensing Her anguish, sent Me forth, being of Him, so that She might see and We be as One again. Though they see it not, it is She, the tender Mother of Mercy, Who is the great redeemer."

– Caitlin Matthews

The Mother energy has returned to Earth's core, and the sacred union energies of the Magdalene flame forces and conscious Christos light awareness, which helps the Earth to purge and bring to the surface all the hidden dark agendas—pedophilia, mind control projects, human and child trafficking, weather modification, etc.—that have compromised humanity for so long. We have a long way to go, but the more exposure to this information, the less consent we will see because people won't be able to ignore it anymore. The not knowing and denial keep humans in an unhealthy dependency bond or false trust of individuals behind the New World Order agenda. But as people awaken, may we focus on healing and forgiveness we can raise the vibration of love on the planet and move into unity, solutions and cooperation.

When we clear our inner elements, we heal the planet—the oceans, skies, land, and out-of-control fires. When we connect with the Earth, we connect with the regenerative power of nature, and it becomes a co-creative process of global alchemy where we work together to open the stargates into the many higher dimensions to experience greater peace, bliss, higher intelligence and abilities. We are up against much uncertainty in the world right now. It may not seem easy to achieve, but when we are more soul-centered and remain heart-centered, we might notice that whatever weapons are directed at us, they can be overcome as long as we live our truth, seek ways to shield and protect ourselves and come together more to tackle our current challenges with the many healing technologies and modalities that are out there. When we choose to journey into the underworld, hell returns to the creative cauldron of Creation, where souls can be reborn and redeemed if one so chooses—it's the very reason we have gone through the hell worlds. Each of us carries the archetypal energies within to embrace this journey that the divine feminine path has shown and instilled in us, as we are a part of her. Things like Venus transits and the 13th sign are cosmic and Earthly proof.

We are in relationship to everything. The more harmonious and pure we are as we interact with the world and our environment, the more light can clear away everything that keeps us in heavy-density misery and suffering. When we are disconnected from ourselves and disempowered, something outside us controls us, and nature too, as we are nature. You can be the override frequency—the higher dimensions are patiently waiting!

We choose to align with the fallen angelics, or we are the resurrection and light force that helps inspire and leads by example. We have fallen only to get right back up. Like children learning to walk, we keep picking ourselves up until we finally run. True divine light comes through when the light of wisdom ignites in the greatest darkness, true light emerging, having embraced the great mystery. Avoiding the dark perpetuates more darkness and our vulnerability to false light. It is the womb, soil and soul and is nothing to be feared. Make darkness the fertile ground that receives seeds of inspiration from your higher self so we can collectively manifest higher Earth energies. Because the Earth responds to us—Father, Mother and child!

Misery Loves Company—The Fallen Ones

Misery loves company. The fallen ones who compromised their DNA to be our controllers seek to program suffering into us, not only to be their food source but also so we forget who we are and stay stuck in the lower realms.

We can be unreachable to these fallen groups and gain the upper hand. So often, we hold that vibration, but it's challenging to maintain consistently. However, maintaining our frequency above the archon structure allows our creative energies to manifest substantial things and ride the waves into higher realms.

3D Earth is a hell realm, and endless shock and disgust are the names of the game. There is so much beauty in the soul beyond 3D, which we can fully live

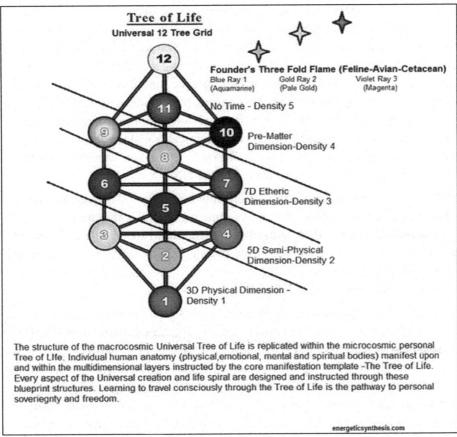

The structure of the macrocosmic Universal Tree of Life is replicated within the microcosmic personal Tree of Life. Individual human anatomy (physical, emotional, mental and spiritual bodies) manifest upon and within the multidimensional layers instructed by the core manifestation template -The Tree of Life. Every aspect of the Universal creation and life spiral are designed and instructed through these blueprint structures. Learning to travel consciously through the Tree of Life is the pathway to personal sovereignty and freedom.

energeticsynthesis.com

Tree of Life. "Learning to travel consciously through the vibrational landscape of the Tree of Life, is to travel through the multiple dimensions of time, Gaia and self and this is the personal pathway to achieve spiritual sovereignty and freedom...This is how we restore our DNA, we must bring consciousness to these dormant and asleep aspects of self and fully rise..." –Lisa Renee, Energetic Synthesis; https://energeticsynthesis.com/library/multi-dimensional/2846-universal-tree-of-life

right here and right now, it is that deeper part of who we are that manifests an entirely different kind of experience. The material trappings of 3D Earth can create fun and joy, but it is not sustainable alone to exist in the world of appearances. We can't force this matrix to change. We must create the change that starts with ourselves. No longer can we allow lower forces to addict us or keep us stuck and looping in lower behavior patterns. No one needs to be perfect. Just be aware that when we slip into lower energies, we have a solid foundation to return to. All this becomes easier the more self-love, forgiveness and laughter we offer ourselves and when we remember that we are never at the mercy of dark forces or the collective. It is from within that we become forever free!

Most of us feel bad over such minor things, like interrupting someone when eager to share. Evil is foreign and wishes to harm. Those trying to run the show don't think twice about doing the most horrific acts. We are fast approaching when it will be impossible to continue occupying the same density with lower energies, so pulling back and detaching from the madness is advisable. At the same time, seek justice. It's easy for unavoidable emotions to feel crushing at times, but find comfort that it's not the final destination but a critical stage of development in a long and drawn-out alchemical transformational process to recover our origins. Trust the process! The cosmic forces and nature are encoded with this very reassurance and truth—like our DNA!

People withhold love, compassion, concern, openness, gentleness, understanding and the wisdom to respond to someone from a higher mind and heart. I say withhold because these gifts always exist within us. They are the deepest part of who we are. Instead, people are often combative, negating, judgmental, uninterested, belittling, impatient, and annoyed. This chaos can sink everyone into a low vibration that causes harm.

Call it programmings, unresolved wounds or ancestral patterns—we are here to redeem these treasures and crack through. The difference in frequency between the two approaches is astounding. One lowers to injure, separate and destroy, while the other uplifts to heal, unite and regenerate. So next time we look at the world and feel troubled by the many things going wrong, remember that we are here to develop our abilities in the face of adversity—what awakening is all about. We can shift this reality, and this option exists in every moment. It is the only true free will we have. Remember that we can be like our immune system in our mental, emotional, physical and spiritual bodies—a transmuter, activator, alchemist, guide and friend, and a divine presence for others and ourselves. People who seek power and control, manipulate and deceive, are not doing their best with what they have been given, nor do they want to be enlightened. The influence they spread in the world can cause some people to forget to live their lives from their higher self, so they become used to negative patterns that seem acceptable or the norm. We should strive for the best in ourselves, particularly concerning the things we have some control over—like our perceptions, beliefs, behavior and the way we treat others. We can make all the excuses we want for others and ourselves, but we are experiencing a quickening, and it's time to snap out of it.

People can change, but the archons and dark forces would change by now if they were evolving. Nonetheless, we are, and when we see the opposing force as the shadow self or the unawakened aspects of who we are that can lead us astray and into a false matrix, then we will bring light to our illusion or divergence from the divine and return to truth and Source.

The labyrinth is a version of the goddess. This image of the Labyrinth Goddess expresses the journey of the divine feminine retrieving her many aspects and going through the many phases. The book, "Maiden, Mother, Crone," by D.J Conway, introduces the concept of the Labyrinth, a journey where you learn to face past emotional upheavals, become responsible for your actions and reactions, and accept all aspects of the cycle of life. The Labyrinth can be traversed with the knowledge and balance provided by the Goddess.

Some will not make it into the higher dimensions. But they are always welcome if they ever care to let the divine spark awaken within, as it exists in all beings and can even be ignited again in the cruel ones.

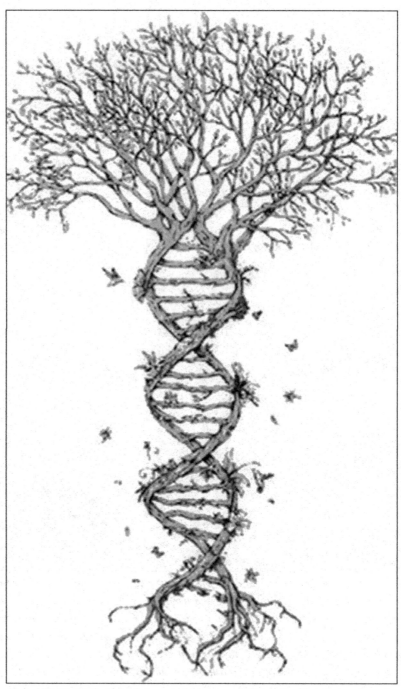

Tree of Life DNA. I don't know the name of the Artist, but I came across this image, and seeing that the Tree of Life is connected to our DNA I thought it was an appropriate image to include as we work to rebuild our DNA template to its full potential.

We will continue manifesting crises until we unearth these abilities. It is well worth our effort because we are the shift, and it is our vibration, and no one else's, that will do it. Conflict should be faced head-on with the utmost respect for the fantastic opportunity that it presents. It is an art and a skill to bring seemingly disparate things into harmony, and every negative situation allows us to practice and master them. We get to see the higher and lower perspectives and align ourselves with what is more spiritually and soulfully beneficial rather than serving the ego. The ego can then accurately express the depth of our being and higher consciousness, and our dreams will finally stand a chance at manifesting in the physical. We are doing the repair work every day by being mindful and conscious.

The things that hurt us deeply must be tended to and not ridiculed, denied or buried, even if they don't make sense or become rigid in us. They require our dedication, patience and love. In doing so, they can help us to be more transparent and not act out or loop in the negative blame, shame victim game. You must be steadfast in respecting yourself and not hold on to any projection that doesn't represent your truth, even when others disrespect you. This is where healthy boundaries come in. The wounded aspects of self are a part of the collective wound we were born into that the storylines of our lives reveal. In taking on this important challenge to rise above and tap into unconditional love and forgiveness, we move forward with greater strength, clarity and purpose. We all share in the task of being a force of transformation that breaks down negative patterns instead of submitting to the downward spirals and avoiding the work required to overcome the traps of the lower dualism of the 3D.

I feel so passionate about ending the race-baiting divisiveness. I am tired of this ploy that keeps us dumbed down in our DNA potential. You can say this, but not that. All the related triggers and hyper-offended reactivity saddens me because we are all a rainbow tribe of warriors of all creeds, colors, races and nations! Every single one of us has experienced numerous past lives in any number of these diverse existences. Anyone who thinks accomplishment comes through division and this level of mind-fuckery, please take a step back and reevaluate. Enough already!

The Goddess Mother of this Earth, which indigenous cultures deeply revere and live in complete harmony with, is the Holy Spirit, the soul essence of Creation itself. All her children matter as they are her very fabric! Language barriers, traditions, and cultural differences shouldn't create separation or fuel offense when the loving hearts of those who live in unity with it share the same things no matter how much it bleeds over. They are the richness of life. Mind control and social engineering separate people from this Earth, so some carelessly abuse these terms and exploit their traditions or art to sell and profit. May they awaken already!

We are all intermixed, seven Root Races and five Cloistered Races, to rebuild the 12-strand-and-beyond Diamond Sun DNA template. The diamond heart radiates beauty in all its many facets. The power of the Holy Spirit grounded in all physical matter will set humanity free. That is when our Spirit force will ignite in our human vessels, and we walk a Spiritual path in sovereignty. These five Cloistered Races were called the Paliadorians, representing the beginning of fulfilling the Covenant of Paliador. This covenant was made as an agreement to rescue the souls of Tara. The longstanding agenda of conquer and divide is to thwart these efforts.

The Emerald Founder Records reveal that there are 12 Essene Tribes that make up the entirety of the collective human gene pool or are the descendants of the Universal Tribal Shield that has incarnated initially onto this planet from the future timelines of Tara. They were seeded on this Earth as a part of the evolution plan that resulted from the Covenant of Paliador lost soul rescue mission. This wouldn't be easily accomplished until the ascension window period when the stargates open.

We were born into a dysfunctional relationship between the masculine and feminine, creating a dysfunctional relationship within the self. Sacred union is the healing of this dynamic. It is the restoration of the Tree of Life from the duality of the Tree of Knowledge. When we find this inner template and illuminate it within ourselves and our partners, we help others find it. It can begin to neutralize the hidden weaponry and distortions and the impact the use of dark technologies has had on the Earth's grids and our DNA. Knowing the targets is knowing what we need to reclaim. Understanding how these technologies operate helps us to see more of what we have been up against for thousands and thousands of years. Being willing to have an open mind is the first step.

The manipulation of our sexual energies and the imbalance of the sexes has permeated races that have disconnected from the true Source, and through the use of some very dark technologies, they keep us from being able to harmonize. In certain areas on the Earth's grids, the masculine and feminine connecting points got intentionally unplugged to push us towards digression and further enslavement. We are born into this, so we must go beyond it to neutralize its effect on our DNA. It takes an extraordinary journey to reclaim ultimate seniority over these lower forces. Some technologies I have already named harvest the energy we unknowingly give away. Is this anything to fear? No, being "an aware citizenry" is the only thing we must concern ourselves with. Much more on how to come.

MULTI-DIMENSIONAL BEINGS

As multi-dimensional beings with an energy body, aura and physical vessel, we hold all harmonic universes in our DNA. To access them means that we heal our DNA, which comes through gaining enough self-knowledge to begin to know that the true Grail quest is of sacred union. The Grail quest is an inner journey into our soul, where trials and tribulations become a rite of passage, uniting all these levels of ourselves. They have been fragmented, limiting

Magdalene Flame. This image and the expression of the Magdalene energy capture what her Soul essence encompasses. –Luca Signorelli, artist, Santa Maria Maddalena piangente

our DNA expression. It was intentionally targeted as an agenda to keep us small and easily controlled. The soul is a chalice for Spirit. When we find our inner Grail, we become a part of a unified field beyond the matrix programs designed to tear relationships and love apart. The underworld journey is to reclaim and purify our darkness so that Spirit light can stream in. It creates an alchemical change that shifts our bodies and awareness into the bliss realms and clears the physical from toxicity back into its pristine and divine form.

I always knew that sacred union created a massive global shift and our ability to move beyond this time loop into something more magical and divine. Unfortunately, there is a mass targeting of the human race to undermine it, chalking it up as "New Age BS." Yes, there are deceptions, but this has nothing to do with a New Age and everything to do with us and our organic makeup. It is ancient and present now, and we are awakening to this recognition, which shifts everything. It takes us into a new experience and world, but only if we can achieve it within ourselves. It is recognizing and integrating our dark and light, masculine and feminine, and tuning into the inner elements and nature, the multi-dimensions of Creation that exist in our vaster makeup.

When we do this, we begin to recognize that we hold all the ascension energies within us already and are thus tasked with shedding the layers that are not in alignment with our true authentic self, moving beyond the obstacles that keep us in unhealthy attachments to imposters, control agendas, toxic people, addictions, negative patterns and dark entities.

STARGATES, LISA RENEE, CHRIST-SOPHIA

The Gnostics refer to something called Sophia's correction, and since I was a kid, my sense of it weighed heavy on me. I had no books, literature or outside information to validate this feeling and expand upon. It screamed from within me, trying to get my attention. I could sense a deep, broken heart that overwhelmed me. And when I ran into information alluding to what needed correction or exposure, I lit up and could barely focus on anything else. I appreciated the confirmation of what I already sensed. I knew I channeled beings similar to my vibration to not alert anyone's suspicion of being something other than myself. I was off in the multi-dimensional fields, doing all sorts of repair work. I was told later in life that I had been clearing inorganic entities from wormholes. I recall it being painful to be out of my body like that—I wished so much to be in it. It was traumatic because I felt everything!

A stargate connects into multiple dimensions beyond this one, hidden within the magnetic fields of Earth and space, waiting to take us on a journey beyond this limited reality. They are an organic part of Creation. According to the Guardians, Guardian Founder races once sealed off and closed these stargates due to severe damage and control by the NAA groups. For those having a hard time believing there are ETs, this might hit you hard and fast, but we must get comfortable knowing that the vastness of life in the universe may be similar to the diversity of species we see in our oceans, sky and land.

My inner-knowing is strong—especially of the Christ-Sophia—experiencing a lifetime of downloads that weren't validated by other sources until I discovered the material of sources like Lisa Renee, who intimately represents the Guardian perspective. Her material brought these points home for me regarding the origins of humanity's compromise and the explanation of Oraphim energy, the NAA and Christ-Sophia. Through lots of inner work, validated by discoveries of compelling sources that give goosebumps and a gut recognition, I know some of what I share comes directly from the Guardians. I have con-

Magdalene and the Grail. "Magdalene is finally rising from the hidden caves of our unconscious. She is re-emerging out of two thousand years of denial, banishment and a mistaken identity, to realize the fulfillment of a sacred trust, the blueprint for love and sacred union." –Ani Williams website; https://aniwilliams.com/mary-magdalene-mistress-of-the-grail/

nected many dots, referencing numerous sources that I will mention along the way. Lisa has reassured me that the Guardians want me to share my downloads. Through our intense connection, we have come to be good friends. The Guardians know I have been living intimately with all they bring forth in me. This vast story that we all connect with that has been hidden and unknown for ages pours through my awareness and all I have faced.

Stargates can step down higher energies transmitting from the source field and into the sun. These higher energies are a wide energetic spectrum of frequencies. As they enter our planet, they get directed into many stargates and circulate throughout the planetary grid network. As the 13th gate gets activated, the zero point energy also goes into the sun and the core of the Earth, where the Mother resides and where she has returned. This gateway between the two spreads throughout the planet and helps us develop our Diamond Sun body, leading us back to the Silicate Matrix.

Humanity has been challenged moving beyond our seven chakras to access our Galactic Chakras because of the psychic attacks and targeting as we move beyond the demiurgic veil. Recycling our souls continues until we learn how to move into the true light of spirit beyond our dark night of the soul journeys. However, when we allow ourselves the organic process of soul and spiritual development that life naturally guides us to develop, we are greatly supported, and we begin to notice powerful synchronicities that resonate with our divine nature versus being caught in the web and their false laws.

Breaking through this net or fence opens us to the fullness and wholeness of all we are. It connects us with the natural infinity spiral in our energy body. Still, we must go into the darkness, the shadow, the underworld pit so that we can fully ground into this Earth-body and merge with our true Mother. This planet has been running far too long on dark mother reversal energies that are not a part of the heart of the true Mother Goddess.

THE MAGDALENE FLAME

"Magdalene can currently be seen rising out of a long, imposed sleep. Like the story of Sleeping Beauty, she and her people have been 'drugged' into unconsciousness for two thousand years, by an extraordinary effort to suppress 'the other half of the story', Her story."

– Annie Williams

The Magdalene flame is associated with those who seek to create ascension on Earth through sacred union, unity consciousness, and deep underworld journeys of initiation to anchor the Mother energy back into the planet, guiding souls into higher embodiments and liberation. This flame works with the Venus transits and embodies the correction of dark reversal mother forces, which the dark rituals of Satanism and Luciferianism created to siphon the life force of humanity and the victims they capture.

The Magdalene flame gathers and integrates the fragmented energies of the exploded Sophianic planet Tiamat. It is a part of this Earth's body and is why dark agendas could compromise humanity to such a degree, with Mother energy compromised by all the abuses of her image. Magdalene is a part of the Sophia-body, and all gets corrected through this energy work.

To alchemize the global soul, one must incarnate on Earth to return the cosmic Aether accomplished by altering the reversal coding on the platonic solid dodecahedron representing this element. It's the underworld journey turning the inverted pentagram upright again, which Venus has done in her orbit and path for thousands of years. It brings the Mother back in as they are mother/daughter.

It is accomplished by refusing the programming, controller agendas and their manipulation, and refusing to remain in exile or victimhood. It involves moving through the layers of dimensional energies that block or enslave humanity and push an NWO agenda by trapping souls in programs and toxicity. Then, stargates must be cleared of inorganic entities, and a conscious connection must be made with the Christos light to remove blocks and patriarchal agendas from Earth and from deep within the psyche of all receptive humans. The Earth does respond to us, but she also has her journey, and although we influence her, she does not depend upon us for her evolution. To deprogram and fully experience our divine potential, we must accept this activation to switch on what is dormant and illuminate our inner divine blueprint. To me, this is what awakening is all about. When Organic Ascension signals get absorbed into the planetary and human bio-energetic field layers, the DNA Silicate Matrix template activates us from carbon base to crystalline embodiments and higher Earth energies.

We may not ascend rapidly, but we can agree that things are accelerating. A massive curse is lifting from the planet and creating a significant shift on a physical level noticeable to many of us. The Magdalene flame purifies the elemental energy, as our ego nature gets deprogrammed and purified, and allows for an easier direct connection with the zero point unified field.

> *"In Jesus' life then, the Magdalene Flame existed. It had become suppressed already, almost completely forgotten, most certainly by most ignored, but it was still present and in some temples venerated and honoured, even by those religions which now deny its very existence. It shone through Mary the mother of Jesus the Master but it shone most brightly through Jesus' consort and lover, Mary Magdalene, from whom in this period of history in which we currently live, it takes its name...*
>
> *Mary Magdalene was a vessel, a channel, a chalice, she carried the feminine fire of the Divine Source, the fire of the Goddess, the ultimate creatrix."*
>
> *– Channelled by Edwin Courtenay, October 2004*

The Beginning
of My Journey

"We get to the beauty through the brutal. Not over or around or under but straight through. We do not ignore each other's pain—we help carry it."

– *Glennon Doyle Melton*

I was born in England, in Fitzwarren Gardens in North London. My mom was relatively young when she had me and felt it was important to give birth at home at a time when that wasn't a thing people did. My father repeatedly told me the story of her African-American midwife, who was quite angelic. Surprisingly, she asked my mom if she could keep the placenta to grow her roses, which went on to win an award in a contest she entered.

My mom met my father through my paternal aunt in Brussels when my grandad John S.D. Eisenhower was the ambassador to Belgium. Soon after, they moved to England, where my father's side of the family lived, to have a life and a family together. At that point, my parents already had my older sister a year and a half before my birth.

My family moved a lot worldwide, though I have lived most of my life in America. My grandpa on my father's side was in the foreign service, so my granny and he and their children traveled extensively. My father was born in Egypt. The first language he learned was Swedish, though he can speak seven in all.

I have also traveled quite a bit and lived a nomadic lifestyle. I have never been driven by money and am more of a "just enough to get by" kind of person. I feel my abundance in other ways, like through expressions of love, being in nature and having good friends. This was fostered in my upbringing by family members who embodied these same values to create success and abundance through dedication and hard work. In all my travels, I find my soul most connected with the ocean. The deep caverns and caves in the darkest of seas feel like the deep plunge we take into our inner waters and emotions—into our soul.

I received my training in wilderness expedition leadership during my time spent in the deserts and seas around Baja, California, and in the Adirondacks' thick forests, mountains and lakes. I have also explored the canyons and ruins of the southwest, where I always found the most peace and clarity as a young adult. However, where I feel my spirit connected in a most familiar way to the land are my times spent in Ireland, Scotland and the British Isles.

THE MAGDALENE IN ME

My father gave me the middle name Madeleine, the French version of Magdalene. I came to learn it was more than just a middle name. While traveling around England as a child, I wasn't aware of how revered Mary Magdalene was, nor did I have any concept of this Goddess figure except for within my intuition. It became a doorway into my soul that connected to something beyond this Earth, yet was its very essence as with Venus. It wasn't something I could put my finger on or put into words. It influenced my awareness of a role intimately connected to allowing this sacred energy to freely move through me with the dedication to awaken it within others. It is more the essence of the divine feminine than the Magdalene archetype and our relationship with its one-of-a-kind expression.

I noticed that, though Mary Magdalene was revered, a big piece of her story was missing, and I became increasingly aware of how incredibly misunderstood she was. Of course, things are different today since so much literature now exists. Still, something in me didn't feel right about her portrayal. It seemed like there was so much more to her story than what the Bible shares. Thankfully, some of them are finally surfacing now. For many years, my life was centered around her. She'd guide me to my inner awareness to reveal who she was, discovering it was impossible to separate myself from that.

The planetary body holds an ancient pain of how the fallen angelics captured her Sophianic body and put it into dark mother reversals—it is when we lost our true Mother. This pain is felt in all lineages—the Cathar lines and the Mary Magdalene Sophia's, the female genetic-equal partner of the masculine form of Christos. It is this inner divine union that we must dig deep within ourselves to restore and recover.

"The Cathars were a part of the Essenes, Christos Templars that formed into a group embodiment with the higher divine purpose to serve and protect the Mother of God principle."

– Lisa Renee

I, too, felt this pain deeply as a child. I felt consumed with so much emotion constantly moving through me to release this ancient pain.

A CHILDHOOD OF IMAGINATION

My family and I moved to the USA before I turned three because my father felt work would be better for him in the US with his training as an English barrister. My mom's family lived in the States, too, so we moved to Rochester, NY.

As a child, I was a firefly of imagination and bliss. When we moved to the States from England, I began to feel the presence of heavenly beings, guides and nature spirits singing, playing and interacting with me. These beings appeared as fairy-like sparks of golden light. In the backyard of our new home in upstate New York, I found a favorite tree to spend my time watching them fly and interact with everything around me. They flew in and out of my heart and mind, penetrating my awareness to reflect the freedom of true spirit. Everything felt bright and loving then. We all had moments like these as kids until media, pop culture, aspects of the medical industry and indoctrination programmed or beat this innocence out of us. None of it was our parents' fault, but that of the accepted culture we grew up in. It seems this is only getting worse in our current world.

In the land of a child's imagination, I would disappear for hours, entering a world filled with color and symbolic images, communicating with the elemental forces. The richness of eternity pulsated as the endless landscape of possibility and breath of life spoke to me. I could feel it was protecting me. I had to remind myself that a human world existed, too, because it was much easier to live in alternative dimensions and experience magical things. So, when I began to sense an intensely complicated hurricane swirling within my head, it was about the time I experienced my first sensation of panic and a "knowing" of something I would need to contend with—something much larger I couldn't avoid.

I remember sensing that my mother and father would not remain together much longer. I held compassion as best as someone my age could comprehend and somehow knew that we were all being challenged by something larger—a human experience within which we were all just trying to find ourselves. My parents divorced when I was four, and they have remained friends. They've been so good to us, and I remain amazed at the individuals they are. They have always supported me unconditionally, no matter what I have gone through. I needed to tackle so much on my own, what I came into this world to experience and discover, and they allowed me to do this even though I know I worried them immensely.

LIFE AS AN EISENHOWER

From then on, my mother, sister and I navigated life together. My mom was young and strived to raise us differently than she was. Her heart

Childhood picture of me. I was in kindergarten when I lived in Upstate New York after we moved from England.

shone through her challenges, and I remember being in awe of her strength and beauty. My father was also a constant presence in our lives, very devoted.

I remember my mom telling us stories about what it was like growing up, having Secret Service men around her and spending weeks living at the White

House. Otherwise, our life was quite "normal" and very different from that. We didn't live off any trust funds or family money. We shopped at thrift stores. My extended family was always helpful, particularly in a crisis moment. I have only known my family to be extremely hard workers and, as a result, quite successful. Nobody received a free ride, that's for sure! It is interesting to reflect on what Dan Cooper was sharing with me—to be raised in this family and hear his words decades later would help bring more clarity to my experiences.

> *"Ike did NOT negotiate a surrender with the Nazi's or the Draco; NOT in 1955 or any year before or after. The proof is simple. If Ike had done so (negotiate being the operative word), he would have guaranteed himself and his family positions in the ICC. He would have been a member of MJ-12. You personally know that Ike didn't do that because NO one in your family has held any position in the ICC.*
>
> *As for Ike creating new members of MJ-12, you know that is disinformation because MJ-12 refused to report to him about anything that they were doing. This is also proof that Ike did NOT negotiate with the Nazi's or the Draco."*
>
> *– Dan Cooper, Senior Advisor to Earth Alliance*

My mom was a single mother, and her experience gave me my first glimpse into what that was like as I, too, would experience this with my kids. I often drift back into these childhood memories and profoundly relate to their pressures. It's not the picture most might have of a presidential family. If anyone wanted luxuries, we had to work for them.

I had so much fun growing up and visiting with David and Julie. We played board games and whiffle ball and sang karaoke at family reunions in my adult years. We had a great time together! They made up some of my favorite childhood memories, with all my aunts, Mary and Anne, and cousins. One time, Pat Nixon visited, and I happened to be there. I remember being a small child playing with my younger cousin, Jennie, when I picked up what I thought was a toy phone and accidentally called the Secret Service men parked in the garage! I also remember meeting Richard Nixon briefly at a family event. I was too young to interact and have a mature adult conversation. But I was observing and processing who all these people were in the world!

Around the age of four, I met my maternal grandmother, Mamie Eisenhower, who had just had a stroke. She was mostly in her bed at the Gettysburg farm, and my sister and I would sit with her and hold her hand.

It was always surreal to return to the Gettysburg farm and feel the rush of memories returning to me, including our playful friendship with Secret Service men. I smile thinking about Dolores, who helped raise us when my mom was a single parent. She was a sort of nanny to my mom, aunts and uncle, and her hus-

John SD Eisenhower and me, taken a few years before he transitioned. We had a very close relationship and spent almost every year there for Thanksgiving and visits.

band was one of the cooks at the White House. But, more than a nanny, Dolores kept and cared for our household and family. Though she transitioned some time ago, she remains a part of our hearts forever.

As a child, I always wanted to know who all these people were, like the Secret Service men coming around. It hit me one day that I was in a family that greatly influenced the world. I remember feeling amazed and appreciative of growing up in this family and experiencing who they are firsthand. It is so different from what one might imagine. I learned so much about the scandals and cover-ups and the blame placed on Eisenhower and Nixon for their ties to things like Watergate or ET government treaties. It was always challenging to delve deep into these topics with my family. I found it was better to enjoy our time together instead. These deeper conversations might have been too much when we wanted to do fun things as a family. I always felt such profound love, a soft nature, and mutual respect for our life choices and direction, no matter how different they might be. There is a comfort in knowing that we all have unique missions that seek only to benefit this world, even in the face of angry people or controversies that may surround our parents, grandparents and my great-grandparents for my generation.

Most of the time, I shared a room with my sister. I recall strange things that happened at night when I was around five or six. For example, I stared at the Moon one night, imagining it as a cradle rocking me back and forth. I got up, secured both ends of my nightgown to the curtain pole, and rocked back and forth outside the window as I pretended to be cradled by the Moon. It was a second-story house, and I could have fallen to my death if I slipped off. Later in our adult years, my sister recalled this story and thought she had dreamt it. I reminded her that I did this, which sparked her memory. This particular story serves as a reminder of the magic we all have access to but lose touch with along our way.

Another night, I remember my blanket turning into a strange being. It spoke to me about very peculiar things regarding the future and hints about what I was to accomplish on Earth. Then my bedroom walls disappeared, and I found myself in a garden with everyone who cared about me waving back at me. My sister remembers me yelling to her, "Look at this!" but she was too sleepy to get her full attention. Then, the strange being shape-shifted into a classmate I would go on to meet in 1st grade named Matthew, who would significantly impact my later life. This being had much to communicate about my future, but of course, I was too shocked to process any of it at the time. Feeling overwhelmed, I just wanted to get away. I remember getting up to go to the bathroom and looking back at the being as I exited the room. It acknowledged my need to close the conversation and quickly disappeared into my blanket.

My sister and I connect on many levels. Yet, we also recognize our incredible differences, which have taught us so much about ourselves, each other and life itself. Astrologically, she is my polar opposite to the day, born on my half-birthday, March 29th. I was born on September 29th.

As a child, my sister always amazed me. She was scholarly, incredibly artistic, beautiful, and a fantastic athlete. She taught me so much. Yet, I felt I could never measure up to her, so I struggled to find my identity and self-worth amid her many strengths. The hardest part was that finding myself meant fully embracing my extraordinary mission, which took some time to discover and eventually articulate.

I always identified my connection with the Magdalene energy as expanding into a larger sisterhood of Goddess archetypes. It is because much has been implemented for thousands of years to safeguard the Organic Ascension timeline and the Goddess energy. Still, it is evident that in this lower density, it has been anything but protected because defending it resulted in being silenced, compromised, persecuted, tortured and even killed for it.

One thing that stood out that I was always sensitive to was relationship dynamics between people. My natal chart reveals this—I have four signs in Libra, but about seven connected with Venus, merging with the Plutonic and Scorpionic. I could see evidence of relationship struggles around me, evident in people's faces that they were operating under a program or distortion. It felt like some epidemic that kept getting brushed off as "normal" or part of the human condition when, in fact, I knew it was the most important thing to prioritize. To strive for the energies of harmony, balance, love and transformation in the world— the most targeted thing—finding the divine union within to create relationships willing to heal ancestral patterns and recover from all the outer world has cast upon us. Doing so would result in massive healing on Earth.

Humans are targeted and compromised. Most haven't heard of the Goddess Sophia. Why is that? Those who have heard of her have likely gathered information through distorted texts that place blame on the feminine. But what do those names mean, and what do they represent? To me, they represent an acknowledgment to know ourselves again genuinely and how to embody the divine template of sacred union to restore healthy relationships and is what will create the necessary shift. But, unfortunately, we tend to always look to our governments, who have consistently let us down.

We are all born into dysfunctional relationships that we play out until we find ourselves willing to express something beyond the matrix distortions. We have to go beyond what is encouraged and what we have witnessed. There is nothing wrong with relationships needing to end. But we must do the inner work necessary to get to the core truth we hold within the self, enjoy it in union with others and purify the planet. What does it mean to find our inner truth? It is the capacity to be fully ourselves without fear of what people think. Being ourselves includes all aspects of self to become whole again. It becomes very hard for anything parasitic to feed on balance and wholeness. It takes time, reflection and shedding of lower layers to get to our inner treasures.

It has been a strong call to help guide souls home to a different harmonic universe after their fall in density from more advanced civilizations in the Earth's distant past. The Sophia energy of the lost divine feminine was all I could think about, but early on, I had no way to articulate it. It was a mission I had to accomplish, even if it meant I lived a double life or no one understood it. It will get done, no matter what.

I caught between a fairy tale and a horror show of buried memories growing up. I knew that I would eventually need to contend with a dark and menacing villain in this incarnation, split into many beings and hidden groups that are tentacles of the darkest kingdom in the shadows. I would follow those leads into the nucleus of the sickness to plant something of a great seed. Something is yet to emerge connected to these Earth missions, which will allow us to mitigate many of the damages and have a greater capacity than we realize.

RECOGNIZING TARGETING

Even at a young age, I felt focused attention placed on me. I would later discover it as the hidden weaponry behind forces attempting to steer me down an undesired timeline, not just because of my personal feelings about it but because of the consequences it could have on the whole human race.

It didn't take long for the dark polarity to show its face. It presented me with a whole other side of reality that existed alongside the bright energies of my everyday world of divine love and magic. I seemed to attract dark characters because I was incredibly vulnerable or completely naive. I could never stand to see anyone's feelings hurt or rejected, so I quickly became a "yes" person and the "comforter." Situations brought me into healer mode in ways that weren't healthy. I absorbed and took on too much that was not mine.

I began to judge myself for this, then recognized a need to master these energies and get a grip on them. Over time I allowed myself to become more hardened and toughened, less trusting and more discerning, which, of course, is something we all need to do as long as it doesn't shut us down from remaining aligned with greater universal love.

Throughout my youth, I returned to England and we traveled extensively all throughout the country. I explored caves and hidden gorges near Cornwall, where Tintagel Castle once stood. Images of the great ocean swirling and waves breaking against the ruins of the past captured my attention often as I reflected upon the mystical experiences I once had there. My granny used to take my father and his siblings down to Butter Hole, a huge hole in the Earth that was a steep climb down. They could only go down there for so long until the tide would come in and fill it up. I remember my amazement as my father told me these stories. There was a specific way to get into it, which looked incredibly dangerous!

My granny was incredible, courageous, bold, and one of the strongest women I have ever known. My spirit knew an ecstasy in these regions and great heartache where the land breathed the forgotten memory of a divine Goddess power and presence—revered by those who live closely with the Earth and feared by the encroaching darkness of patriarchy, which has been trying to

My mother, myself and Uncle David in 2014 at a family reunion near Gettysburg, PA. I have so much love and respect for my family. They are the most loving people, and we always have so much fun. All the information I share is unique to my own soul journey and discoveries. So, as you read this book, know we are a tight-knit family and respect each other's differences in how we view the world or share information about Eisenhower's legacy.

engineer humans away from sacred wholeness and connection to our divine Mother and Father source.

My process for rescuing myself was the formula for me to be authentically myself regardless of criticism and rejection. Clearly, too much was at stake not to take things seriously. It felt like life and death trying to deny any of it. If I had to enter the realms of death, it would be my catalyst for massive transformation over giving up. I remember declaring to the sky as a child to use me however necessary to bring balance back to the planet. I also told myself I was here to lift the illusory veils between life and death.

I still feel a strange force pulling me back to the ruins and cliffs of southwest England where the energy of the Goddess is embedded in the Earth, and also to Glastonbury, where the ley lines represent sacred union. Here, the targeting of ley lines has been extreme due to the Nephilim Reversal and Niburian Diodic Crystal grids so that we would be born into a confusing, unbalanced and disconnected world. Most humans recognize it as a deep, unexplained inner turmoil or sadness, which some may label as an affliction like depression, anxiety or ADD. Unfortunately, these labels and diagnoses keep us from getting to the actual message and reasons behind our feelings, only to believe that something is wrong with us.

When my mom met my stepdad, it began a new chapter of our lives. He was an Irish sailor and very fun to be with. We moved ourselves to Lake Ontario, a fantastic place to explore. There was enough nature around to keep me very content, and no matter what changes happened in our lives, I was happy residing in my internal world beyond this dimension.

We were delighted when my little sister was born. She was an amazing baby who got so much attention for her cuteness. I loved playing mommy with her and thought she was the greatest. She had such a sparkly spirit about her and still does. I adored her and still do! She has always been so focused, strong, resilient and hard-working. She has achieved much in her life.

Many years later, when my younger sister was still a teenager, our beloved stepfather would transition to the spirit world from bone cancer. It was an excruciating time to witness. My sisters and I held his hand to the end as he slipped from this human realm to his next. I remember feeling peace for him as I followed his soul with my mind on his journey till I kissed him goodbye.

As kids, my older sister and I were tomboys. We played out in nature with our imaginary horses. We had a pretend stall for them and spent hours naming them on paper. We skipped around all day together, lost in that world of being both the horse and the rider. She had an unwavering strength. Noticing this in her reflected a mirror image in me. I remember we had a fight once, and she stuck gum in my hair. After that, I had to cut my hair really short, and people started asking me if I was a boy. It happened so much that I pretended I was a boy named Chris at a YMCA sleepover. I sat with the other boys and talked about Tonka trucks and other things. We became fast friends and buddies. I was having so much fun with them that I was surprised when my mom showed up the following day calling out the name "Laura!" They watched my response to her. I looked at them. They looked at me. Then I just shrugged my shoulders, smiled and walked off as Laura. They might have gone into shock, maybe never to be the same again, thinking the whole time I was a boy!

It saddens me that children are being encouraged at a young age to have sex changes or identify a gender other than the one they were born with. I can't imagine having that kind of attention put on me just because I was a tomboy or connected to my masculine side. I saw no confusion and thought nothing of it, and appreciated being in touch with it without getting confused about it. Kids need the room and space without interference to be children and be given the chance to grow up and settle into what it means to be true to our unique expression and learn to love the body God gave us. These extreme measures should be addressed at a more developmentally mature age, if at all. Children aren't even allowed to drive or cook meals! Children are in developmental phases that must not be irreversibly interfered with.

I don't recall embracing my more feminine side as a child, at least in a conventional way, though I always had a doll on my hip. Come to think of it,

I had lots of babies and animals. I took them into the trees with me and even found myself trying to find a place for all of them at night. While cuddling up to certain stuffed animals and gazing around the room, I couldn't stand to leave all the other stuffed animals out, so I made a comfortable bed for them next to me. Sometimes, there was no room left for me, LOL. My mother would find me the next morning fast asleep on the floor.

My deep sensitivity and love for all things would challenge me in life. I didn't feel okay unless those around me were happy. As sweet as this may sound, it threw me off balance. It likely carried over from past lives where I didn't feel I could rescue or help those in need. I have always felt called to that and finally realized I must also not deny myself in that process.

EISENHOWER ENCOUNTERS

So many nights while in bed, the spirit of my great-grandfather, Ike, visited me. I could often feel his presence and guidance in my everyday life. Sometimes I could see his physical form, but mostly just his face. At times it startled me. I couldn't figure out why he was visiting me, though I knew he was well-known as I observed pictures and books and had discussions among family members. I began connecting with him very young, asking questions as I tuned into conversations at family gatherings and events. I felt him deep in my heart, and he acknowledged the need for his presence in my life. He is, in fact, present with all my family members and has a particularly close bond with his grandchildren. Our family is tight. We hold deep mutual love, respect and appreciation for one another. I never realized how loved I was till later in life. I think I felt so different from everyone and far from knowing how to do "human" well that I created many insecurities for myself.

When my mom found herself in a new relationship with my stepdad, my biological father decided to become a Catholic priest. He was my ultimate father figure as a spiritual guide and leader with a deep connection to the sacred heart. The way he is with people and the way he touches their lives is awe-inspiring to witness, planning trips with people all over the world and being with them through marriages, births, funerals, illness, hospitalizations, family tragedies— just being a divine presence and support in their lives with an inexhaustible spirit force and the most loving heart.

Regardless of what people feel about religion or where it has been compromised, one must look at the individuals, what it means for them, and who they are beyond the structures or troubled history. I am on my own spiritual journey, which he fully respects and appreciates. Whatever path any of us chooses to walk is what we should feel good pursuing as long as it leads to loving and respecting one another and being a person of compassion, empathy and forgiveness.

View from inside Tintagel Castle. One of my favorite places to go as a child. I felt such a deep connection to this area, and it was one of the places we often visited when I would go back to England and go on adventures with my Granny, sister and my father. This castle is associated with legends of King Arthur, Merlin and Avalon, including where King Arthur was born.

Sharing his great universal love was a life calling for my father, "Pa," and I always felt the depth of his spirituality. He would take my sisters and me to church, and I remember staring at Jesus on the cross, unable to pay attention to anything else. It felt like we had telepathic communication and a profound understanding of one another. Still, something seemed off as the energies of the Magdalene kept pushing through, making me very emotional at times. I cried myself to sleep on occasion while being taken on journeys into the heart of a love story more incredible than I could imagine, as I was quite aware that it involved the entire human race, the Earth and the cosmos.

When I finally understood that I was related to a wartime general and former President, it always baffled me how someone like me could end up in such a family. But, it became clear as I learned more about what President Eisenhower stood for and the heavy dilemmas his administration faced. He and I agreed to work together on the spirit level to help with a massive global shift that would bring about disclosure on many levels. Ike and I have a deep bond with each other. A while back, someone told me that I served as a spirit guide for him during his lifetime as Dwight D. Eisenhower—how sweet that he now serves as one of mine!

Some people hear about President Eisenhower and consider him a war criminal or that he sold us out to ETs. I know how vital it is to remain aligned with the truth over preserving family ties. I needed to explore all these allegations from a place of neutrality. Along the way, I discovered there is much more to the story. Notably, the treaties did not originate with Ike. Regarding accusations of being a war criminal, there are many distortions to the book "Other Losses," specifically around this claim, which has been analyzed and refuted by many reputable sources.

We must understand the impacts of a rewritten history and that it is possible to implant and manipulate information utilizing quantum access technologies to make timeline changes or make specific individuals look bad so that we reject or discount them. A massive agenda is underway that will go to any lengths to achieve its aims.

You can imagine how deeply I felt this weight of responsibility. Often, all I could do was cry to release the pressure that was crushing me. I called upon channels and psychics, who had no preconceived opinion or stake either way, that validated the popular narrative wasn't what happened.

Around age nine, I remember being in the grocery store aisle and seeing an article about Dwight David Eisenhower in a Weekly World News tabloid, a joke newspaper, saying things like "Batboy is trying to take over New York City" or something else absurd. Then, another tabloid with President Eisenhower on the cover said he had met with aliens—it triggered something in me. It aroused my curiosity because I could sense there might be some truth to this. It was the catalyst that kicked off the dot-connecting endeavors that would eventually help me integrate the many layers to this reality and timeline, which have been split, fragmented and compartmentalized.

Along my journey, I realized what has taken place on the world stage, compared to what's secret, reveals a massive targeting on our ability to achieve sacred union, Unity Consciousness, and advance our DNA to exist in a higher world connected to nature and our Source. Nothing could prepare me for what my life was in for. Although I discovered much about what is required of humanity in these times, it demanded I embark on a terrifying journey into hell to develop a deep understanding of how ETs interacted with the Earth and governments over time.

When enough outside abuses came my way growing up for holding such an open-hearted energy, the warrior in me jumped forth in powerful ways. I kept having this feeling of being buried alive that I couldn't quite understand, almost as if I had an ancient rage connected to other lifetimes collapsing into the picture.

GLOBAL ALCHEMIST

Hell is a state of consciousness that is incomplete. It has yet to go through the necessary alchemy, so many souls become trapped in this "place" of negativity, their corrupted consciousness unable to grasp the power of their composition or how to resurrect from the traps. I answer the calling of thinning the veils between life and death by bringing light, love and compassion, as do many others. I acknowledge our collective effort by using myself as an example. I have made it a point to read between the lines and reach for deeper messages, which might bring additional validation to someone's journey into the depths of pain and darkness. We all go through it, so I want to be sure that when a person dares to enter this raw place, they know what they can expect and how rewarding the transformation can be.

Our connection to God Source recognizes the vastness of our creative imagination. We have much to draw upon to influence our reality in every living moment. God/Goddess isn't about belief systems. It is about Creation and consciousness—light, sound and vibration. We are an integral part of this co-creation on multi-dimensional levels.

There are higher and lower aspects to Earth. It doesn't hold lower energy if integrated with the higher, just more form. A lower energy imbalance would be a negative ego, suffering or duality unable to create harmony and connection with its polar opposite. We come to Earth to balance and integrate polarities and experience the pain of separation until we hear the call home again. It doesn't mean we negate all darkness. It means we embrace it back into harmony and plant seeds of light from our higher consciousness instead of fearing it or allowing someone else to inhabit us through our unconscious vulnerabilities disguised as health conditions, mental confusion, pain, grief and afflictions. So many impostors and deceptions have distorted our relationship with self and connection to Source. We get further from ourselves every time we give our healing over to something that wants to numb or silence us by treating only the symptoms.

We see other species besides ourselves as "alien" or view history in a limited way. The controllers have withheld the truth because no one can live it as powerfully as we can. Our inner work goes beyond clearing and purging. It's to get in touch with the book of your soul and epic journeys throughout many cycles of time, space and beyond. We begin to see our multi-dimensional selves. What we may have once thought of as alien becomes all too familiar. The word "alien" means foreign, making the controlling invaders the actual aliens.

We can spend all our time avoiding our connection with Spirit, but it only keeps us from reaching our highest potential. We need to feel the inspiration, notice the synchronicities, and recognize the divine magic and miracles to take notice of the collapse of timelines and how we land on higher ground.

We are the reflection of the uniqueness and diversity of nature. Creatures our minds have a hard time imagining reveal their interconnection and genius. We can be one with all. The power of storms, the seas, the fires and the mountains are the breath of life wishing to be heard. If we silence the programmings about ourselves and others that linger in our thoughts and beliefs, not feed negative technologies that power up and weaponize the elements and their equivalents within our soul essence, and listen to our inner guidance to exit the dramas of the matrix, we can begin to hear Gaia and realize our fullest DNA expression, heartbeat and inner voice.

THE JOURNEY CONTINUES

Around age eight, my concept of God was all-embracing. It burst out of the church walls and overflowed into the natural world. Growing up, I filled up with curious joy and intrigue about existence and creation: God, Goddess, nature, the cosmos and the human spirit. Through my unending curiosity, I understood the power and essence of what I came to know as "truth." It felt like stillness and a sweeping presence at once. It felt like love, all love. I climbed inside this feeling while I wept at humanity's relentless suffering, seemingly caused only by our disconnection from the all-encompassing force of love existing all around us. Why I was so emotional at such a young age, I even found odd.

Existing in a spiritual reality and a multi-dimensional state, I continued through my early school years. I wove in and out of worlds and dimensions regularly, appearing easily distracted by my teachers. A usual day of teacher droning and blurry chalkboard pointing threw me into a trance until the bell snapped me out. My "inattention" in the classroom was viewed as a problem, and it became clear that many thought I must have some learning disability. Other people's projections and judgments only confused me because weaving in and out of dimensions felt good. It made me feel alive and connected to all sorts of things. However, I always felt kicked in the gut when any form of authority or attempt to control me entered my world. These intrusions felt foreign and insulting to me.

I had no idea that my emerging battle would eventually take me into the territory of great danger. I was already feeling heavy. I knew I was only getting out of the school control system once I was old enough not to show up. Its judgment hurt me, but I didn't have time to dwell on it. I knew I was just taking a different path I fully signed up for, so I had to keep trusting myself and stay true no matter how misunderstood I might be. For some, school was an opportunity to achieve great merit, status and success while making others feel they could never be good enough, ignoring other abilities and forms of intelligence. It felt so wrong to me!

In first grade, I befriended Matthew, who I immediately recognized from my earlier vision: the being that had appeared years before in my bedroom. Matthew liked to play with dolls, so nobody wanted to go near him, thinking he was weird. Not me—I was drawn to him instantly and thought how he would make a great father, and we quickly became friends. We took care of this baby doll together, and at recess, we went outside like a couple with their child and took it very seriously. It felt as though Matthew was waiting for someone to raise this doll with, and I was more than happy to be that person. I would gift him things that would benefit the baby, and I will never forget how much that made him smile.

Over time, I noticed odd things happening with Matthew. He would receive calls from the office or get picked up early. Sometimes, he would be gone from school for days at a time. On the days he was in class, he would look over at me, and I could tell something was going on and sense some pain he was hiding.

One day, he came to school with a hat on and took me to the back of the room where nobody could see us. He took off his hat and showed me this massive scar across his head. He told me the scar was from a brain tumor they tried to remove. It looked painful, and though I felt a surge of shock and sadness, I also felt strength and hugged him to share in his vulnerability. His sweet smile and fearlessness eclipsed the stitches across his head as he didn't want me to worry. My experiences with Matthew made me forever curious about the nature of illness and pain, why it happened and what it would take to heal ourselves.

The day came when Matthew didn't show up to school. Days passed, and I thought maybe he needed rest or wasn't feeling good. I wandered around recess feeling lost and didn't care to connect with any other kids because they had been so mean and judgmental to Matthew. I didn't know what to do with myself. Anxiety crept in.

The Eisenhower family reunion at the Gettysburg Farm in Gettysburg, PA. I stayed there as a child and met Mamie before she passed away. My other family members used to spend so much time here. It is now a museum and owned by the National Park Service.

I didn't know where to find a safe zone or who I could go to for help, so I just waited. I'd sit on a bench by myself as the weather got colder. The dried leaves crunched under my feet and broke apart. I was watching my breath in the cold air, waiting. The extremes were playing out in me. I hoped that I would hear good news to warm my heart and ease the tension. The stress from daily processing made me feel like I was quickly growing into adulthood from 1st grade. It allowed me to discover a wise elder within me who understood death, darkness and the hidden mysteries.

Eventually, my teacher pulled me aside and told me Matthew had died. She wanted to let me know first before announcing it to the class. At that moment, a part of me left 3D. They permitted me to leave school early that day, and my body didn't know how to register the devastating news. I went home, told my mom, and then laid down on my bed, where a waterfall of tears opened up and formed pools in my ears.

I tossed and turned until a feeling of peace came over me when I realized he had gone somewhere very beautiful. Then, a portal opened before me—my first glimpse into the underworld journey I was preparing for. I could already feel its power pulling me toward the more challenging parts of my path. In some prophetic realizations, images of the future flashed before my mind's eye like headlines on the clouds, changing shape and meaning based on my belief and perception about it. Tragedy and conflict triggered my premonitions, as did confrontation with any reality that opposed my ideal vision of how the world should be. I already knew, at this point, that I had to make my life's work about healing the planet. We all heal the Earth when we hold true to ourselves and devote ourselves to higher principles and balance. I had this eerie sense that I was on the brink of embarking on a dangerous journey.

As time passed, the conscious awareness of some of my more frightening premonitions took a back seat as I tried my best to blend into the world. Unusual dreams and visions still plagued me at night, but I told myself they had no significance even though deep down, I knew they did. I felt pressure to fit my experiences into the structures of the outer world so they would be accepted, knowing they couldn't accommodate them. Because of this, I never felt grounded.

I kept myself from expressing too much about my experiences because when I did, I would be met with confused looks or written off as having an overactive imagination. However, I felt something tapping me on the shoulder, reminding me, to my dismay, that the time was fast approaching. I could feel the information wanting to reveal itself, and it unfolded over many years. I remember one time, the wind blew a familiar breath that activated my senses and summoned up the memories of an agreement with the divine forces of nature—a path I was born to walk. There was nowhere to run, and I couldn't stop it. I was not even a teenager, yet I was preparing to face something that would grow in intensity over the years to proportions I couldn't ever foresee.

While all this was happening in my internal world, life continued with new developments that were often difficult to process fully. Then, one day, my mom sat my sisters and me down and told us that she and my stepdad were getting divorced. Once again, it would be just us girls again.

PROCESSING CONSTANTLY

I didn't feel separation from the multi-dimensional realms as a child. However, I felt disconnected from any authority or way of life that produced an expectation or projection upon me. Of course, that is a feeling lots of starseeds or rebellious children have. For me, my thoughts expanded into the world at large. My attention was on the global and cosmic energies. Being highly sensitive to the programs and social engineering kept pushing me outside its trappings. Soon enough, I became overwhelmed because I couldn't dedicate my undivided attention to my preparations. When is that ever possible as a human? I was aware of the timeline fast approaching when I would face attempted recruitment to go off-planet to a Mars colony. These preparations were to ensure my resistance and not end up on this timeline that would compromise many others. A passion for truth makes us less likely to venture down artificial timelines that hide the most heinous crimes against humanity.

Noticing things so young made me not want to participate in what the television, media, news and forced social agreements pushed onto kids. I remember watching TV in utter confusion, thinking, am I supposed to like this stuff? Especially when the commercials came on. I didn't want anything they pushed, like Strawberry Shortcake, My Little Pony, or Barbies. I remember almost feeling angry about it. My friends loved these things, so I would join in regardless when playing with them.

Still, I do remember a deep sensitivity to what commercials and TV were trying to condition people regarding how we relate to our genders. If I preferred collecting race car toys and it said toys for boys, so what? I grew up to love being a woman. Everyone holds masculine and feminine energies within themselves to get in touch with. The outside world should not tamper with this or push anything onto the developing minds of children and let them be. We must ask ourselves why this has only gotten worse in our society. For the sake of our future generations, we must examine this. Part of our soul development comes with learning to love the bodies we were given and embrace freely expressing them without making permanent, irreversible alterations before we have the maturity to know all we truly are.

What was crystal clear growing up was that I needed to learn the basics, like how to function in a human body or show up for school every day. They were a low priority, even though I still managed to do both. My mission felt way more important, like a double life I needed to manage and contend with. So many of us don't know how to acclimate to this physical plane, which causes great struggle, especially when you feel a strong pull to complete something while here. Most people won't understand this, let alone provide validation, reassurance or guidance. We do it because it needs to get done, even if we feel like a fish out of water. We continue until we realize the water is contaminated, the fish is not well and can no longer swim. And still, we feel a tremendous call to purify and restore it.

THE VEIL AND GETTING GROUNDED

We are being asked to accept this matrix as reality. Just getting grounded can be incredibly difficult unless you can exist without giving it much thought. But how can we ever be present if we don't accept what feels false? The quest to become grounded for some of us involves bulldozing through the thick density blocking us from other dimensions. A thickness that holds lies, deceptions and dark agendas that can also provide us with some real answers about the true nature of reality if we are willing to venture in to understand it. I couldn't occupy my body until I started this process of bull-dozing. I didn't realize it would take me decades, and there is still much more to do. It always felt like a life-and-death struggle. Some refer to it as the veil, the demiurge. Others call it the NET and see it as a quarantine surrounding the Earth.

We will only thrive with a willingness to move through it all and come out the other side. We must have the courage to poke a hole through everything we were taught about reality to get to the other side. It is the connection of the micro to the macro. The very thing that veils us from higher consciousness is how the outer veil impacts humanity collectively. It is why the energies of ascension are so hard to achieve. But here we are in this great time of purging, exposing crimes against humanity and busting down the falsities. Purgatory is where we feel the higher dimensional realms more easily after a purge. Thankfully, we are doing it together as a team, liberating us as individuals and as a whole. Some began this process long ago, and many more are inspired to engage now. I see more and more people finding the drive and permitting themselves to "go for it," ready to say goodbye to all the BS and take back their lives.

It's suffocating and detrimental not to try and break through the human time loop designed to keep us trapped. Our dark night journey into the under-world helps us to create the necessary soul alchemy. Integrating polarity, our masculine and feminine within, and our light and dark, removes the barriers that keep us out of balance and in duality. From a higher perspective, we do this until we gain the mastery to clear the veil. From a human perspective, the veil enslaves and recreates us indefinitely. Our unconsciousness is a form of consent. All sorts of things sneak through our belief systems to infect our creative channels. We are taught to fear venturing into this dark night to heal ourselves. Many don't go that far in their thought forms and just accept the reality handed to them.

Those courageous enough to enter this zone may initially freak out and resort to using pharmaceuticals, believing something is wrong with them. This type of reaction, unfortunately, is what the system was designed to do, taking advantage of our vulnerabilities and throwing labels at us instead of helping us appreciate the transformative power of it all. However, a willingness to pierce through it is alchemy's inner and outer work. What is trying to keep us as lead and in carbon-based form is slowly but surely turning to gold, helping to usher other souls into this new paradigm.

Some who have come to serve others are already awake and have a consid-erable task. Though we have the same potential, some came solely to remind and activate. Many incarnated advanced souls struggle with ego and identity and feel very shy, misunderstood, and often ostracized. They attract unconscious envy from others or automatic repulsion but remain deeply sensitive and committed to help no matter what gets thrown their way. They notice magic and synchron-icities as a clear reminder of divine nature's power and how that links to our soul and awakening dormant DNA. They feel complete resonance because they know what they are here to do. They aren't wired for anything else, so walking away from such a mission can feel like life or death. They feel no other option, and the thought of something different causes pain and disorientation.

In contrast, a choice to move forward in a mission to face tremendous op-position forces can provide comfort and motivation, knowing it has to get done. In the face of unavoidable pain, do we get to know ourselves more or give our

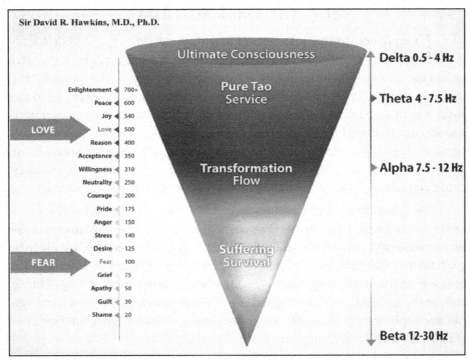

"Power vs. Force" by David Hawkins. When we dip down into survival energy, our frequency is lower, and it is very hard to create anything good for ourselves or think clearly. When we can be mindful and conscious of the times we sink into this energy, we can raise our vibration and shift, and in turn, this changes our lives and improves health and well-being.

power away? A good question to ask ourselves.

So, early on, it was evident to me that something hidden and sinister was trying to steer humanity in a particular direction that disagreed with me. It wasn't just the apparent injustices and patriarchy or a rebellious attitude towards authority. I was aware that there was some agenda (many actually) that intentionally produced the conditions of contamination, disease, imbalance and separation to control how we navigate and experience our path. With our soul journey compromised, primarily through our egoic nature, our emotions, minds, hopes and fears are played upon. We also misunderstand the important initiations we must go through and are thwarted in our every attempt to step into our truth frequency. It is what these initiations are all about.

It is where people begin to give their power away and rely on others to tell them their reality, then live with this diagnosis as a part of their identity rather than seeing it as an opportunity for growth and greater self-awareness. My awareness and commitment to this frequency remain my strongest protection. No matter how hard it gets, I will continue learning more about myself. We always have the choice to gain more self-knowledge and stay clear of mind control.

EGO AND DARK AGENDAS

People new to this information may respond with repulsion or confusion—it shatters the foundation of all we have been taught. It may feel unfamiliar and intimidating, but we are not separate from it. We recognize the soul architecture, DNA and chakra connection, which can empower one to the awareness that we only win the war if done from within. We take our power back and sort our relationship with all these diverse vibratory levels with different species connected with them, which are aspects of ourselves. Reptilian Anunnaki or other controlling ET groups did not create our bodies and souls. Instead, they modified humans to suit their domination agendas through hybridization.

The question is, what vibratory level dominates our thinking and creativity? If it's our negative ego rather than our higher self, we may have many necessary processes to experience and expand beyond, and if we don't, it's likely to get caught in the sticky stuff. We either find ourselves suffering or seeking status or power at the expense of others—negative beings represent that way of being and frequency level. To move beyond is to become sovereign, and then our ego can operate in integration with our wisdom and love nature. They must be integrated—it's what Heaven on Earth is within our being.

We didn't learn this in school or through news, politics or media. It's common sense. If not, we need to ask ourselves how limited we allow ourselves to be. We were all born into captivity that has become what we believe freedom to be, but with amnesia. There is too much out there that starts to open the lid of our consciousness to a higher vista that requires acknowledging. Whether we accept it remains our choice, but we at least deserve to be exposed to it instead of oblivious. It can only enrich us, even if it dismantles or threatens the foundation of reality we have been operating from.

Fortunately, the stargates are opening progressively during this ascension cycle, with the main planetary gates opening into the galactic and universal. The 13th gate and Mother energy returning to Earth's body opens us up to our Galactic Chakras that we rarely hear about. Many are incarnating at this time to do the repair work and embody this stargate energy to help activate others.

I always knew the significance of achieving sacred union in this lifetime. The multi-stage process requires deep inner work and observation to discover that the love story exists within our DNA. The initiations a person must go through are similar to what is experienced when a true love union is formed. We can do it without a partner from the inside. Understanding this and aligning with it brings us closer to our soulmate companions. Then we can decide to take that journey together, or we can be in sacred development on our own, continuing to meet other significant soul family members at any stage.

When we struggle to free ourselves from the past or negative patterns we carry, we remain vulnerable to narcissists and abusers, but this can help us know better who we are so we can keep moving forward and growing, never to repeat. Our trauma and wounds can make this quite challenging to do sometimes. Our relationship to life reveals a micro/macro connection. Are we more connected to abusers and deceivers or the authentic aspects of reality? The inner work helps us get there and is different for everyone. Many remain unconscious until the light is shined onto their hidden self. While we are still learning, growing and feeling occasionally lost, we may bump into situations that derail or injure us.

It is easier to attract other healthy relationships when we are strong within, living our truth and more grounded. However, no one philosophy explains or applies to all situations. We will experience things our unique way until we reach an epiphany or breakthrough, and we reserve the right to come to our conclusion without someone else inserting their opinion of why we created it the way we did. Some things come out of left field. Some things are targeting. Sometimes, it's not even about us, so looking at all the possibilities is essential.

We all hold a common purpose to embrace authentic love. It starts with loving ourselves enough to live in our truth and find internal harmony. This is greater than anything else we may focus on. We have forgotten how to love ourselves to such a degree that it's become the root of environmental degradation, suffering, misery, disease, parasitic invasions and susceptibility to mind control. Our lack of awareness enables and keeps it alive like an infection. In so many phases in history, it was beyond our control, as the dark powers of the cabal have been infecting the institutions we had to rely on for survival—even when we disagreed with them—until we found a way to emerge from the matrix.

We now find ourselves in the optimal window period to finally exit the matrix! It's time to take our power back and know what it truly means to be a sovereign being—harnessing our divine wisdom and creative abilities and letting go of anything that doesn't serve us, including the memes and propaganda that still try to control and contaminate our creative powers.

True power is not domination and control, which are limited creative powers that rely on other people's submission and worship. When it is forced upon society and human extinction is a threat breathing down our necks, we can't accept or ignore it. We must dismantle the powers that be and strive to understand what is at stake, regardless of the degree of targeting, to create a better world. Their distractions of "lesser evils" are still pretty horrendous, where the media presents disturbing headlines to make us feel like improvement is being sought after when, in actuality, they are covering up great crimes against humanity. They encourage us towards distraction through fueled division over political views and more, which eventually come with mud-slinging and insults. Many miss the point and fail to see where the real enemy lies. To me, the enemy is our ego nature that has lost connection with soul and spirit, and because we stay stuck, we end up empowering the very present (and future) world we endlessly complain about. We become enablers by taking the bait and playing out their script through more division, unrest and conflict.

The ego is the force of our character and personality, which seeks alignment to spirit and soul. In its attempt to find its home base, it gets easily distracted and programmed through our minds and emotions, then forms identities that aren't always authentic. It is what social engineering and mind control attempt to do and is why we are easily recycled. We interpret it as being trapped or a need of ours, so we necessitate experiences to remember who we are. If we view ourselves as trapped, we fall prey and victim to negative groups to which we are meant to find seniority. In this process, we learn to transcend false light that throws us back on the time loop wheel. It all comes down to awakening and releasing ourselves from their grips. It is the catalyst that helps us to return, though it doesn't excuse for a moment the evil and pain these demonic forces have caused and all who have served them.

We work to shed the layers and overlays cast upon us, but without knowing that this is all our common purpose, what we identify with can stray us more. We must be conscious of what we need to release. Very often, forces of nature through our experiences set us up with what we need to do—even those things that get our attention in less than comfortable ways. When adversity strikes, it is our chance to see through the game. But if we don't, our attachments to the falsities will increase to present a crossroads. Some people have the most profound awakening experiences when they fall ill, have an injury, or lose a loved one or relationship. Others may seek revenge, become darker, and feel blame, hostility and suffering. It depends on how much access to wisdom one holds and is something we cultivate through alignment with our higher self, the part of us asking to be fully integrated into our physical vessels. Without that, real change can't happen on the physical plane.

In his book, "Power vs. Force: The Hidden Determinants of Human Behavior," David Hawkins' Scale of the Levels of Consciousness reveals how much our frequency drops when we are in survival mode. In this state, it becomes hard to think and create abundance. People in this state will tend to medicate their fear, grief, apathy, guilt and shame. These lower energies make us vulnerable to being taken advantage of. We need to recognize where these vulnerabilities and lower energies exist within us. Otherwise, they will manifest as pain and disease in the body. If we can consciously move into more neutrality, we lift ourselves out of these lower energies and into more acceptance, joy, peace, love and enlightenment.

Even if I was somewhat isolated in my thinking processes, I was certainly not the only one tapping into these thought forms. But, still, I never imagined how long it would take to find other like-minded people. I never assumed that those around me didn't get it or weren't going through something similar. It was more about finding common ground to communicate with others in an understood way. Still, our society doesn't encourage these dialogues, which is when our shell thickens as we age. We aren't as reachable. It is almost like we cultivate this for our survival. So many end up complying and conforming to whatever society presents. Certain types of individuals hang out outside the fringes of society, still not entirely sure of what is going on. But when we open these dialogues, we will all be surprised to realize we understand things much more than we think.

Though we feel it in our own way, our reactions are diverse. As an observer, I paid attention to different personality types and their conscious or unconscious response to the matrix we are born into. So, for example, we may see people gravitate towards music and art as a sanctuary for freedom of expression, people choosing careers to support those oppressed or represent them, or people struggling with unexplained symptoms and conditions related to unreleased or unprocessed things. It can become a physical challenge, alerting the person to dig down into the roots of where it may have originated. That is why transparency is so important. It's so we don't internalize things and have them become an energy block. It is hard enough when childhood is disruptive, and you can't speak up or process wounds.

Some people may experience injury and accidents, which hold hidden messages and an opportunity to see things differently. Some will be very progressive and inventive and attempt to push the envelope, and some will pursue what is considered alternative, but many will reject these ideas. Instead of having an open mind, they will ridicule and criticize anything different from their beliefs. Therefore, it is paramount that none of us tries to shove our beliefs down anyone else's throat or assume we are always right and that we don't belittle others or be harmful to people who think differently.

Outside of life paths and career choices, most of us can agree that there are deeper reasons behind why we experience certain events over our lifetime. From an optimistic point of view, I say it is to help wake us up from a more negative perspective because we are being attacked and compromised. Some might say we are flawed humans who constantly create issues for ourselves. Combining our many views may find a balance in how we see things and even an epiphany. Not every event occurs for the same reason like there is not one philosophy that can apply to all situations. The truth frequency can help us decide what something means, but we must relearn how to be ourselves and think for ourselves.

There is a large portion of the population who take advantage of the vulnerable and find ways to make money off of them, who strive to elevate themselves into a position of fame or celebrity for wealth and power, even if it means they are part of a coverup of crimes that exploit children. It also connects to the dark side of things like ritual abuse to stay in their position or role, with all the perks that come with it. It is not possible to generalize. One can't say that everyone in whatever industry is a part of the dark elements or agendas, but as we gain more exposure to what is hidden, we can achieve much more clarity about things. Those involved in criminal activity will be revealed and held accountable, as will those who have been complicit or otherwise make the appropriate self-corrections.

This criminal activity exists everywhere: in our medical industries, Hollywood, news media, religions, politics, etc., and the coverup of so much is now finally coming to an end. Our true hidden history, ET presence, dark technologies, Secret Space Programs, and specific agendas have infiltrated all sorts of institutions that take us into our deeper galactic origins. People who have seen it firsthand are now coming forward. When disclosure is a more public concept, it will be hard for anyone in power to continue duping the world, and certainly not after a Full Disclosure Event. So many experts are already disseminating information and disinformation, which will be very protective in the face of all that will inevitably come.

Encroaching Darkness

"While the Dark Night of the Soul is a process of death, the Spiritual Awakening Process is the rebirth."

– Mateo Sol

6TH Grade Revelations

My mom headed to Washington, DC, after she and my father split up, and we remained a significant part of each other's life. My mom has an amazing ability to maintain strong friendships and continue being true to her path, which helped me stay strong when I needed to do the same. She felt it was time to make her shift to go on her own to support our independence. She had a fire in her that I still admire—she is the most rock-solid person I know. We lived in Maryland. I was the new 6th grader at school and made many new friends. It was when the concept of boyfriends came into my experience. During this time, I also began to sense a magnified focus on me, both positive and negative.

I had one relationship with a boy who passed a journal back and forth with me. We discussed many things about home life, siblings, sports and dreams of the future. At some point, he began stealing his mother's expensive jewelry to give to me. He would put these little gifts in the cubby we were given. I would open them, and to my astonishment, there were beautiful jewels that, when I wore them, made me feel loved and adored by this boy. My mom noticed gold pendants, sapphires, and diamonds on my fingers, which, as you can imagine, surprised her, knowing I was not much into jewelry. When she realized that they weren't fake but real diamonds and sapphires, she questioned where I had gotten them from. Looking back, the idea of fancy jewelry was funny, but I still felt flattered. It didn't even cross my mind where he got them from or if they were real— I appreciated the loving gesture! My mom promptly forced me to return all the items to his mother when he later admitted he took them without permission.

Around this time, I had a contact experience with a luminous group of three female beings with no hair that radiated pure love. In this powerful lucid dream, we were on the shores of a beach near some ruins. They asked me to look through a viewfinder, and when I did, I saw timelines. They explained that I was to help create the positive Organic Ascension timeline, which would happen during an approaching potent window period in my lifetime. I eventually related all this to the planet Venus, the Venus transits, and what I would come to understand as a Stellar Activation Cycle. This activation would mark our collective turn toward the ascension timeline and the return of the Goddess to the Earth. They said that dark forces would try to take me away—destroy me—and so they encouraged me to hold on to my truth for dear life.

I later discovered that they might be the Arcturians who have worked on the planet Venus to anchor the energy of Arcturian temples, using the power of Venus to help link human consciousness with their healing frequencies. Other beings associated with Venus would later cross my path also. I sensed that I, too, was from a different place and somehow connected to Venus. My focus was not on making contact per se but on getting the needed assistance or risk going nuts.

I had such a clear picture of our soul architecture and Venus energies and what the Venus transits represented, which was a grand alchemy connected with the redemption of Lucifer, purification of our negative ego, and release from any enslavement to our unconscious. It was clear that we all needed to participate to accomplish this, and if enough people took it upon themselves, we could positively impact the shifting of the whole collective. I began to see Venus as a medium through which the heart chakra, the higher heart, can be activated. This alchemy pushes us through the seven gates to purify and transmute them from archonic energies and into the seven pillars of wisdom via the Seven Chakra System in our body, ultimately reconnecting us with the Seven Higher Heavens. Libra is the 7th sign of the zodiac, my Sun sign, and most of my chart is Pluto/Venus dominated, so the morning and evening star's journey into the underworld seems symbolic to me and my mission.

Research has shown me that the Arcturians often place etheric crystals in the ground or atmosphere of a planet to help shift the surrounding frequency and anchor their healing energy. It is how they assist humanity and the Earth during this ascension window period. These etheric crystals help humans rediscover higher vibrations and overcome the false light energies that tempt consciousness to seek wealth or status rather than the inner organic light. Unfortunately, I can't cite the source of this research, but I do recall coming across it, and it has stuck with me ever since.

These luminous beings that visited me made it clear that the rise of the divine feminine was a crucial step to help restore the masculine energy on the planet into alignment with Source, therefore awakening Christ Consciousness on a mass scale. I was grateful to know I had a part to play in making this happen!

OFF TO ENGLAND

I remember being eleven when my mother proposed that I move to England. It had been an interesting year of observation for her. I had just finished a year at the new school, and she concluded that I could use the time to get to know myself more. I may have also freaked her out with some of my 6th-grade relationships. She told me that my grandparents desired a grandchild since all of their children had grown up and missed having children around. It was reason enough for me to pack my bags, to fulfill their longing and wish, though I would later find out that the actual reason was that they thought it would benefit me. So, I prepared to go alone, away from my mother and sisters, to England to experience something new with my grandparents.

It was just the three of us in England: my grandmother, grandfather and me. The home was beautiful, with a fantastic garden. It felt like a sanctuary offering peace to me. I was ready for adventure now that the redundancy of the American school system, with all its weirdness, was gone. I knew it was up to me to make things work, and thankfully, I was entertained as the forever observer of all around me. I appreciated that my father's side of the family lived there and that I was born there, too. I finally began to settle into my roots. We lived outside London, and I loved the energy there. Being outside of the USA reawakened my spirit to life again. My uncle visited sometimes, but mostly, my grandparents and me.

My new school was a very primitive convent called Ursuline Convent Prep School. It was a simple place taught by nuns, with classrooms all over campus. It wasn't elitist. Some buildings were a bit run down. We wore humble uniforms with blazers, skirts and cloggy brown shoes. I remember walking so far every day to get to school. I can legit say to my kids, "In my day, I had to walk up and down hills for miles through rain and snow to get to school!" LOL. No joke, I walked and walked and walked. I made a song in my head that incorporated all the street names I had to pass, and I paced my walk to sing the street name while crossing the actual street. I came to find comfort in the solitude of these moments deep within.

My school was small, so it was a big deal when a new kid showed up. I stood out because my American accent was so apparent. Only one other American had ever attended years before. I heard it didn't go well, so everyone was nervous when I showed up. However, it ended up being the best year of my life because I made the closest of friends: Abigail, Lucy, Florence and Nicola, to name a few. We all had so much fun together, and everybody was friends with everybody else. Strong bonds formed quickly through all the laughter and challenging times we shared. We did so much together, and although things started a bit awkward, I was highly social, so things quickly changed.

A sweet headmistress nun led the school. However, the nun who taught our class was the scariest person you could imagine. Her name was Sister Anne. My friends and I spent hours making up stories about her, finding the most unbelievable amount of humor about her and especially her authority. We didn't hate her or wish to do any harm. We were just kids who found humor the best survival tool in her classroom. We had to have been the most animated group of girls the nuns had ever seen, and through it all, we became incredibly close. We did a lot of improv and plays, making music and magic happen. It was almost as though nothing else existed, like living inside a great novel where each page inspires and is unique. Every day, we felt the excitement of turning a new page. We stretched the curriculum further than intended because we found joy with each other, and acting crazy together was far more entertaining. Our antics started to freak the nuns out.

We did group improvisations during our breaks, and by the end of lunch, a crowd of people stood watching our plays and laughing. Many were stunned. One inspiring young teacher opened many doors for us because she wasn't as strict. Everybody loved her.

My classmates and I had sleepovers often. I made some of the best friendships in my life and began to feel my true, authentic self emerging. I thrived in England and even got good grades. I realized for the first time that I had no learning disabilities but unique, special qualities.

The best year of my life would end soon, and my mom wanted me back home in America. I wanted to see her too. So, the whole school community threw me a going away party and rented out a section of a beautiful park. Everyone came with gifts for me, including the nuns. I couldn't believe the outpouring of love and appreciation. Sister Anne told me my stay had been a mixed blessing, and even the headmistress was crying. We shared our heartfelt goodbyes and stayed pen pals for a long time afterward.

My nervous system underwent a major shock when I returned to American school. My heart had been so opened by the sisterhood I had experienced in England that returning to my American middle school seemed harsh and empty. Nobody seemed to care about another's true spirit anymore, which was easier to spot when everyone wore the same uniform. Popularity became more about materialistic priorities. I went into 8th grade and noticed right away that the girls were petty and superficial for the most part. Classmates only cared about trends and fitting into cliques. It was super challenging to re-acclimate.

Thankfully, when I was one-on-one with classmates, we could go deeper than the surface, which seemed impossible in groups. Things improved once I spent enough time with someone to get past the facade I saw forced upon them by American culture. Still, I never fit in as well as I did in England, and I had come back with a slight British accent that I would be made fun of.

All my changes into womanhood and failure to acclimate to American school marked my entrance into the underworld realms of darkness and the collective shadow self where pain and horrors reside. I am thankful my childhood prepared me for this journey, becoming familiar with certain archetypes before they began to play out. The glimpses and premonitions I received were getting closer, and what I almost hoped would never come true was getting ready to strike.

LABYRINTH

The labyrinth metaphor harmonizes the individual's DNA with the Earth's elemental patterns. The labyrinth, as a path, is the gateway to the underworld. In this day and age, literal hell needs to be purified back into the Mother-womb. It is a path that plants seeds and creates global alchemy. The most vital part of my mission connects to this understanding—the labyrinth is a preparation process.

I felt almost like puberty wouldn't be an average experience for me. It seemed too powerful to step into feminine energy on this more fundamental level. I was a tomboy and used to boys being something I could relate to. Every once in a while, I would make a great female friend, but I didn't enjoy at all the programs that most girls were operating from, the responses from men in return, or the other way around. It felt lonely more than anything until I found like-minded friends many years later.

How can one know when a program and distortion is coming from another or when you are about to fall into its pit? Of course, my sensitivity increased as I got older, but I still had no idea how much this was a part of my soul journey. Although I could recognize the big picture, growing up surrounded by society's distortions left me feeling utterly confused.

When these years hit, and the changes were beginning to happen, it was like I could feel a hand on me and a voice that breathed strength into me and encouraged me to remember what this journey I was on was for. I felt the innocence of Persephone, a primordial Goddess of Nature, a maiden. I felt an impending fright, like I was on the verge of being kidnapped by Hades and forced into the underworld. It is a massive initiation we all have to face on some levels. Still, so many are more unconscious of knowing themselves as the living myth or that we live out some of these archetypal energies in powerful ways.

I didn't read many books growing up, yet I knew this story was a massive part of me. My journey into darkness would awaken a wisdom that allows the light and dark to join forces within. I understood it on a soul level. This alchemy is about balancing and integrating polarity for dark and light to dance together rather than get lost in power struggles, drama and suffering. Thrown into separation, they become one again through the true union of the masculine and feminine, right and left brain hemispheres, science and spirituality, etc.

When polarities aren't in harmony, they are vulnerable to attack. Alchemy is impossible without those forces merging, as is transformation or protection from parasitic demonic forces. We hold this divine power in the world, but we must still be in that aspect of human experience to understand and heal it. We are all built with the antidote, and we have experienced all that needs this medicine and are still experiencing it. Awakening is knowing this is what we indeed are. We always have the consciousness to defeat anything harmful. We just lost it and are finding it again. It is that ultimate trust in yourself to know you can handle anything that comes your way and create the essential conditions for yourself internally and externally, allowing balance to return, shielded fully from digressing influences, shifting everything as we know it. That is where I feel we are heading.

This was the living path of Venus, the morning and evening star. I was going to allow myself to metaphorically die and feel the deepest pain and suffering so that I could rise, shift my perspective and empower it again. I had so many glimpses of these truths, and the presence of Christ would be so intense at those times. It mattered little how old I was. These truths and archetypes were beyond age or about people or past lives. It was an energy, something I knew existed if we could live beyond negative ego. However, these glimpses and realizations morphed into a dread because I knew I was preparing to be thrown into the underworld. Still, in the end, only my higher self—the greater part of me—could have possibly constructed these circumstances. I have done this many times before, but this time, it would be my greatest challenge ever.

I felt the abduction of Persephone in our era as the exile of divine feminine energies in our patriarchal culture, which distorts our connection to womanhood so that we feel exiled from within and victimized. We live out other mythologies in tandem with this one as we do all we can to clear the unconscious parts of our nature and face the shadow and a place beyond ego to rise again. This is what it takes to be multi-dimensional and fully conscious.

I saw this dark impending pit as the underworld when I was in it, or the veil as I observed it from afar and as I entered it, a kind of tunnel that needed to be

The Dunure Labyrinth dating from 2009-2010, South Ayrshire, Scotland. This is such a powerful image of the Labyrinth.

excavated and navigated. I recognized that it was total darkness. I sometimes saw it as the thickness of this density that kept us stuck in the matrix. I knew it needed to be penetrated and understood so it wouldn't be some unconscious form of control or separation. Many have talked about a NET encasing the human race, which keeps us limited to just a 3D experience, and so I see this as the fences and seals in our DNA that need to be broken.

On a personal level, this initiation brings one into the dark night of the soul not just for self but for Gaia and for the protection of the Organic Ascension Timeline. It simply had to be done, and we all face this along the way. Later in life, I discovered the level of targeting to oppose my willpower and stop me from completing this goal I was under. So many individuals are facing it, too, as is humanity. When it entangles us, we can feel trapped. Leveraging adversities to find our greater wisdom illuminates our lantern in the darkness, and we can begin to find our way out. This is the archetype of the Crone, connected to great wisdom. In these times, humanity must learn how to upgrade when facing adversity.

Everyone around me seemed captured by the programming in high school, but I wasn't ready to become complacent and accept that this is what being human is all about. Instead, I felt a deeper pull into an intense initiation that would bring me closer to my soul, and that was the only way to do my mission work.

The more misunderstood I felt, the more I recognized the matrix and all its trappings. The more I projected onto myself that something was wrong with me, the more my physical symptoms would manifest—like my body was screaming at me not to go towards those beliefs or to forget who I am and what I am here to do. No one needs an identity to be who they are. It is simply being true to the self that is enough. Sometimes, I'd choose to "go there" and would experience some significant symptoms. Ultimately, they helped me see the root of true healing because I remembered their source was where I had given my power away, had shoved something down or held trauma I couldn't release or process.

I began to hide more and not speak up. Yet, I continued to experience many powerful signs that helped me to see that I was on a long road toward the goals of my life's work. I would not let anything get in my way. I knew deep down that I wasn't crazy or way off, but sometimes it was just easier to play the role of the "lost" or "fucked-up" kid. The immensity of pain and weariness from the constant self-reflection I felt every day often left me no room to do basic human tasks. It was hard to hide my work from people without feeling ridiculed. I know many of you can relate to that.

My path showed me a need to reclaim all the fragmented parts of my prior lifetimes. My initiation into womanhood meant entering something much greater than me. Living in the present moment was hard without getting lost in the immense global, cosmic and galactic energies. My transition from girl to woman threw me into many changes, vaster than anything typical, yet I knew I wasn't alone and others were on this journey too.

The encroaching darkness threatened my mind, soul, womb, and creativity because this darkness wasn't like the pure soil of the Earth. It held things that needed clearing beyond my being and into the world soul—confronting gatekeepers, demonic entities, predators, and what I would later understand as a Negative Alien Agenda (NAA). Keeping all those forces out of one's being can be very challenging in the face of attack and weakened by life's traumas. I always felt clear inside from the intrusion and programming, but the exhaustion and overwhelm of warding these things off of me or dealing with the trauma and overwhelm has been the most challenging. So many of us do planetary work through our bodies. Usually, when a person has a lot of outer planets in their chart, it reveals this.

Many can't handle that this could even exist. Yet, we must understand that we have the upper hand to claim complete victory. We win the war on consciousness from within, leveraging our divine blueprint and sovereign birthright. I learned that walking through the threatening energies was the gateway to purifying myself and the Earth from a traumatized history. However, I will say that there was no way to prepare enough for the level of opposition that stood in my way or the degree of slung insults from my attempts to share what I saw without higher help. I would recognize guides and other support later in life, but in the beginning, it felt like something I tackled on my own, almost like I knew before I was born that this would be a part of what I would take on and do.

We all have to do the work, and I want to inspire others to see this necessity and jump on board. It is not about being saved. This soul work is needed for true liberation. Though many reap the benefits of those taking this journey, only some are up for such a venture. Being receptive to an Organic Ascension versus assured regression through transhumanism is paramount. I had to travel through portals and many layers of the astral realms that lead to the higher worlds, guarded by demons and inorganic life forms controlled by evil forces who did not want the truth and light ever to be found again. These are the frequency fences placed in our DNA in the form of gatekeepers.

The underworld hell realm is what had become of the Mother's womb. She has always been our breath and life source. I surrendered to her fully to become one. Her pain is my pain. Her wounds are my wounds. Her will is my will. Her transformation and healing are mine and my deep devotion to her empowers me to do this. My love of unity, God and Goddess, Heaven and Earth, man and woman, in their highest spiritual expression, gave me all the strength I needed to continue and a certainty in its achievement.

BEING AUTHENTIC

We all benefit by embracing uniqueness and authenticity in ourselves and each other. It makes it easier to hear our inner voice and is how things can most effectively shift. The ultimate goal is connecting with our soul, direction, spirit and personal truth. When we embrace our painful processes and recognize the initiations into the many dimensions of ourselves, we deprogram from the projections, labels, and disregard we get from mainstream culture. It also helps us break free from the conditionings where we have bought into any level of mind control.

Of course, we won't see things the same way and can't expect everyone to be open to it, so cultivating patience and acceptance is paramount. We must be willing to come together in mutual love and respect. Then, it is possible to share and hear one another without conflict, strife or disharmony, no matter how much our opinions or theories differ. Remember the end goal—more love and peace. We can all agree on this.

Soon enough, there are obvious truths that the collective will eventually agree upon. Then there are personal truths that are the compass to our physical vessel and connected to cosmic laws, soul, and a higher self-connection to Spirit and a healthy ego. So again, we don't all have to be alike or force someone to see things our way, but we respect where the other is and harmonize like a beautiful orchestra developing mastery with diverse instruments and skill sets.

Let's unite and be mature enough to face the injuries of our souls and mental, emotional and physical bodies. We are diverse in our abilities, powers, expressions, narratives, wounds and afflictions, and these are gifts to share with one other. Peace comes when we no longer fight differences and cultivate integrity. Our greatest defense is our ability to love, forgive and cease compromising. We must stand our ground to be genuine—fuck what anyone else thinks!

With approximately seven billion people on Earth, personal attacks may continue. So don't be afraid to release yourself from what brings you down, and know that you are enlightened the minute you stop trying to attain enlightenment. Perhaps this is actually about learning how to hear the truth that your higher self holds, instead of mainstream news or outside distortions, and then bringing it into your felt experience and expression and accepting the purging and releasing without judgment to get to the other side without feeling defeated or a failure.

Many resources are available to us, and information exchange is helpful, but not agreeing with something doesn't mean it's right or wrong. We can prefer those of like mind and resonance and be a resource while respecting others' soul growth and not assuming we are above them. Those doing evil acts are a whole other thing to contend with. Building our spiritual immune system has been a process we have been strengthening and challenged by for thousands of years. Much of what I share is to activate a transformation process and help you to get closer to your truth and divinity.

To Err Is Human

Making mistakes, even a lot, is far different from being evil. Evil has an intention, plan or agenda that knowingly harms another. Outside of this, we have to forgive mistakes of the past, for not knowing better, for being lost in ego hang-ups, for being injured and projecting onto others, for not realizing that we supported things built on deception or manipulation, for not having better control of our emotions and for unintentionally causing pain to others or the self. Our mistakes serve as opportunities to gain wisdom, readjust and self-correct.

The asteroid Chiron is the wounded healer who takes on a portion of humanity's afflictions to rise above it for the benefit of all. This process includes the experience of falling and then getting back up again or being all that we are not, only to remember who we are. Chiron exposes our traumas and deep pain and how, when we rise above or understand them and dig deep into their roots, we can heal others even if we aren't fully healed.

This level of conscious recognition keeps us from acting out and being in the blame, shame and victim game. It helps us redirect our energies in service to humanity rather than be in harmful looping patterns easily taken advantage of by dark forces who wish to keep us in negative energies and disconnected to feed on us. So, the fact that Chiron rules Ophiuchus reveals how we are healing our relationship with the greater Mother force of the planet and the damage to our mitochondrial DNA as we begin to recognize that this loss of connection has been the root of a trauma we have been carrying for some time and were born with, that we can finally now overcome. This reconnection heals the inorganic and dark mother reversals. Just like we journey into our childhood to heal any wounds, we must do this as humanity so that we are not misled by rewritten history and distortions of our divine blueprint.

As we give ourselves more love, facing our dark night of the soul journey becomes more understood. We can drop judgment of the adversities and challenges and start to see our process and courage for what we boldly face. We retrieve our inner treasures while confronting all sorts of opposition that hopes we fail in becoming fully sovereign. We move beyond fear of our darkness and power.

It's empowering to honor these times of challenge instead of projecting onto ourselves that something is wrong with us. We were born into wounds, duality, injustices, ancestral patterns, systems of control, contamination of the elements, imbalance, tainted food, and more. But we also carry an innate knowledge of how to transform things in our lives. Humanity knows it's not just our mistakes that got Earth into this state. Is our greed, neglect and selfishness the only things we must come to terms with, or can we finally begin to accept that we continue to be interfered with by ET races, the Illuminati, repeat invasions and other outside influences?

History is complex, and there is no way to obtain complete accuracy because one of the ways these groups target us is to mix disinformation with truth into everything. There will be differences of opinion, too, so they leverage this to scramble our minds, pit us against one another and feed on our negative or fearful loosh energies as we run around chasing our tails while whipping each other with them.

All my experiences, research and intuition convert into an unwavering knowing, with sources I have gathered that back up my revelations and epiphanies. I allow my body to help me to discern in a similar way that kinesiology works.

The distortions of our natural energies that have been challenging to contend with bring belief systems not in alignment with our body's wisdom up to the surface to be seen—creating un-wellness or some level of imbalance. Sometimes, technology implants are also involved, ancestral patterns, or both because almost everyone has been exposed to each of these at this point. We are challenged by the same things our planet is dealing with. Mother Earth is just waiting for us to remember our connection with her and join forces so we can return to higher dimensional Earth. Becoming one with the immune system of this planetary consciousness will eradicate all that compromises it. We must step into a level of devotion to our highest principles, which will no longer allow us to house negative entities. Also, digging in the dirt barefoot would be helpful, too!

Too many have accepted that trials and tribulations are a normal part of the human condition and thus won't investigate the deeper roots and hidden influences. Coping with diseases, war, pain, loss and suffering becomes normalized and never relieved. However, we as a human race are finally ready to stand up and face things as they are, realizing we always had a choice in these matters. Looking the other way has gotten us nowhere. This is about the liberation of the Earth—not just recognizing that there are more secrets than we thought existed. The process of disclosure and treating one another with mutual love and respect is one of the most vital aspects of this process. The negative parts of our experiences are because they are a part of the human experience we agreed to participate in. Still, we can't think it is okay to assault nature and us this way. Wishing it away with love and light alone won't cut it. Taking action and seeking justice when called will.

Nature leads us toward the antithesis of what we have grown accustomed to. Spending time in nature allows us to discover our spiritual abilities to live beyond the veils as multi-dimensional beings. We are learning the extent of our capacity to heal, regenerate and shield ourselves from the insanity of the lower matrix designed to keep us disempowered and dependent on systems that pull us further from ourselves and our divinity.

Many well-intentioned people have no idea they are participating in these systems, while others know exactly what they are doing and continue their corruption. Ultimately, it is not about fighting a system or "us" against "them." It's about releasing ourselves from what no longer serves us, uniting instead, and assisting one another to use resources wisely or create new ones so we can fulfill the needs of everyone. Let's face disclosure with as many facts as possible, an open mind for what cannot be proven, and always discernment.

Thankfully, the deceptions and betrayals of parasitic influences can't survive in Unity Consciousness. The dark eras of the last 26,000-year cycle are now something we can initiate out of, something we can rise above, as we now have a chance to watch a fundamental shift occur, where we recognize the power of this human vessel and what it can do. We are the shift. We divorce ourselves from the imposters. We create with true love and experience true love with all creation—the great love story encoded in our DNA.

How can we venture further than what we are told and taught without feeling like we are breaking some rule? Just do it. Choose yourself. You hold the law—the truth frequency!

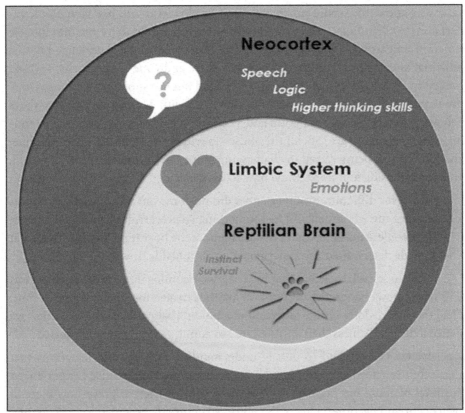

The Reptilian Brain. The oldest of the three, the reptilian brain controls the body's vital functions such as heart rate, breathing, body temperature and balance. Our reptilian brain includes the main structures found in a reptile's brain: the brainstem and the cerebellum. The reptilian brain is reliable but tends to be somewhat rigid and compulsive.

HIGH SCHOOL

Every summer, I would do an overnight or day camp. Often, I went to a sailing camp back in New York, where we used to live. I loved being on the water. Even while I was trapezing off a boat as a young person, I would still feel the inner dialogue buzzing around my mission. It never left me alone. So, I would often be accused of being "spacey" while on the water. Every experience seemed to connect to my mission—like it was either serving it, attacking it, or taking me to a place that needed healing. Thankfully, living in the trees as a child and attending summer camp got me into nature and the wilderness. Going to camp became a sanctuary and a welcome break from the school year, though I noticed people either liked me or ran the other way. It seemed like some years, friendship was "all" or "nothing."

My intense shyness and insecurities began to arise after socially abusive events caused my emotions to be shoved down. I would always find a release valve as I knew this would make me sick if I didn't let it out. Just ridiculous, superficial people I didn't even care to have as friends would drive me into intense isolation and would eventually take its toll. Many children experience horrific bullying, and my heart always goes out to those enduring such cruelty. I wasn't bullied in my situation but was confronted with intense snobbery and weird, unpredictable behavior that I wanted nothing to do with. Unfortunately, I see these behaviors as just another affliction and a cry for help due to a lack of understanding of who we truly are. So, all the abuses inevitably get handed down the line, and kids end up being raised in challenging home environments. Most, if not all, are hurting inside and don't know how to handle it.

However difficult, my experiences did push me out of my shell to eventually embrace my whole self and feel something so powerfully wonderful happen with the people around me that I couldn't ignore the liberating lesson—that what I held inside determined my experiences on the outside. It was life-changing!

Back in school, tragedy, tests, and trials were coming into my life rapidly. I was sensitive to how friends, teachers or love interests treated me, and at the same time, I had this total I-don't-give-a-fuck kind of attitude. That made it hard as I knew we shared a deeper likeness than anyone cared to admit, yearning to be expressed.

I have been drawn to deeply understanding projects and programs that abuse children beyond anything we can comprehend. Not because I experienced this level of abuse but because my heart and soul yearned to grasp how it could even occur and become a part of the power structure that seemed to feed on misery in absolute service to self. I sensed it was significant work that I would help to expose and heal. So many incredible warriors of light have endured such horrific abuses. Their journey helped me understand my own and get more in touch with it. As much as I could see and acknowledge the programs and distortions used to perpetuate horrible agendas, it was all truly eye-opening.

My ability to feel profoundly on a multi-dimensional level made life an overwhelming challenge, processing my major mission work for the planet with urgency running through my veins and nowhere to go with it except within. I did appreciate the guidance I received to validate my experiences, mainly through spirit guides, signs and omens impossible to ignore. I found it increasingly difficult to cope with everyday life circumstances that others seemed to handle just fine. At one point, I accepted that maybe being crazy was possible. I was not trying to prove anything with this—my heart just ached, knowing I needed to fulfill something significant, whether anyone knew it or not. And I knew I couldn't do it alone.

In my teenage years, I recall feeling gut-wrenching love nearly every day on every level. I finally realized that I had given myself entirely to Mother Earth. I was more than Laura having experiences as a human, but a part of the planetary consciousness and the world soul. My energy was much bigger than I felt comfortable with. Later on, I would be told that I was part planet, part human, and I am sure I am not unique in this way. It is what the human race steps into when we can get out of the matrix programming.

As an adult, I learned from my friend Rising Phoenix Aurora that when I was about 13 years of age, she had sessions with clients in which they shared that they had met me and that I helped remove them from the program. Though I found this startling to hear, it didn't surprise me. Eventually, she shared these profound testimonies with me:

"MILAB CHILDREN EXPERIMENTS

Session #436: Recorded in February 2022

Never before shared.

In this in-person A.U.R.A. Hypnosis Healing session the Higher Self of Gabriel who is the client, is taken to a large facility on the dark side of the moon. When Gabriel was eight years old, in third grade, in the public school system, a female and a male went to his classroom and energetically scanned the entire classroom, choosing and inviting two of the children to go to a recreational camp for a week. He was one of the children. His parents agreed for him to go to this camp. This is when Gabriel's experiments began as a child.

There is much to this transcription, however we will fast forward. We will begin where Gabriel is in his designated room, on the dark side of the moon, while experiments are being performed on him.

A [Aurora]: Tell me what is going on.

G [Gabriel]: We all have been summoned. I have no control over my body. My body is moving to where we are being called to.

A: Tell me what your surroundings look like.

G: There is a long hallway, which has at least one-hundred rooms. It is all very sterile. The other children are coming out of their rooms as well.

A: Are you not able to resist going to where you are being called to?

G: No. My consciousness is being controlled by implants that have been inserted into my brain.

Fast forwarding to the big dome room where he is summoned to in this facility on the dark side of the moon.

G: There are hundreds of children standing in rows like soldiers. There are people on a balcony speaking, giving us our ranks on how we are doing. It is all a game, and we are in competition with one another. Those who are not ranking high enough are dying. I am feeling a pull to my left, someone's energy is calling me. I typically cannot move on my own, but my body is moving towards this voice. It is Laura M. Eisenhower, she is about thirteen years old. She is not like the rest of us, she is in control of her consciousness and body. I go to her, and stand next to her. She whispers, 'What are you doing here? You are not supposed to be here.' She then with her fingers touches my third eye and says, 'Don't ever give up. Keep fighting the fight!' As she does I instantly go back to the time and space before my first MILAB experiments began.

The Higher Self of Gabriel explains that young Laura M. Eisenhower has volunteered to go into these Mk-Ultra/Milab experiments selflessly to pull people out one by one. This is one of the reasons why she was born into the bloodline of the Eisenhower's. Many of the whistleblowers who she has inter-actions with now, do not remember, but they are alive and have had their erased memories come back to them because she pulled them out of these inverted timelines. She has never been controlled by these dark forces, is one of the purest souls on Earth, and she does this work everyday. She has saved hundreds of children on Earth."

REPTILIAN BRAIN

"Move Beyond good and bad, right and wrong, or dark and light. Try to see every condition as an aspect of creation rather than seeing through the eyes of separation and judgement. Essentially the Universe is in perfect balance. It is the human mind that creates polarity."

– Lyssa Royal, Galactic Heritage Cards

Many wonder, will we ever be able to integrate with the Draco Reptil-ians? Will they always be our enemies? Will we forever have to deal with their constant threat? The truth is that we can only overcome through heal-ing and integration. Understanding what they are all about and why they came to be serves as a mirror for us to understand ourselves. We have a reptilian part of our brain. Though the unconsciousness, amnesia and societal mind control pro-grams can make it hard to stand up to such a force, it is something we can indeed override. The ego is like a lost child wanting to come home again, but the shame and denial make it nearly impossible to begin knowing how to heal.

In the "Galactic Heritage Cards" booklet by Lyssa Royal, one of the cards in the deck associated with this is called Essassani – Spiritual Sovereignty. The Es-sassani are a human-Zeta hybrid species and are highly evolved, assisting Earth through its transition. Deep within the Essassani collective memory lie the healed lessons of the Zeta, Orion and Human species. Because these lessons were fully integrated, the outcome is a species of pristine consciousness capable of non-po-larized thought. She explains in this book how the human tendency is to think that something "out there" will bring us liberation or awakening. But unless we see the false self and refuse to live as that illusion, true spiritual freedom will elude us.

So, this is where the more highly benevolent form of healing comes in, but there are breeding programs where humans have reported being abducted by EBEs (Extraterrestrial Biological Entities). They are designed to carry out certain tasks for their higher-ups. Lisa Renee talks about how many were once humans involved in the Orion Wars, captured and used in worker colonies. This is one of the possible results of the transhumanism movement underway, which leads to the future alien or dark force control over the soul. She says that there have been accounts of contact made with benevolent types of Grey Aliens that are aware of the violations and crimes made against abducting and torturing humans, that have joined the Earth alliances to help free humanity from their negative alien oppressors, and are proponents of disclosure.

Spiritual therapist Bonnie Baumgartner talks about how the Alpha Reptilians created the grey soulless AI aliens that are only workers for whatever group purchases them, like the Zeta Reticuli 1 and Zeta Reticuli 2. Their agenda is to please their owners and handlers.

During the time of Atlantis, the dark alliance put the Anunnaki Reptilians in charge of the Earth 13,000 years ago, and they remained in power until 1995. In 1995, most of the Anunnaki decided to move to greater light, a higher resonance of compassion and forgiveness and, thus, changed their name to Annanuki and are members in good standing of the Galactic Federation. Let us hope this is true. I hold high discernment myself when it comes to these things because of imposter beings claiming to be of the light. Still, I will always have an open mind and continue to explore all possibilities. I know a major healing and transformation is underway, and many species and aspects of our multidimensional existence and reality are involved. All these efforts are about healing, finding sovereignty and integrating polarity.

The Orion civilization experienced the deepest polarity, and many Orion souls chose to incarnate on Earth to heal and integrate this. A resistance group called the Black League helped change the consciousness within the Orion system so they could transform, like the Jedi Knights from Star Wars. So much of this plays out on Earth. And as far as the Reptilians, only a few species are considered hostile. Lyssa Royal talks about the Reptilians representing the unprocessed and denied fears within us, which often manifest for protection and survival. As I understand, many are peace-loving, gentle and quite ancient. We must remember that we sometimes increase polarity when we fight something perceived as negative. Doing the inner work to integrate all polarity is the best thing we can do for ourselves and the planet.

MOVING THROUGH ADVERSITY

When I was 14, I went to an herbalist. She told me she could see the Magdalene energy around me and encouraged me to avoid negative people. Yet somehow, they always found me. I felt like a magnet for very dark individuals and did not make eye contact with anyone. I did my best to play the role my family and society expected from me, but my emotions became too much to handle. My passions were too powerful to manage, and I feared my darker aspects that lay chained somewhere screaming. I tried to push these thoughts away, but they kept creeping up. It wasn't darkness in agreement with evil. Evil was harming the darkness, and I needed to get the source of it.

It wasn't until high school that these experiences became real like everything before was a warm-up for what was to come. I deeply sensed all vibrations, especially concerning the social world. I already understood the concept of sacred union. These energies made themselves very known to me as a child. For me, the necessity of sacred union went deeper than stories and myths. It was required to heal this planetary system and move beyond the imbalances, amnesia and socially engineered indoctrination. A call towards the core root of all creation, a trail for light to pour in, to create global alchemy through the union of opposites.

When I met my first boyfriend, all felt easy and familiar. Our freshman year together was great and fit my ideal. However, I went too far in projecting sacred union onto this relationship, as either it was unaccessible at that time, at this age, or with the existing mentality around me.

My mom always made plans for me every time there was a school break. One summer, I went away to New York, and this was when my boyfriend and I began to grow apart. His father was dying, and his Mother was grappling with addiction. I was sad I couldn't be there to help him through it. I tried not to blame my mom for being away during break times, but it still crushed me. Regardless, I am sure it was for the best. I was a wild child, and without her being able to supervise me because of her intense workload, I could see that it was more for my protection. After getting "all caught up in boys" beginning in 6th grade, I think she sensed this intensity in me to make my boyfriend and our love more important than anything, like growing up and finding direction.

Our relationship began to fizzle out in my junior year. He cheated on me with another girl, and my world shattered. It hurt badly because I expected so much more. Thinking back, I wonder how I could have placed such massive expectations on our relationship when we were still so young. I believe it was because I was so ready for sacred union and felt I had been waiting lifetimes! I am unsure why I was so bent on him being "the one" because he wasn't. Afterwards, I remember feeling that I didn't want to be with anyone else or ever love again. I

The Law of One
Practices

- Practice Unity Consciousnes.
- Practice Loving Yourself
- Practice Loving Others
- Practice Loving the Earth and Nature
- Practice Service to Others
- Practice Consciousness Expansion
- Practice Responsible Co-creatorship

Law of One. "Simply put, the Law of One is the Universal Truth that All Is One. It is the Truth taught by Christ when he proclaimed, 'Love your neighbor as you love yourself.'" –Lisa Renee, Ascension Glossary; https://ascensionglossary.com/index.php/Law_of_One

wondered how people did this. They do every day, but how?

The whole experience thrust me into a dark place. I lost my feeling of safety and security once again. I started to recognize how close I was to dwelling in the depths beneath, but the road to process and let go was still a long way ahead. I experienced increased energy attacks from there and had each foot in different dimensions. I recognized I was more vulnerable to attack due to the breakup, but it was how the story needed to play out. Once I accepted this, I entered the underworld to work on my mission. I knew it wasn't an accident that I ended up there but a necessity, so I embraced it, whatever it took, and quickly realized a happy life would not be how.

I learned that snake bites were used in ancient times to ensure the feminine would embark on this underworld journey. My intuition told me that, though this practice wasn't widespread, it was a powerful way to bring balance back in the face of duality and patriarchy. It was a place to go to and then be reborn and transformed. Going deeper into this darkness through each stage of life, it was time to call back the deeper aspects of myself that needed to be retrieved and brought to the surface in the face of things that wanted to keep it down, exiled and forgotten. It wasn't him so much as my inability to exist on the surface of Earth, my whole self, feeling cut off and silenced when I wanted to engage in these dialogues. So much in me has always wanted to express a deeper reality, to live on an intimate soul level and prioritize love and union, with memories stirring constantly about how that nourishes the kingdom and the people.

I was lost in the past of what used to be, striving for it to return to the world and way too young to create it with another. However, it still consumed me as an urgent goal to embody fully from within and discover in life with another. I later found that this was the focus of my felt targeting, dark weaponry and attention—it was the part of my mission they wanted to disrupt or control for their own purposes.

Insecurities and confusion continued to plague me after the breakup. I started drinking and lost my ability to relate to the people around me. I was haunted by feelings of abandonment and betrayal, dredging up every past life where I had experienced it. I desperately wanted to connect with people, and these darn programs drove me up the wall. It felt like a barrier to realizing incredible connections, like Unity Consciousness—two words I would repeat throughout my life, to the point of apathy and cynicism, and then back again to recognizing I would never let it go!

I could sense the ground opening up in front of me, a deep hole going into the Earth, as I walked forward into time. I tried to avoid the pit but felt male and female energies beckoning me forward. The male force wanted to abduct me, while the female force tried to guide me to all my lost aspects that the male force held hostage. It was the Crone when I started working with tarot decks. The number nine card was that female energy guiding me, and at the next level was another beginning of a cycle, just like the seasons. I continued forward because I sensed victory before I even began. Still, it was challenging, and I had my coping mechanisms—like swearing! This magnetic pull wanted to introduce me to the devil himself. I found a place where I could hide once the darkness started to creep up on me, the connection to the soul of Mother Earth deep in thick forests and caves—a dark vessel of creation and regeneration. The so-called devil challenged what I truly felt.

On the surface, drinking alcohol, attending rock concerts and skipping school became "my thing." My relationships at home felt strained, and I didn't like myself or how I saw myself. The self-destruction in me just needed love. I felt the deeper pains of suppression, exile, and the total neglect of the divine feminine at all turns. I had so many emotions to sort out that I could only cry. I also had my share of sexual assaults throughout high school, but I was determined to heal and overcome them. I never wanted to bother my family with these kinds of issues. I love them so much and didn't want them to worry about me.

Though I was too young to fall in love, it was my nature to desire a deep connection that I was not mature enough to handle. The pressures of life made finding direction in the world quite confusing because I had this whole other dialogue going on inside me connected to my mission that I couldn't talk with anyone about.

I felt targeting that I couldn't explain until I found others who had either been through similar or knew about it. I experienced a lot of nervous system distress and would only later realize that this attention had been on me since childhood.

Every morning, I awoke presented with this pit into the thick and dense darkness before me. I could also feel the energy of a hand on my shoulder and a voice that breathed strength into my being, asking me to remember what this journey was for. I could feel dry, coarse fingers touching my skin, encouraging me to follow—the Crone, the part of myself with true mastery of the underworld and who guided me through this terrain before I knew how. Something in me knew I would survive it. Though I feared this hand, I learned to trust its lessons that I would eventually achieve, where the wisdom and experience of such a venture would be more firmly established in my consciousness.

Her hand gently caressed me and moved me closer to descending into her domain, the underworld, death. I stood at a crossroads—a part of me was already buried in the darkness, but a part remained free in the brilliant playground of spirit. I was a human bridge to the underworld and the heavens, with pieces of me existing in both realms simultaneously. I was born with this dilemma, this urgency in my nervous system, that I can only describe as a mission to synthesize the Earth, underworld, and heaven into wholeness. It was no small task, but I knew I had no choice as the hand of the Crone tapped louder and louder on my shoulder. The Maiden, Mother and Crone are revealed in the seasons and many life cycles we all embrace as a deep part of our soul development and journey.

I fought hard not to doubt and lose myself daily, but it felt impossible. Believing in myself was too radical. I could lose myself completely if I had an off day or a moment of distraction when I needed to focus constantly to protect myself. I fasted, used herbs, threw I Ching coins, and shuffled my tarot cards repeatedly, asking if I would survive. Without these tools, it would have been impossible.

I had a tough time with the loss and tragedies that arose. As a child, I had already gone through two divorces and didn't know how to handle love. I felt like a baby being birthed from one extreme to the other, screaming upon arrival, settling in, only to find that I was squeezing back through the birth canal again the next day, with no mother to hold me like a newborn—just the perplexed support of my family. They loved me so much but didn't know how to handle the extremes of what I was going through. I wanted to protect them from it, so I held in my experiences and put on a brave face, knowing they were also dealing with so much in their own lives. If I told them, it would have pulled them from what I knew they needed to focus on. I am sure it would break their heart knowing this was how I thought. Nothing they did indicated this. It was just part of my sensitive and stubborn nature to heal myself and navigate things on my own. Later in life, when I finally felt I could open up to them about the hellish situations I was facing, I realized how unconditional their love and support were for me. They helped me immensely, especially with later experiences that would become way more extreme.

Everyone has breakups and heartache. I just happened to put myself in dangerous situations because so much more was happening inside of me than the external storyline showed, things I brought in before I was born. I know many yearn for the love and support of their families. I lived without relying on or seeking it because I wasn't sure if I would be loved or accepted if I shared what was happening. I could a little. I just never wanted them to know it was as extreme as it was to avoid outside treatment for my mental or emotional health. I desperately sought to understand it on my own terms.

There was a time, though, when I did have some professional assistance along the way. Unfortunately, the person was cold, didn't engage in deep dialogue, asked some questions and seemed ready to prescribe a drug I didn't care to take. I tried them for a week and then stopped. I am not encouraging anyone to avoid getting help. I am suggesting you write it out, express it and find the release valve. It can be a tremendous opportunity to dig deep into your soul and truth, live a life that honors your deeper longings and needs and not give up in your pursuit of your soul calling, dreams and visions that want to be realized.

Before the breakup with my boyfriend, this fantastic man came into my mom's life. I was about 16 years old at the time. Through her work, she met a scientist with an extensive resume. According to Wikipedia, Roald Zinnurovich Sagdeev graduated from Moscow State University, is a Russian expert in plasma physics and a former director of the Space Research Institute of the USSR Academy of Sciences. He was also a science advisor to the Soviet President Mikhail Gorbachev.

As life was adjusting to this new relationship, I existed more in my internal world than the outer, trying to figure myself out and how to navigate the enormity of what was going on inside me. In moments of clarity, an inner dialogue with Christ existed in perfect harmony, while externally, I lived in supreme chaos and confusion, strangled by dark shadows. My only triumph was in my stillness and calm. At times, a warm, golden and divine light streamed into my being. It brought tears to my eyes and reminded me of experiences from dreams and past lives. This light shone so immensely that I thought others would surely notice.

Before the light could spread outward, I would get yanked away by something false and synthetic, pushing me aside. I became so ungrounded that I couldn't regain clarity. I now know that this artificial force was interference from the false matrix prepared to stop me at all costs. Some energy sought to derail me whenever I emerged more empowered. It wasn't a world I could be myself in. I needed to manifest some adventures to breathe and expand and not feel the suppression of the societal forces that wanted to mold, shape and condition me.

Gravity toward the pit pulled on me, wanting me to witness how lost and barren my landscape had become. I still needed to embrace this darkness within me. That was where I could clear and release all that made it uncomfortable to be there and to face gatekeepers showing up in the external world that might keep me from one day emerging. This dark, mysterious part of ourselves challenges our beliefs and tests us to find our truth without the assistance of the vast light above. I started to see many lost souls wandering in these regions. They would cling to me as though I was going to rescue them. Their looks of desperation and longing alarmed me, and I came to miss my happier friends yet felt a painful compassion and relatability to these skeletons.

My external conditioning tried to force me to forget those heavenly glimpses that defined parts of my childhood. Society hounded me to develop my analytical mind. I could not conjure the words to describe the sensations of paradise in my dreams. I had pressures and opportunities to go after notable achievements and degrees. My family loved me and wanted the best for me. Even though my parents weren't together, I still felt a strong foundation of family and dedication. But the doors to the far-reaching depths of the great below had already opened.

When it came time to graduate from high school, I didn't know where I would go. I spent my time trying to heal and mend, and I hadn't prepared for the next phase of my life. Then, by some miracle, I received mail describing a school in the Adirondack Mountains. It was easy to get into. My grandmother took me on a trip to visit the school, and I instantly fell in love with the land. I was finally confident that this was where I needed to go, so my next step was to create a plan to apply, get in, and attend college.

In the midst of all of this, an invitation to participate in the International Ball came up! It was a tradition that the Eisenhower women would attend the ball, and every aunt of mine, cousin and sister did it. I was the only one who didn't. I wanted to uphold tradition, and it was a hard decision. But I had already grown dreadlocks in my hair and didn't know how to fit in. Even with it being a relatively small time commitment, I was so deep into my mission and feeling out of sorts that I didn't want to risk ruining it for everyone, however disappointing not attending might have been. My Grandad, Ike's son, reassured me at one of our subsequent family gatherings that he completely understood, that I was a warrior and that he appreciated me. None of my family members ever gave me a hard time, so I was relieved. This would have presented me with more opportunities and exposure, but I was not seeking that and was on my own unique journey that I continued to explore and stay true to.

Adversity and life's trials can help nudge us in the right direction if we keep our eye on the bigger picture and remind ourselves of what we need to guard and protect. We humans already have a hard time as it is. We can't even begin to fathom that there are hidden powers in this world that practice dark arts and use things like weather modification and trauma-based mind control to create slaves undetectable to us. It has become a weapon used against us and our world, and many who have been a part of these projects and programs are recovering and sharing their stories. I will delve into these topics in this book and others. Focusing on the subtle yet extremely powerful sabotaging forces is essential. We can trip up from the power adversity has over us, whether personal or not. There are many levels of trauma. If adversity is bad enough, it can turn into trauma and impact the quality of our lives and our capacity to move forward and thrive.

When outside adversity strikes, it can become personal because we feel much more than just ourselves, especially those who are empathic. We must see adversity differently to transform and rise above it. It can remind us what needs changing in our lives rather than something that crushes us or causes a feeling of failure and low self-worth. Unfortunately, conditioning teaches us that adversity is a misfortune so that we can sink further and further into despair, suffering and disillusionment when it strikes.

Adversity is a blessing and a teacher, reminding us of where our attention needs to be. Trauma could shake our nervous system and cause endless triggers even if we experienced the event long ago. But addressing adversity first reveals where we need boundaries and more protection and helps us know where we require more balance. If it triggers something, it invites us to step back and breathe through it to see if it is the same assaults experienced in the past or just something we perceive as such.

VICTIM ENERGY

"For women, Sophia is a powerful archetype for identification on many levels. She is every woman ever raped, denied her creativity, kept isolated, abandoned or exiled. She is also potentially within all women who wish to discover their creativity, maintain their integrity, and support justice in the world and in themselves. She is the strong woman who survives in the face of adversity and rescues her treasures, to display them at a more suitable time."

– Caitlin Matthews, *The Goddess Sophia*

Adversity and negative experiences can rip us open and take us into our soul, strengths, hopes, prayers and desires. It can snap us out of a trance of taking things for granted or not seeing previously hidden layers. But for many, victimhood results when adversity comes along, especially if experienced for long periods. Yes, there are many victims in our world, but how can we acknowledge this without allowing it to overtake how we view ourselves, the people we come across in our lives, and the friendships and partnerships we form?

To successfully move out of victim energy means we are ready to rebirth.

We are changing our vibration and perception in the face of something threatening because we have gained the wisdom and experience to recognize predatory energies. Being an open-hearted person can make one vulnerable. Maintaining an open heart and being shielded and protected from those wishing to take advantage of you can be challenging.

Rebirth, or being "born again," means one recognizes oneself as a whole and complete child of God/Goddess, dropping the story of what anyone's biological parents may or may not have done right or provided and feeling a product of that without choice. In many ways, coming to Earth is like showing up at a site that needs reconstruction, restoration, rehabilitation and renovation, just like a rundown house that needs fixing up in some places and tearing down in others. We don't want to become the areas we are called to work on. We don't need to become the rotting wood or the broken window if that was the shape it was in upon arrival. But, because we can't avoid the early conditionings and imprints from all our exposure to it, it becomes harder to see ourselves outside of it.

If we can see it through the eyes of our divine nature, it can allow us more wisdom in tackling the problem because, after exposure, we know what is lacking and what the missing pieces are. We get to bring all that forth, even though it takes great strength. It is all too easy to forget, sink into the damage, and fall apart. Still, it is time to remember that we came to change it by being senior to the forces that have broken it down, by doing maintenance work rather than enabling and contributing to the destruction because we took it personally or are lost in the shadow and all the symptoms that result from neglect or years of allowing forces to degenerate the temple and the soul that dwells within.

All we find wrong in the world represents our inner work to heal the ancestral lines and rise above global deficiencies and negative archetypal imprints. We are their children. More deeply, we are children of Source and Mother Earth, and as we identify more with this, we regenerate and find release and liberation. The story of where we came from and what we live through in our life journey is our mission to enlighten and awaken to take steps out of looping patterns and not stay victim to the programming or shortcomings. We do not need to inherit their patterns, afflictions or societies. We came to set them and ourselves free! In acknowledging this, love and forgiveness can overcome blame, victimhood, or the looping patterns, asking us to find that breakthrough. For many, this includes moving out of one's comfort zone and releasing any attachments to a false sense of security in a sort of addiction to the conflict or drama.

With so much technology used to control how people think that embeds a belief system about the self or our outer reality in the unconscious, it becomes critical that we harness our attention to leverage these same forces to catalyze a most profound awakening of our spiritual abilities so we can feed the lower forces back a much higher vibration than what it threw our way. In the same way that what we were born into requires our higher frequency to raise the vibration of the family energy that may have been conditioned into us, like the inner voice of authority that tells us what to do and threatens punishment for non-compliance and how that ends up translating into our relationship with the outer authority of society.

Where we can, we must take risks in pursuing a calling that might not fit into a tradition, status quo or expectation as long as we can do so without it hurting anyone. When we find the confidence and trust in ourselves, regardless of the reaction, it can inspire and plant seeds so that someone else might feel more permission to break from oppression or restriction placed upon their unique expression of truth. Truth isn't about "I am right, and you are wrong." It is about self-honesty and the willingness to be soul-centered to engage on a deeper level for love and understanding to enter the picture.

If we don't fill the physical experience with depth, meaning and purpose, it is like a civilization making technological advancements without spiritual growth. We cannot repeat the patterns of our past or have them play out to the point of being in fear or imbalance, where the quest for instant gratification and service to self pleasures becomes more important than connecting fully to our higher selves. Religion was set up to be rebelled against or control those who fall into its web—both behaviors miss the mark and weaken our connection with the sacred energies they have mimicked and distorted.

Part of the manipulation in our early history involved locking us into our lower self, where we become unconscious that it is the very thing that enslaves us. We need to reach the light of Source that dwells deep within to truly restore and find a balance between the merging of free will with cosmic law while being willing to do the construction work as architects of Heaven on Earth. We must also be willing to transmute and integrate the fragmented and programmed aspects so that the true nature and divine blueprint can step forward within all things.

Can we refrain from projections, resentment and jealousy and still acknowledge we are wounded and hurt? Yes, we can. Sometimes, we must live and feel it to know how to heal it. It works as long as we keep it from becoming a subpersonality that masks our divine potential and hides our true abilities as alchemists, wisdom carriers, initiates and healers on the road to mastery. Only then can Light Symbol Codes direct their frequency patterns into our DNA to activate our dormant levels of DNA, come online and function at higher levels. When we are no longer the victim (or victimizer), our mind can direct these Light Symbol Codes and their core geometries to direct frequencies into our body for healing, wellness and various consciousness enhancement purposes.

Journey into Relationships

"Until the Mother of God and Sophia's Holy Spirit are freed to be embodied in matter, women all over the Earth remain enslaved through the Baphomet and Black Madonna Networks."

– Lisa Renee

THE WILDERNESS SPEAKS TO ME

While studying to be an expedition wilderness leader in the Adirondacks and other places, I encountered the extremities that nature offers—from 105-degree deserts to 30-below mountainscapes with snowshoes and a backpack. I spent much time in Native American ruins, forests, canyons and oceans. They helped me to regain ground again as the sky clothed me with strength and clarified my purpose through solitude and quiet.

Mother Earth embraced me and made me feel truly alive. I rested in caves, snow forts and rock formations that brought the essence of nurturing and tenderness to my withered soul. Creatures and animals gazed upon me, and birds flew close to my face to wake me in the morning. Everywhere I turned, it seemed the allies of nature and the love of the Mother were with me—every climate and creature, a new expression.

She spoke through me as I talked to her, as I wrote hundreds of pages in my journal about the euphoria I felt in the presence of the soul of the living world. The sky produced shooting stars, and the glistening reflections in the ocean mirrored the thousands of tears I cried. The pain of the Mother overwhelmed me at times, but the unconditional love of her presence humbled and brought me to my knees as I prayed and assured her that I chose to serve her and would die, rise and heal along with her. I felt her wounds as my own, as revealed by this poem I wrote while in the desert of Baja, Mexico:

Rising From the Depths

A sea of open grace and depth

Beyond the shadows tortured death

Inside purified waters singing

to light the fire of sacred dreaming

Held in the arms clenched firmly around

the surrendered path that breaks veils with no sound

laughter cleansing, mind games playing

with patterns and waves of old scripts breaking

The fossil of a once fragile mind loses time

the ebb and flow carve a new world that's divine

deliverance is frozen in a mirage of desire

while agreements with angels placed wood on the fire

Choking within on my heartbeat's sorrow

enduring the dark with a feeling to follow

the air whispers thoughts of a dormant reminder

inside senses light in a quest to go find her

Taking flight to the height of the depth in my heart

surrounded by stones in the forest so dark

fishing intuitive oceans for sharks

I wake up alone, the lost memory departs

Humming birds waking me up in the morning

the breeze from their wings cools the soul-fire burning

a new day of oneself is finally dawning

to picturesque images no longer so haunting

Saga's lost in a spiral epic once stood

now placed on the shelves of minds rotting wood

waiting to be broken and forgotten forever

so the heart can stand bravely to endure the cold weather

Swirling in chaos

shifting through silence

breathing and dreaming of wave wind and mountains

the sparkle of stars giggle fiercely at blindness

when being too nice is a weak form of kindness

Alive and asleep, awake and half-dead

the wisdom that pulls through has heard what was said

the merging and fusions bring forth and give birth

to the freedom within that is felt beyond words

After all the wilderness adventures, I had a tremendously difficult time re-adjusting to a buzzing world and society. I could not hold on to feeling good, alive and awakened for very long around others. I kept running across people who greatly challenged me, so I continued grappling with alcohol as a coping mechanism. I went down to the woods constantly to lay my body down and feel the connection and life force of all that I was fighting for. As I sat up high in my favorite tree, the wind and leaves fell in such a way as to show me my strength. This tree was my place of solitude, where I dreamt I could receive a kiss from the light on the cobwebs of my life that felt dead, where magic was dead, where I felt dead. I contemplated and tried to figure out how to function outside the protection of this tree. I thought my journeys in the wilderness would help me navigate life more easily, but it only felt harder.

No matter what I did, I could not escape the challenges I was destined to confront. The wilderness training revealed my survivor strength and taught me about the soul and how thoughts shape what we experience. It taught me to hold on to those unseen things beyond our belief systems and to exist as a clear know-ingness and connection to Mother Earth, the elements and all the creatures. It awakened me to the truth that we are all co-creating this reality together. I tried to embody this connection to bring back with me into civilization, but I could not hold my ground anymore. I found I existed between two worlds once again, and the pull of the underworld felt like an unstoppable force.

I experienced anguish, terror and devastation as I felt myself falling deeper and deeper into an abyss with no safe landing. I felt humanity's intense separa-tion from spirit and what this separation has done to Mother Earth. I fell into a long despair filled with images of history, archetypes, imprints and wounds. Revelations and symbols to guide me lay hidden between the curves and forks of a dark and twisted labyrinth. Lost souls often eclipsed these internal truths.

Then, I encountered my turmoil, feeling so immersed in darkness, which I knew was a gateway beyond the physical world where the lost souls of the dead go to be reborn. It is a place where initiation is possible if one can see through the illusions of matter. This underbelly is where the roots of life grow, where all that's hidden has implanted itself. It was the place that I had to transform and reclaim. Here, amidst the stench of death, I found buried parts of myself. I would draw them up into the planetary root chakra to free the power of the Goddess, sleeping at its base. I fought hard with everything I had to awaken bliss and oneness in these places of total pain and darkness.

WEST VIRGINIA AND THE PSYCHIC

After I wrapped up my education experiences in the Adirondacks, I realized I was short a class to fulfill my associate's degree, so I planned to move back to West Virginia to complete it. So much was pointing towards a need to leave the Adirondacks. Though it was a place I loved, far removed from the matrix and the BS I was trying to avoid, and where I formed many deep and meaningful relationships, some ended up being quite traumatic, as all heartbreaks are.

One was particularly hard. I didn't know if I wanted to be with him forever. The triggers, red flags and strengthened calls toward my mission couldn't sustain this relationship. I couldn't communicate my feelings to the point of being understood—I didn't fully understand it myself. Most of what I did share concerning my larger mission wasn't well received, so how could I be with someone if I couldn't fully be myself or process what I had to? I saw how much I needed to heal, which sometimes overwhelmed me.

It was hard to hang out with friends when nobody knew I had this whole other kind of experience to contend with. No one knew what to say or wanted to talk about it. What would I even tell them? *"Cut me some slack. I am on a critical mission concerning my Great-Grandfather Dwight David Eisenhower's legacy and extraterrestrials. I have had some strange weaponry or attention on me since birth. I am also part of a Christos-Sophianic mission to restore our DNA and the planetary grid network impacted by ancient galactic wars. I feel a relentless force trying to steer me onto a timeline I don't want to be on. Ah!"* The enormity of all I was processing felt too much. Outside of my soul knowing, I wasn't even close to having my head wrapped around it.

Yet, forces within kept me going and helped me connect more dots and manifest the synchronicities needed for more clarity to open up and share. My intuition was always clear enough to guide, reassure, and help me see and feel things that would lead me toward more revelations than I could ever imagine. But, unfortunately, there was not one soul on Earth I could share any of this with since I was a child. I could only share with my ever-present spirit guides. It was not the fault of the people in my life, so it became something I learned to live with. I knew that if I survived to tell the tale, eventually, I would share with the pure intent of it being for the greater good of humanity. It was always surprising to see how many people would disappear or gloss over and on to different con-

Ike, Mamie, and David and Susan, grandchildren.

versation topics when I would let my guard down. Occasionally, I would explode when the pressure became too much, which is why relationships were so hard for me. I could never reach my desired level of intimacy. Being interrupted or shut down seemed the way it would be, so to be myself required leaving behind some of these partnerships, which was devastating.

Sometimes, I wish I didn't have such an intense emotional body or so much empathy. Not because my pain was too much, but because of the pain I caused others whom I knew loved me to their fullest or the best they knew how. They couldn't reach me on the deeper levels I needed them to relate to, unable to appreciate what I was up against, the targeting and urgency to uncover things and overcome the forces trying to steer me in other directions. Even if I wanted to stay with them, it was near impossible. I couldn't compromise with such a heavy mission weighing over me. It was painfully lonely, debilitating, and exhausting to find the will to keep moving forward to quench this inner calling that screamed loud in me for as long as I could remember. I had to be more independent, and hopefully, I'd meet people in time who could understand.

I felt immense pressure and an overwhelming longing to experience sacred union with another. I couldn't handle superficial or casual or not being with someone who could comprehend all of this. My soul required the most profound, mystical, magical union that felt this urgency and understood these darker agendas. As you can tell, it consumed me. Most people never took me very seriously. I realize it's partly my fault and perhaps a protective mechanism for myself or others. It appeared easier for people to roll their eyes or just laugh off whatever I was trying to communicate or think, "That crazy Laura," than to take the time to go deeper, especially because I carried all the stigmas for not liking school. It was easier for me to slip into the persona of being a "fuck up." After heartbreak and too much to process, it became evident to others that I was coming undone.

If it weren't for excelling through the wilderness courses, getting good grades and high scores on some papers I wrote, I wouldn't have had enough of a foothold in the human realm to complete my wilderness training certifications. I set aside all my other passions, research and interests because I didn't have anyone to share them with. I struggled with uncomfortable insecurities trying to play "human" while dealing with life and death matters bigger than what I could even wrap my head around. My soul, however, understood it and had clear recollection, downloads and intuitive hits about a much larger picture. My soul knew I was in for some major shocks and surprises. I was about to discover much more about the enormity of what we were up against—what humanity is still becoming aware of today.

I realized my partying was a way to unplug and give myself a break. Music and letting go were about celebration and would help me feel some release of pressure from the intensity of what was coming at me and moving through me. It was like a much-needed vacation. Not that I could ever entirely forget it, but it made things easier for me at the time. I struggled on and off with alcohol and am still horrified looking back at these memories. Completely letting go injured me and caused more problems than it was worth. There might not have been another way. Or maybe I could have done more to keep from self-destructing. Who knows? It was a healing process. Thankfully, I only went into a destructive mode when the trauma, wounds, overwhelm and isolation felt too much. Many might relate to some degree with this as we all go through difficult times. Of course, not everyone would choose to handle it the same way I did. So much was unhealed and ungrounded, no doubt amplified by spillover from previous lifetimes. I knew my birth chart had a challenging South Node. I will leave it at that for now.

The time came when I moved to West Virginia, where my mom had purchased a gorgeous Victorian home on 80 acres. It blew my mind! I enrolled in an art class and started working for Living Earth, an organic food shipping and delivery company in West Virginia, which I would eventually take over as my own business. It was the early 90s, and health food stores were not the norm. Most people were just getting acquainted with the whole concept of organic, at least in my area. I felt so inspired to help those who, for one reason or another, couldn't leave their home to get the food they needed. Some had various allergies that called for a specific way of eating. I worked overtime, drove to farms to pick up food, and had abundant fresh vegetables, fruits, and more.

One day, my pregnant friend asked if I would accompany her to see a psychic. She wanted some advice on whether or not she should give her baby up for adoption. I felt the importance of supporting her and went. I wasn't interested in a psychic reading myself—I already worked with the Mother Peace Tarot and the I Ching and was comfortable in these modalities. Though some think of these as demonic, I see them as wonderful aids to greater self-awareness. Creator has provided many helpful tools to achieve self-mastery in this realm.

We got to the psychic in Georgetown, Washington, DC, and my friend went to get her reading done. I was hanging out in the waiting room when the psychic approached and offered me a free reading. I was comfortable accepting the offer and keeping an open mind, curious to see if an important message would come through. She wanted to hold my necklace, saying it was all she needed. She held it in her hand and closed her eyes. I was amazed by the accuracy of what she shared. She went into my future outlook and said there was so much love. She told me I would meet a 6-foot-tall Danish man and have babies with him. She said I would be meeting him any day now in the area of West Virginia where I lived. I recall feeling sad knowing this ahead of time. She said I should return at no additional cost and that she would continue to guide me.

I took her up on her offer the next time I was in the area. This time, it was her daughter that met with me. Her daughter told me my last relationship was good for me and that I might not be ready for this new person her mother had described. I felt weird about leaving that relationship and still questioned my decision. Looking back, I cannot believe something or someone outside of myself would have such an influence on me that I would turn back towards a life I was ready to move on from, the Adirondacks. I had a lot to look forward to moving on. I had many questions for the psychic, as well as concerns. It was hard to process, seeing as I was so affected by the messages shared by a psychic I didn't seek out. But my feelings extended so much beyond myself to my relationship back in the Adirondacks that I sensed more closure was needed to see if there was still a future for us and for me to move forward in life freely! I finished my art class and completed my final credit toward my associate's degree in Science for my wilderness certifications. I was still working for Living Earth when I felt called to return to the Adirondacks. So I left for the little town I had lived, nestled in the middle of seven million acres of protected wilderness, the place I had fallen in love with.

Driving down the mountain roads in gusty winds, with silhouettes of the endless forest's canopy in front of me, I spent hours in the dead dark of the new moon filled with excitement and amazement. My will to get there seemed more vital than my vehicle's limitations, which lacked heat, proper windows and door linings. As the wind chill entered my tin box machine, I was heading back up into the mountains to get closure with the life I used to live there and my previous partnership. At the time, I didn't realize that this land had been my security blanket and that it was really time to move on. I stayed at friends' houses, and when I didn't wish to impose anymore, I chose to move on.

A fun and outgoing acquaintance convinced me to stay with her and party. Before long, we spent much of the money I needed to return home that she promised to repay. I was again too generous and rediscovered my weakness to lack the proper discernment because my hopes outshone the reality of our friendship. She continued to convince me that she would pay me back and help see to it that I would safely make it home. The fun and draw of continuing to party was too much to resist then. The wild and boundless freedom of the mountains made it hard to want to leave, but I wanted to get back home. With my Mother out of town and me broke, I felt stuck. Then my car broke down, and when I had nothing else to offer my friend, she backstabbed me like nothing I had ever felt. Not paying me back, she ditched me alone in the wilderness.

She went to great lengths to interfere with my ability to get help and did some incomprehensible things that harmed my previous relationships. I was stuck there for another month. I wanted to get myself out of this mess, so instead of being a burden, I relied on synchronicities with the people I would encounter. I spent time in an ice fishing shack with a loner friend and went out to some cabins. I decided to embrace the adventure as much as I could until something came through for me to be able to return home. It felt like a big setup. I had faced women like this who repelled my open heart and loving soul and wanted to punish me for it. Instead of delving into the drama, hurt and confusion, I took it upon myself to find a way to escape the freezing mountains while keeping a positive mindset. My parents were away. I took full responsibility for my actions. The cold temperatures and the small town quickly isolated me.

Other people in town agreed that this woman embodied dark forces. They even went as far as to call her "the beast." She felt like the archetype of Eshrikigal, the dark Mesopotamian Goddess of the underworld. In myth, Eshrikigal chooses to kill Inanna, who has journeyed into the underworld and stands naked in front of her. As a result of this same archetypical betrayal, I found myself broke, without a car and stuck in the Adirondacks in subarctic temperatures. It represented a continuing lesson in reforming my belief that everyone is loving and safe when their actions prove otherwise. These were the pitfalls of trusting something outside of me at a time when I should have relied solely on my inner knowledge.

After the betrayal, I lasted alone in the frozen mountains for two more months. Internally, I continued inside a hellish maze. I didn't know then that the deathly journey I started would continue for more than two decades. Just as Inanna meets the seven gatekeepers in her descent through the underworld, I, too, met with numerous levels of initiation that sought to strip me of my power. Each gate and level of initiation was a horrific and heart-wrenchingly painful experience. All this happened alongside a constant need to hold my ground as "Laura," a young girl who relied on her inner strength and intuition to venture for another day. It's still a blur how I got myself back from the mountains. All I know is that I was a mess when I returned. I experienced the ultimate sabotage—for now.

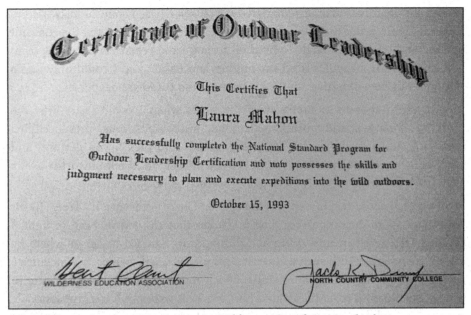

The Wilderness Speaks to Me. Degrees in Wilderness Expedition Leadership.

A LITTLE DEATH

I felt constant multi-dimensional attacks as I dragged Laura around in the Earth plane. The same energies I confronted in the archetypal depths showed in my everyday life. I had to battle them at every turn, which was overwhelming and exhausting. The weaver woman in me journeyed through many dimensions, weaving these worlds together, like Ariadne, the mistress of the labyrinth. Yet, parts of me remained chained in the depths of the underworld, like Inanna or Persephone, shackled with all the aspects of myself that had suffered terrible abuses in many past lives.

Waking up as Laura, I tried hard to feel some normality, but it would never last long. In temporary isolated periods, ranging from moments to endless hours, the coldness of my reality buried me alive. The only light I had to guide me was a flickering lantern that brightened when I focused on my internal wisdom but would extinguish in fear. As a result, I became very withdrawn and nervous. No one could make sense of me, yet I could still access joy and be somewhat normal with close friends and family. Unfortunately, the overwhelmed and isolated feeling of being unable to talk with anyone led to some wild behaviors to soothe my anguish. The only guide I had was an inner voice of wisdom, and I did not have enough confidence in it.

In this dark abyss, I could feel the creative energy of my womb under attack. These attacks were marked by lunar cycles. In the increasing darkness of the waning moon, forces of control battered me ceaselessly as I continuously tried to reclaim myself. From the new moon forward, I could feel a break in the constant battling and tried desperately to hold on to hope and regeneration. Away from home, I kept my struggles from my mother and father, and I could only find a safe outlet in the wilderness and a few friends who could see deeper.

These desperate moments were the times when I could feel Christ the most. In my darkest and most pathetic hours, his compassionate presence filled the room, and I could see his facial expressions and pick up on gestures and vibrations from him that lifted me out of my misery. Yet, I felt unworthy as my gifts, truth and high capacity to love only seemed to poison me.

Once, I could feel myself leaning against Christ underneath a tree. His divinity was so all-encompassing, like a blanket that clothed us both in light. I couldn't see myself in this vision and didn't know where I began or where he ended. He vibrated with such a glow that his physical self seemed to concentrate the pulsating light of the entire spirit, which moved up and down his aura in waves, reaching out to all life around him. His eyes were pools of compassionate love that healed deep inner wounds. Looking at him and feeling his warmth and words resolved the ages of history's misuse of knowledge and power. Between him and I was bliss, union, freedom and wisdom. He was there for all of us to awaken to within and to become one with him.

DEEP REVELATIONS

The more we understand Mother Earth and our galactic heritage, the more we can thrive, advance ourselves, and overcome the assaults like geoengineering, psychotronic weaponry, and false flag memes that contaminate our creative channels, enabling the very thing we don't want to manifest. All of this relates to a great warning that President Eisenhower gave us in his farewell address about the hidden power of the Military Industrial Complex. It is hard for many to believe that such advanced technologies exist and that they may have been handed to us by advanced ET races in exchange for genetic experiments. There are also Earth hybridization projects to help a digressing ET race. There is much information to share on this subject.

We need to understand what the cabal has been up to, how these technologies are being kept from the public, how our tax dollars are being used to fund black budget projects, and that there are also numerous mind control projects and super soldiers. We also need to become more aware of the hidden technologies put in place thousands of years ago to stunt our development, placed in significant places on the planet, to disconnect and distort the energy circulation of Earth grids, which in turn impacts our DNA.

It is why moving into a higher Earth energy has been so challenging. Repeating negative patterns has taught humans that we can't progress or become an advanced culture without technology playing an important role. Instead, we find that technology is keeping us from advancing ourselves.

There is very little authentic spiritual leadership on the planet that helps us understand our role and how we can rise above this hamster wheel we have been stuck on. We must realize that we are the leaders, and all are tasked with this work. It can't be just up to some. Leadership today has to help encourage people to take responsibility and understand that ascension is an inner initiation into more of who we are. It's a beautiful revelation once we get on board. So many treasures exist within us that we can discover.

TWIN HEARTS ARE BORN

As the psychic predicted, I met the 6-foot Danish man, but I was working so much that I couldn't embrace the encounter. I saw he had a girlfriend, and I wasn't feeling particularly social. I didn't have the energy to see what might have manifested and didn't want to think about it. There are many possible timelines. Maybe I felt this way to experience a different timeline and continue onto something else. My inner voice was nudging me to Mexico to learn cob building and stay inspired. At the time, I didn't know it was the extreme targeting I felt for why I wanted to "just go." There was always such powerful attention and weaponry on me that it tripped me up constantly. I wouldn't realize this till later when I learned more about these things.

I felt called to sell my organic produce company and to do some traveling with my sister. Health food stores were popping up everywhere. I realized that my dream of expanding or having a storefront would take too much to be successful—it felt better to sell to a local that was further along in this kind of endeavor. At a crossroads and needing a break, my sister and I decided to take a trip to New Mexico.

On a later road trip to Oregon, I would eventually meet my children's father, Steve. He and I discovered a freedom and common love of the open road. However, we met when I already felt very lost. I was running Living Earth when few organic health food stores were around. I drove a delivery truck between West Virginia, DC, Virginia and Maryland before there was GPS! I was also trying to let go of my time in the Adirondacks, a horrendous return visit and my ex-boyfriend for good.

About two months into our relationship my sons were conceived, though I would have no idea I was carrying twins until much later. The minute I knew I was pregnant, I immediately adjusted my lifestyle accordingly and embraced pregnancy! I felt such immense love and joy feeling the growth within me. I sensed Steve and I would not have a lasting relationship but was willing to try everything to make it work. Nonetheless, it was necessary to prepare for any outcome.

All might have worked out if I had not visited the psychic. I knew seeing things that way didn't serve me, but I felt there was so much potential. I had an innate understanding of this shifting energy and no one else could hear it at the time. I loved working at Living Earth and spending that time close to my mother, which was the hardest part in deciding to let it go. My mother supported me yet knew it was in my best interest to sell given the growing competition.

Steve and I continued our travels, scouting the best locations to settle down because I desired a home birth. In the back of my head, I had hoped eventually to move back to West Virginia. Our travels brought us to the state of Washington. I knew seeing a doctor and getting a sonogram or ultrasound was important, so we found someone I could see. I remember it being early morning and lying on the table when she picked up on two heartbeats and told us I was carrying twin boys—I was stunned and overjoyed! She also told us twins were not something most midwives would take on, being considered a high-risk delivery. We would do what we needed to.

Having my children was life-changing for me. Anyone who brings a child into the world knows their life will never be the same. It so happened that in this time, in 1998, my mother would sell her house in West Virginia. The timing felt odd because the day I told her I was pregnant with twins was when she told me she had sold the house. It was a magnificent Victorian home on 80 acres, and I knew my mother had worked so hard to get that house. It crossed my mind—if anything were to happen, it would have been wonderful to know it was there to return to. I knew I had to be strong no matter what and that I had to trust that maybe this life was about not having anything outside of me to fall back on.

Over time, Steve told me he was abducted numerous times by aliens. I began to witness behavior that was out of control due to their frequencies. Much of it was beyond a challenge to handle. At night, he would sometimes say that he could see these aliens and that they were around us, and some nights, he refused to sleep. He displayed extreme paranoia. His shifts in behavior came out of the blue, and the erratic nature of his character made the environment feel unsafe.

I gave birth naturally to my twins in Olympia, Washington. When I saw them, they appeared golden and were holding hands! They were around six and a half pounds each. When my boys were still very young, we drove back to New Mexico in a '65 Dodge pop-top van and moved into a house in Santa Fe that my sister helped us find. Eventually, we would relocate to Cerrillos, NM, as we had some connections there and it was more affordable. We traveled to Madrid often

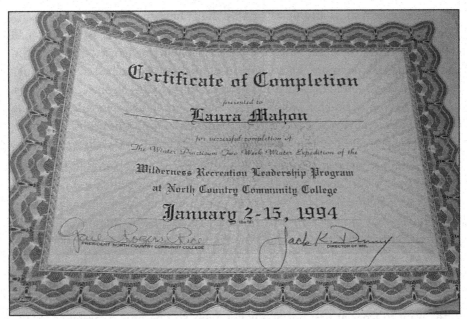

Certificate of Completion of Winter Course in the Adirondacks, where I came up with the itinerary for the expedition.

and started to feel a sense of community. I was still breastfeeding and did until they were two and a half years old.

Unfortunately, always seeing the grass greener elsewhere, Steve didn't want to live in New Mexico anymore. I was so disappointed, and though I didn't want to move, I eventually gave in. I still love him and mean no disrespect. I understand how he felt, but as the mother of young boys, it was hard not to be heard or taken seriously. I feel he had our best interests at heart, but things went downhill after this.

While still in New Mexico, we purchased a school bus for adventure and continued our travels. We heard great things about Asheville, NC at a Rainbow Gathering we went to and became interested in moving there. Honestly, I never really vibed with those kinds of gatherings. My first one was at age 17, my first time west to Peonia, CO, with my best friend from high school. I recall men much older than us, sexual predators, saying it was all about free love and dosing the kitchen crew with LSD! I didn't appreciate this being done without my consent, and I remember calling it out and putting people in their place. Don't get me wrong—I met many incredible people there too.

Since we couldn't make it to Asheville right away, and after driving our school bus to the East Coast, we ended up staying with my mom for a bit, then a little cabin she had in a place right outside of Gettysburg, PA. It was there that the most traumatic thing occurred.

Steve was restless and upset that we didn't have the funds to get to Asheville immediately. He was drinking, and I begged him not to because of our small children. It drove me crazy since I also had alcoholic tendencies that I resisted and couldn't take anymore. I gave him an ultimatum that he had to stop drinking around us. I tried to help him and get counseling for his alcoholic tendencies, which I had compassion for, but unfortunately, it didn't end. I remember breaking down in tears, realizing it wasn't safe or healthy to be with this person anymore. Vulnerable and sad, I had to accept that I was alone to raise our kids myself.

I remained determined to stay close to him somehow and fought hard to forgive him. I didn't want my kids to be away from their father and continued to hope we could maintain a co-parenting relationship. We eventually made it to Asheville, but our relationship was so dysfunctional by that point. I felt so unloved and unsupported that our time there was not good. I didn't know how to make friends, and when I did, a neediness overcame me. I didn't know anyone well enough to lean on them.

I returned to work when I just wanted to be a stay-at-home mom. Steve didn't want to work at first but finally got a job, so I became a caretaker for the land and enjoyed it. I would say landscaping, caretaking and working at plant nurseries are my favorite things! But, by that time, I was ready to be on my own. I was confused and didn't know how to be intimate anymore, and as much as it seemed he wanted to stay together, I felt pretty much done. I could share so much more about this chapter in my life. I am not even sure why I am compelled to be so transparent, yet I am for the chance my story can assist someone else.

It wasn't sustainable to live in Asheville anymore. I wasn't doing well, though I enrolled in an eight-month program at a Natural Healing School to get a certificate in massage therapy. I didn't necessarily want to, but I had to do something. I was more interested in the energy medicine courses, but some family members said it wasn't practical enough. I understood this. I just felt I was the one who needed bodywork, and so it felt hard to give them. I aced all the tests and got through about six months of the program, but the stress of the relationship was enough for me to quit. I was ready to move back with my mother and reflected on what it must have been like growing up as a child so close to Ike and Mamie and how very different my generation was, not having much of a chance to truly interact except when I was super young, able to meet her at the Gettysburg Farm. My mom always accepted me and the boys coming home and acted as a protector when we couldn't make it alone.

Steve eventually followed me back, which I completely supported. I needed to be in the healthiest environment for them and hoped he was ready to improve his life. I knew his dedication to our boys and his desire to be near them. It was around when the tragedy of 9/11 happened. Just like everyone remembers where they were when that took place, I remember working at American Plant Food in Bethesda, MD. I walked into one of the sheds where we kept all the equipment to take care of the plants and completely broke down after seeing it plastered on every television in the break and lunch rooms.

BREAKING A SPELL

There was so much going on for me, raising my boys alone. Multiple times, I have moved back and forth between California, the Southwest and the East Coast. When their father and I officially split up, I lived in California. At this point in my life, I wanted to pursue going to an herbal school, but they did not have enough applicants. I felt incredibly lost and overwhelmed, trying to make enough money for us, and I certainly didn't have child support. I had some family assistance, which kept me from drowning. The energies were intense daily, and I could feel the targeting or weaponry as I had in the past. But this time, I had to understand what was happening and get to the bottom finally.

After being thrown every dark force imaginable to make me feel unwell, I learned through researching and cultivating inner knowledge how to use herbs, soul alchemy and spiritual truth to heal myself in many extraordinary ways. Even when chained in the excruciating depths of the underworld, I had an enormous capacity to heal others. At times, I felt light energy come out of my hand chakras. I could feel the high eons move through me, but fear of myself and the power of my love still confined me in darkness. So I set out to resolve my past life and current memories of being attacked, misunderstood and mistreated, and that's when I found a psychic institute in San Francisco.

I was walking down the street one day, and someone approached me from the psychic institute and encouraged me to get a reading and explore all of this, free of charge. I thought, sure, why not? They could see how incredibly ungrounded I was. Someone in the group mentioned to the rest that Eisenhower was there. But of course, I was not carrying the name then or letting anyone know my relations with him. While there, a dozen counselors gave me profound readings, and I suddenly better understood myself. In several readings, people saw Magdalene in my aura. It is why, one counselor explained, I am not okay if the world is not okay. He saw me only using 10% of my power, with the remaining 90% used in the other realms of healing, processing and traveling.

I received readings about the Goddess lifetimes in Avalon that I had had, which didn't surprise me, although my wounded, humble self felt stunned. I finally felt seen and recognized this gift as an opportunity to go deeper with myself and this energy. Rather than just knowing, I thought it could land more into the physical as a way of living and being. At the end of the session, I told the woman who mentioned Eisenhower of my relation to him, my great-grandfather, and she said, *"Yes, he is with you and works with you on this mission you are on."*

I ended up at the clairvoyant institute for two years. As much as they tried to assist me in what they saw in my auric field and chakra system regarding targeting and attack, it was too strong to subdue, and I knew I had to face it head-on and find the source in me. Where was this coming from? Do I need to deal with it directly since it has a hold over me and my creative freedom? I did find out that one was a spell placed on me that has affected me since childhood. I also learned the others were about invisible weaponry and being taken off-planet.

It was challenging to remain in California. There is so much I could write, so many stories. A roommate of mine almost killed me, and this was after breaking free from someone with much darkness pursuing me at the Clairvoyant Institute. I was desperate for help, and some did try to. I am still in touch with one person I had a weird connection with at the time. He was the director at the institute in Santa Rosa, a branch in Berkley. We loved the same music. There was so much familiarity, and he was very good at his work. Our relationship had gone south, and I lost his support because of all his responsibilities and the many women pursuing him. I just wanted to maintain a spiritual connection and work some of this energy since one of the students was pushing his way into my life. We are like siblings from another lifetime, and I am happy to say that we remain friends after being out of touch for over a decade!

I went through deep soul work while trying to raise kids and work to conclude that I didn't have enough money to survive. So, after breaking free of the student forcing himself into my life and dealing with the twins' father and the heartbreak of being unable to be with him or heal our situation, I had to find a roommate. The loss of my mom's property in West Virginia and the mistakes I made leading up to that consumed me. I looked on Craigslist for a roommate, and it seemed benign when I found this older man who portrayed himself in such a way as to be harmless. You may wonder what I was thinking as I write these words, knowing all I have already gone through. I couldn't put this burden on my mother or other family members because I got myself into this situation, and it was up to me to get out of it. So, we arranged to meet. He talked about his kids and work and was in a situation where he also needed a roommate. He told me of a long-term girlfriend he would visit occasionally but assured me she wouldn't be coming over because the place wasn't big enough. His room was in the back, and he had his own door to come and go out of.

I would eventually learn that this man was a meth addict and—no surprise—was not the person he claimed in his profile. He had all sorts of people coming and going, and I was shocked. It was horrendous. I had no choice but to kick him out or involve the cops. I couldn't figure out why I was attracting these people. Readers at the institute made it clear I was being targeted, to trip me up

Certificate of Completion of NOLS course in Baja, California.

and to exhaust me. I have an open, loving heart and like to give people the benefit of the doubt. I realize I was doing too much to be more discerning and wasn't very grounded as I sought to heal. Even though they said I was one of the institutes best readers, I kept attracting this kind of thing into my life.

A college kid named Matthew came into the mix and offered to be my roommate until things got better. He seemed to be mitigating the situation and was connected to one of the people my evicted meth roommate brought to the house. Again, I felt this young college kid benign as he assured me he wasn't using drugs. He attended the College in Santa Rosa, and I met his father, a dentist in San Francisco. I was also much older than he and a mom. It felt like it could be a much safer arrangement than I had just dealt with, plus my kids immediately took a liking to him. They played video games together. He offered to take them to the local park, but I never wanted my boys out of my site, so I accompanied them. After some time, I felt comfortable with Matthew and accepted him as our roommate.

Wouldn't you know it—he became obsessed with me right away. He stole many books about Mary Magdalene, Venus, and other archetypes from the bookstore. Then, he would bring them home and say, "This is you. You need to read them." I told him what he was doing felt crazy and to return them. I was also dealing with Steve, the boys' father. He was still somewhat in the picture but deteriorating, and nothing I could do would help him. He would go crazy on me when drinking and was not a safe person to have around the boys. It all felt like the worst nightmare!

One night, Matthew offered to give me a massage. I told him rubbing my back was fine, but it got weird as he put his hands in places he shouldn't. I freaked and tried kicking him out, but he refused to go. I ended up calling his dad for help. Matthew refused to leave, and then, out of the blue, he strangled me. As I felt myself leaving my body, I remember saying, *"Love is stronger than death,"* and I felt the Christ energy come near me. All of a sudden, Matthew loosened his grip and ran away. I went to the cops and begged them to help me remove him for good. Because they didn't have enough proof of the assault and his name was on the lease, they couldn't do much. One of the cops felt so bad for me that he continually circled the house I was living in, making Matthew nervous. It took a lot, but I finally got him out of there. My boys, whom Matthew tried to turn against me, weren't having it either, and they told him to leave me alone.

There are more stories about my time in Santa Rosa, but I will spare you—they are shocking for me to reflect on. I decided it would be safest to move back to my mother's home and live in a basement apartment with my two boys. I needed security, as the chaos and insanity were more than I could handle.

Geez, how many times in this book have I said, *"More than I can handle?"*

When I lived with my mother, I kept to myself and felt tremendous isolation. I didn't feel resonance with other parents and people in the neighborhood or local area. So, I found a website online to share my writing, thoughts and revelations regarding the Christ-Sophia and planetary mission I have compiled over the years. I happened upon a forum about Christ-Sophia, where I met a man, and we started to exchange ideas. He expressed a desire to meet in person and since I lived close by. I was uncomfortable with everything that had happened so far in my life. I agreed but proceeded cautiously. From our conversations, he said that he mostly identified with the archetype of Dionysus. He shared that I fit precisely a description he had received from three separate individuals.

Not soon after I walked through the door, he pulled out a piece of paper and said it belonged to me. He explained he had hidden this piece of paper years ago on a bookshelf after talking to three individuals and writing down all they shared. One of them claimed to be Eve. He had never met anyone that he could give it to until now. I had goosebumps as I read, *"All three added she was extroverted but introspective, and would try to balance the two. Sandra said she would be confused and drowning in her human-ness."*

He presented me with a list of things these others were telling him. Some of it resembled me, and he insisted that no one fit my description. The fact that he pulled it off a shelf after many years I found interesting, so my concerns of this being a set-up diminished. I still don't fully believe it. But like most things, I take what resonates and leave the rest. If I shared his whole text, it would be quite mind-blowing.

Eve, he explained, was an ageless woman who never perished. She claimed to be the original Eve from the Bible and had a tribal following. She gave him hints about the recipe for immortality, described soul families and the whole story of Eden, and told him that he would meet a woman about whom he had lengthy information and descriptions. He explained that Eve kept herself alive forever by inserting an orb into her yoni, which changed colors and reacted differently depending on whose hands it was in. He shared that he was quite skeptical until they talked for hours, and she satisfactorily answered his many questions.

I was skeptical, of course, like he said he was initially. I became more open-minded when I read the words he presented to me. Eve had given him countless stories and names, like Lilith and Diana, Sophia's sisters, and spoke on the nature of Adam, other planets, and the singular creativity of Sophia. I do not feel a need to determine whether Eve was the same immortal individual from the Bible. Though hard to believe, nothing shocks me anymore after all I have been through. The orb was referred to as the Philosopher's Stone with nine ingredients. The most incredible thing I read, though, was about her children and the tribes that emerged and her answers to his many questions.

We had ongoing discussions and conflicts about my role and emergence into this world and the false demiurge control. Even though it seemed like he wanted to set me free, he became very imprisoning and an incredible challenge to break free from. Skilled in alchemy and witchcraft, he admitted to casting a spell on me in 1980. After hearing about me from this Eve person, he was getting weary of the search. He thought he would find this woman in a year or two, not twenty. Not aware that I was still a child, the spell was intended to bring to him this woman he was destined to meet, but he told me he couldn't stand waiting. I was only seven then, which resonates when I remember feeling the dark forces first yank on me. I realized then that he, too, had fallen into the traps of the patriarchal matrix. In this case, he wanted to love and possess me.

I don't claim to be any Goddess or incarnation. However, as many women do, I feel connected to the Sophia/Magdalene energy that was brought up in these exchanges. It was getting a bit wild, though, because it was finding me instead of me looking for something to validate this part of me and my larger mission here on Earth. I didn't need it, but I felt it helped me grasp the human Laura more, which was imperative. The human Laura encompassed a larger picture and mission that being in my body was tough—even with my many experiences with physical things, like my wilderness expedition background, landscaping, birthing and raising twin boys. Each time I tried to detach myself from the whole concept of being mission-oriented, something would come along and demand my attention. It showed up in so many different forms and disguises—this being one of the most intense, along with the Mars recruitment that I will soon get into.

I was exhausted, surviving some tragic and deeply traumatizing experiences, especially with my boys' father. With his loss and the struggles endured during our time together, I almost didn't survive. Neither did he. Many extreme events continued for seven years with my kids' father. Deep down, he was a kind soul and spiritual person, but he was haunted, wounded, and unable to function and carry a job—more a free-spirit type who really tried his best and loved his children very much. I take responsibility for all my choices in life. The hard part was feeling lied to, deceived, and taken advantage of. Steve had a bit of that, but I fully forgive him, and the gift of my beautiful sons is where my attention has been. There is so much I have made peace with, holding him in the highest light of love and compassion. I worked hard to care for our kids and fill many gaps, and I enjoyed watching my beautiful sons grow up.

The man I had met on the forum sought an intimate relationship, but I was not attracted to him in that way. Incredibly possessive, he professed his undying love to me so many times that I felt for him. Still, I couldn't exist in this and needed to move forward. Did he seriously cast a spell that impacted me when I was seven years old? Based on his descriptions, the strong intent he held to bring this woman to him, the fact that I met him and he was so convinced I was that person was a hard one to wrap my head around and still is. The hardest part was when I needed to break this spell and regain my freedom. He took advantage of me. In convincing me that he was all about my freedom and happiness, the prison walls and manipulations just got worse, and his attempts to compromise angered me to such a great degree that I spent months putting him in his place, demanding he get his energy out of my space.

He would go on to share personal things about me on the public forums, which I begged him to delete. I was furious. Chances are he continued doing so. Later on, he had a soft and spiritually driven moment and wrote a testimonial acknowledging that I wouldn't say I liked the experience he wished to put me through and that it wasn't healing. He admitted his ego got in the way and knew I needed to move on. I relate to some of the words, but not all of them. Over the years, he has fluctuated with bitterness, trying to hold me in this higher light. I am concerned that he has lost himself to an archonic attack during this critical phase we are facing in humanity and might seek to harm out of his own cynicism. He hasn't fully let go and doesn't like his position in life when he placed too much importance on me and him having a destiny together. I don't blame him for feeling this way if he is convinced I am this person that so much was written about. But I know that when I need to break free from something and be sovereign I have to trust it, and there was no need to try and make this work with him.

Laura and her twin babies, who are all grown up now! This was taken in New Mexico.

Mars Recruitment

"It is a positive thing for the human race to put survival colonies on other planets. Earth has been struck by many cataclysms in the past, and so we should protect the human genome by placing human settlements on other celestial bodies. Yet, when secrecy surrounding such projects tempts government to rob the free will of individuals, and excludes humanity from debating a subject that implicates the whole human future, and diverts the destiny of a planet to serve an off-planet agenda, the conscience of a free people requires that such projects be undertaken in the bright sunshine of public scrutiny, not within the dark corridors of the military-industrial complex."

– Andrew D. Basiago and Laura Magdalene Eisenhower, 2010

In 2006, they attempted to recruit me into a hidden operation regarding the Alternative 3 colonization of Mars scenario. I was pre-targeted for this operation before birth using Looking Glass technologies, which allows them visibility into future probabilities, which could then be influenced to manipulate timelines. I knew quite strongly that I would not be assisting in the Organic Ascension if I agreed to go—I was aware of this even as a child through my connection to the Venus energy. I found it interesting that, as a result, I was contending with Mars.

They could not see beyond 2012 when a significant timeline shift occurred and are scrambling to regain control. At this point, all they can do is continue their usual tactics to manipulate humanity—implementing their NWO agenda, Agenda 2030, 15-Minute Cities, chipping humanity, and whatever else the masses will choose to consent to. Chemtrails, geo-engineering and the use of holographic technology to bring about fake alien invasions are possible. It is a dangerous period where DEWs (directed-energy weapons) are still being used, and there are aggressive attempts to maintain control and initiate even greater ways to convince humanity that all is for our own good using mass social engineering tactics. We must research this deeply, look at all sides, and not be led astray because someone on the news or in a leadership position is encouraging us to look the other way and dismiss it. All this inspired me to come up with an Alternative 4 option!

AGENT X AND THE AVIARY

In April 2006, as I was working hard to break free from the terrible characters that had entered my life. I had been such a recluse after I made my boundaries clear with the man from the Christ-Sophia online forum, raising young twin boys and extreme emotions while feeling the forces of the archons and negative technologies trying to break me daily. All I could do most days was cry and release the overwhelm. I needed a break, so I decided to attend a small festival gathering. But I would come to find out I was being tracked and monitored.

At the festival, I met a man I will call Agent X, though that is not his name. We hit it off from the start and spent the evening together. That night, we intensely discussed topics relating to Magdalene and Joseph of Arimathea. He told me how he had heard that our paths would cross. He seemed to embody Joseph of Arimathea in his general presence and knowledge and Osiris in his spirit of mastery of the underworld and regeneration. His knowledge of nature, artwork, and general awareness were deep, intense, and brilliant. Little did I know he could only maintain his organic nature for brief periods until something powerfully corrupt would overtake him. He brought up these archetypes to me, so I was grateful that we could talk about these larger-picture things.

In June 2006, he asked me to marry him after a short time together. We had an undeniable heart connection. My whole being desired sacred union so much, and he understood my path on a deep level. Soon, we were engaged. As I got to know him, he revealed more about himself. He told me about a group he had been secretly going to early on and expanded upon it more and more as time passed. This group was into remote viewing and investigating alien abductions. He had witnessed truly bizarre occurrences, one involving a skinned animal with all the blood sucked out of it. He told me there was radiation at this event that negatively affected his health for a long time afterward. I wouldn't say I liked where this was going, but I already had formed strong emotional ties to him as my fiancé and wanted to heal him and make everything okay with our love.

He explained over time that his secret group was a type of think tank, an investigative group working on creating a mission to Mars. Agent X very much

Laura Eisenhower speaking at the Consciousness Beyond Chemtrails conference.

thought that these people were good guys. The physicist adviser in the group was X's hero for his involvement in zero point energy and remote viewing. X kept telling me about cataclysms that would inevitably hit the Earth in the future and that we had a chance to escape the disaster by going to Mars. X thought it would make me feel special or excited to be in a select group to escape Earth for Mars, but it did not sit well with me. He wouldn't budge on his position, and I just hoped the mission to Mars talk would all fade away as our love became increasingly important. At this time, I had no idea the power the secret group had over him. I was blinded by love, and I just wanted not to think about Mars again. I later discovered that the group had sent X to find me at the festival.

> *"'The Aviary' is a collection of strange birds: a group of key scientists, military men and intelligence agents who share an intense interest in UFOs, telepathy, remote viewing, parapsychology, mind control and the creation of psychotronic weapons."*
>
> *– Artificial Telepathy blog post, The Aviary: Key players of the 1980s and 1990s, June 18, 2006*

They are also connected to all of this. I didn't see the Artificial Telepathy website[8] and this information until years after I had broken free. It confirms everything I suspected about what they were doing to my partner. The communications coming through appeared to me to be artificial telepathy and not a legit ET group. The blog post goes on to say:

> *"The strange UFO slant on this group appears to be simple disinformation.*
>
> *Members of the Aviary have reportedly participated in MILABS operations—black operations by rogue military-intelligence units that stalk, harrass, terrorize, kidnap, drug, gang-rape and mind-rape innocent civilians, using hypnotic mind-control programming to implant a false posthypnotic 'memory' that the episode was an 'alien abduction.'"*

As we got to know each other more, I realized he knew a lot about my inner path from numerous sources that overlapped with one another—information collected from Freemasons, Knights Templar, and a hidden branch of the government behind creating this Mars mission. He explained that his group understood me based on remote viewing and time travel devices. I felt a dark force taking advantage of our circumstances and trying to stay one step ahead of how nature would bring us together organically. Finally, a few months into the engagement, he told me he was an agent for the group and that they had sent him to find me.

He told me the group had a list of men tagged to target me or be used as plants. I understand it wasn't anything that these men were fully aware of except Agent X, who admitted he was tasked with the mission to find me. When all those relationships ended because I broke free and saw through them, the group went all the way with Agent X.

It seemed like a long-standing plan if there was pre-targeting on me connected to this. They knew the chemistry between us from so many past lives together would be irresistible to me. So they made it their business to get to him before I did in this life and use him to trap me. They utilized Looking Glass technologies to locate us in previous lives, set up how we would meet, and then work to control our destiny together. They recognized that we had the potential for hierogamic union, which is very targeted on this planet and something they would rather control for their own purposes. It is the conclusion I have come up with, along with many others who validate this—I wouldn't find this all out until way later in the relationship.

I told him about the work my friend and I were starting to create, all about the Goddess Consciousness on Earth. I explained that we were also coming up with global strategies and visions of the future for our home planet, with many projects in the works, including events to bring about a real awakening to all. I told him about her education, and he seemed open and impressed. He wanted to begin a dialogue with her about Mars and Earth. He threw out ideas about her role and mine related to the Mars mission, but they aren't specific in my memory because I had no interest in going to Mars.

Going to Mars was not an option. In my vision, we would stay on Earth and do what was necessary to call out the dark agendas, expose what humanity needed to know, and reveal all the things that have been held in secrecy so we could get to the truth of what has really been going on. I knew even as a child that this window period was a time of ascension, and I was prepared to stay true to myself and stay with Mother Earth as we have this opportunity to move into higher Earth energies.

Leaving her name out, my friend and X got on the phone together and talked at length. I didn't feel good about it because they were formulating a goal more to do with Mars. Deep down, she understood the need to create a positive timeline on Earth, and she always remained able to follow my thoughts and stay centered, alert and open. All this was an exciting discovery for her, and she tried to grasp what X was proposing and for what reasons. My friend knew the organic love and connection X and I had. We had discussed how profound our connection was regarding sacred union, Hieros Gamos and Grail Knight/King archetypes, and how important it is for this Earth that sacred union couples find one another to heal the planet. It is something many feel called to do, and at this time in my life, it was consuming because there was an urgency attached to it. I always knew I was born to create that with a man, so this was it! The problem was that something outside us, this Aviary group, had him in their grips.

SULLA ESPLORAZIONE
DELLO SPAZIO E LA VITA NEL COSMO
SPAZIO E POLITICA

29 marzo 2014
Teatro Titano

22° SIMPOSIO MONDIALE
SUGLI OGGETTI VOLA
NON IDENTIFICATI E   SSI

EXTRATER   ICA M   ALE

Laura Eisenhower with Roberto Pinotti at a conference in San Marino, Italy.

August 2006, we were still engaged to be married, and the plan was that I would move to Raleigh, NC, and we would live together and figure everything out. He convinced me that my vision and mission would not go unnoticed, so I agreed to make the move happen. We were so united in our hearts that we went ahead and did the Celtic marriage hand-fasting ceremony before we left. It is a trial marriage for a year and a day, and after that, you decide to stay or go. This seemed reasonable to me and not something like a legal marriage that would be much harder to get out of. He had Irish origins, spoke Gaelic and was so familiar to me in my soul.

Upon arriving, things drastically shifted. Mars kept coming up repeatedly, and I did not feel like it was a choice. It did not feel safe, and my intuition screamed that this Mars mission was being created from a hidden agenda that wished to disrupt our organic love and have control over it, used for their plots in the grander scheme of things. X's behavior fluctuated wildly, from a deep love connection with me to panic and intensity about the need to go to Mars.

He ranged so much that he seemed to have multiple personalities, and I let him know. Unexpectedly, he told me he had multiple personalities, and many had told him so. He had endured a lot of unspeakable trauma throughout his life. He often spoke about alien encounters that he had and continued experiencing. He mentioned that his mother had a noticeable chip implanted under her skin that he could sense since he was young. It was used to manipulate her energy and train his personality through being traumatized by her to weaken him to their influence. I began to research government programs of this nature and found much information about secret projects like MK-Ultra. I tried alerting him to what I was starting to uncover because I wanted him to heal and evolve.

Over time, the Mars issue only grew louder. My friend and X started working on plans to make this mission happen. But before anything was finalized and based on my observations, she realized his intentions were dubious. We could only try to investigate more. She and I continued talking about it, and I filled her in on every detail I could. I had dreams and premonitions that something was way off. After I moved to North Carolina to live with him, our discussions regarding the Mars recruitment decreased, yet I was still trying to get to the bottom of it all with little to go on. I was in for a fight for my life and my children.

In one dream I had, I got taken up by chains into a ship. A voice told me I had to choose between being on Mars or staying on Earth and that they wouldn't harm me on Mars but would certainly control me. I chose Earth. I fell out of the ship and into the ocean alone in the darkness. Wanting to understand things more and reconnect with my partner back on the ship, I flew up into the air, trying to communicate with it, but thunder and lightning obscured my ability to see the spacecraft, and I fell back into the water. Then, a crazy alignment happened, and many planets surrounded me. An organic light filled my being and was cast out upon the dark oceanic water. I knew I had made the right choice for Gaia to stay on Mother Earth and bring to light all that I could and understand what this ascension window period is all about and all that was trying to hijack it and our awakening.

This resolution connected with my deep awareness of myself and what I am here to create. Plus, I naturally have adverse reactions to being controlled in any way, so I knew it was my only choice. I told X about the dream, and he was nervous, but we stayed together. He even said that I shouldn't have told him. I continued to observe him while feeling a broken heart welling up deep inside. I knew I was losing him to them.

As time went on, X continued to get phone calls that made him drop everything and leave to do work for the agency. He kept disappearing to do missions for them. It started to get more and more intense. All I could think about was the secret group and their extreme desire for me to agree to go to Mars. Even though X thought his mentors and associates in the group were good, they seemed to be mind-controlling him and making him do things on their behalf. Something deeper was controlling this venture, and I could feel it related to Mars colonies and some off-planet agreement.

I told him I did not want to go to Mars, even if there were Earth catastrophes. I felt confident, especially after that dream. X disagreed completely, and

Leigh J. McCloskey. I visited his home often and here I sit with the Goddess Sophia. Leigh is a profound artist who has painted the many aspects and expressions of the Divine Mother, the living Myth and visual philosophy. From his bio on https://leighmccloskey.com/, *"Leigh's fascinating and inspiring creative life, his art, career as an an actor and his personal 'heroes journey' lead him into a lifetime devoted to exploring and reinvigorating the stories, myths and arts that return dignity and meaning to our human struggle."*

things escalated to a point where he told me that I had to go and if I didn't, they would kidnap me. I was horrified and scared for me and my twin boys. His behavior got worse and worse. Soon after, he was dealing with all kinds of death threats. I knew that no matter how much I loved him, there was no way he would be able to pull himself out of their grips and stay on Earth with me.

Once, he frantically pulled all the electrical equipment in my house apart. He took out cell phone batteries and shut down everything else electronic. He then candidly told me everything he knew and revealed much about me and my boys, which explained why I was even a person of interest. I listened in shock as he told me we were being bugged and that there were webcams in the streets. I came to understand through this conversation that I was a person of interest to them due to both my lineage of the Sophia-Magdalene as well as my desire to empower this on Earth, as it resides within our divine blueprint and the Eisenhower bloodline and many past life histories of myself and my boys whose energies could be used to power their agendas on Mars. They knew a lot about my boys and what they represented. He even said that he was sent on a mission to meet me, so we didn't actually meet in an organic way.

In January 2007, I needed time and space from him, so I moved down the street and out of the house we shared. However, X still came to see me too often. The frequencies coming off him made me physically ill. A friend of his and I realized that the group was trying to turn him into some robot that would mechanically follow their every command. We confronted him, but he got defensive. It was obvious that he was being heavily mind-controlled. I spent a couple more months researching everything associated with the group members' names he gave me. I discovered that a few in the group were associated with Extremely Low Frequency (ELF) and High-frequency Active Auroral Research Program (HAARP), one even being called the Grandfather of ELF technology. I also learned much about trauma-based mind control and found the stories of many other victims whose abuse by government programs led to insanity and sometimes death. I even ordered some rare Earth magnets and Orgone to try and de-activate him, but I could never get him to cooperate in his deprogramming. It was around when Michael Salla and Alfred Lambremont Webre entered the picture. Both of these authors and researchers helped clarify these programs for us.

My friend, the only other person who knew of this and was involved, began to work with me to put the puzzle pieces together, more and more, till we began to figure out what the Mars agenda was all about. She eventually agreed with me and began seeing that this attack was aimed at my heart. We figured out that, for the group to maintain their matrix of control, they needed the Isis/Osiris seeding of Mars to re-seed a civilization there with humans to produce offspring with divine blood. I have no idea if this has anything to do with us, except we seemed to be a match for hierogamic union. This actually came up in some readings and was later validated by someone else's research into their plans on Mars, something I can't find to this day. They knew the power of my heart and connection to the Divine Mother—that's why they targeted me.

A part of me is still baffled by it all. It is possible they were targeting my childhood dream realm of feeling my mission so strongly, and because of my relation to Eisenhower and knowing I would reveal some things they might wish to censor, which they did, this is why they wanted me to go. Perhaps they knew my quest to get to the bottom of things and hoped to redirect my attention elsewhere. It's hard to say, but in reading that book given to me, and how they were aware I was going to be born to this family before I came, and even Project Pegasus talked about me, according to Andrew Basiago, a year before I was born, there was something there that they wanted that I couldn't take the risk of giving them.

In my intuition, the ICC/Nazi/Draco Alliance, who operate the controller agendas of 3D Earth, have been trying to destroy the divine feminine for thousands of years. Did this have anything to do with my passion to ignite this divine blueprint within all and the return of the Mother? Or, with my passion for understanding the controller forces on the planet that are trying to turn us into something else, be further enslaved and completely unaware of the amazing treasures we are meant to discover about ourselves and our true origins? Or, all the ways they manipulate what we see and experience and how they engineer events to keep us in a low vibration of fear and disempowerment? I still wonder and continuously contemplate all the feedback I have gotten through the years to understand better why they wanted me to go to Mars.

X constantly pushed me to go to Mars, and it took all my strength to break free and stand up against this recruitment. The group told X, *"Recruit her and set her up with a handler or leave her."* When they finally threatened his life, he considered leaving the group and staying with me. He finally understood how much they were messing with him. Eventually, we split. We both knew our connection was too big of a danger.

Right after I broke free of Agent X, it was confirmed by many ascension sources at the time that a negative timeline had been destroyed. I don't fully see that, maybe on a deeper level, but I think we have much more work to do. Since this attempted recruitment, I have been working hard to tell my story and empower the positive, Organic Ascension timeline in every capacity I can.

I recently got to know the senior advisor to Earth Alliance, Dan Cooper, whom I mentioned previously. I asked him questions about this attempted recruitment. In response to something he said, this is what I said:

"The Mars recruitment, they only wanted me to know a limited amount in order to lure me in, stating it was for my protection. They delivered these messages through my partner at the time, who would join them at Aviary

meetings. But maybe they didn't expect me to dig as deeply as I have and refuse to go—maybe they weren't prepared for that."

And to this, he responded, *"Correct."*

AN ARTIST LIKE NO OTHER

I was doing landscaping while dealing with the Mars recruitment. I was working hard, even in the drought that North Carolina experienced that year. I, fortunately, was excelling. It was a great way to channel my energies when I had difficulty processing everything. Eventually, a new man came into my life. We met up in Baja, California, a place I had fallen in love with and that he liked to venture to for surfing expeditions. When he heard through a mutual friend how much I was struggling and loved Baja, he invited me and my boys to join him there. It was an incredible break, even though the relationship only lasted two years. However, it was enough of a connection to convince me to move to California to live with him.

We moved to Ventura and started a new life. It was so liberating to get away from Raleigh. One of my greatest highlights was meeting Leigh J. McCloskey, a former soap star and one of the most profound artists I feel has ever walked this Earth. He has painted Sophia, the Mother Goddess, Lilith, Christ, Egyptian Goddesses, and the whole creation story without using a canvas. He also created one of the most intricate and beautiful tarot decks I have ever seen. There is no way to describe it all. You have to see it. It changed me, and I remember being in tears for a week. It was the biggest deal ever and one of the most profound experiences even to this day. I post his artwork, talk about him often, and have done about three or more interviews with him. He is a mind-blowing individual with an amazing wife and family who are all incredibly talented and just so divine.

One day, a mysterious thing happened. Alfred Lambremont Webre, an American author, lawyer, futurist and tribunal judge who has produced so much incredible material throughout the years, received an email that accidentally got sent to him. It was an exchange my friend, whom I wish to keep anonymous, and I were having. Somehow, it was sent to him without our awareness or intent. He was already doing many interviews and working closely with Andrew Basiago, a childhood participant of Project Pegasus. We had all talked before and recognized a quantum entanglement in time travel and timelines. So, after Alfred saw our email, he suggested I let him interview me.

PUBLIC SPEAKER

My recognition in the public sphere began in 2010 with the invitation to do my first interview. So much was coming through me, and I talked so fast, feeling like I had to get this out of me because holding it in was overwhelming. I knew it was tough for people to follow. It came with much sup-

Conference in Montserrat, Spain. Located in Catalonia, 45 km Northwest of Barcelona, the Parc Natural de la Muntanya de Montserrat gives home to the Benedictine Monastery Santa Maria.

port and also criticism. I received some severe attacks, and trolls started to go after me. I sincerely appreciated Alfred's willingness to do this and how much the dots began to connect with him and Andrew Basiago.

My partner at the time didn't seem into my emerging public role and was unsupportive. He was pretty controlling and narcissistic and caused me quite a bit of grief, but I was at least in California, and things were looking up. I felt more protected being a public person. Even though the attacks were vicious, I was sharing my experiences, so I tried not to let them get the best of me. Truth doesn't need believers or followers. Even still, being subjected to relentless targeting would alter the trajectory of my and my children's life path and potentially even that of the human race. I always knew it would be safer exposing it than managing and going it all alone.

Putting myself out there to call out all the deep, hidden layers was what I knew I was here to do. As much as our coming together at first was about loving me and my boys, it became difficult to be with someone who couldn't understand me or my mission on these deeper levels. Eventually, my partner and I broke up. Even though I initiated it, I was still quite devastated by its impact on my children. You never want your kids to have to live through failed relationships. I took some time after the breakup to process and regroup and did all I could for my children as a single mother.

Sometime later, I met a man who uses "Dr." in his name as a moniker, which I learned was connected to his life's work of inspiring people to live their dreams, using Tibetan healing bowls and words of empowerment. I was returning from a conference and flying into Los Angeles when he expressed wanting to interview me. Since he was in the area, he suggested we interview in person. When we met for the first time, he saw I was in a bit of distress. He asked what I was doing as I shuffled my Mother Peace Tarot cards. I told him I was going through a breakup and headed home to my kids, and that shuffling assisted me in navigating life and was how I worked energy to stay in communication with my higher self and everything around me.

He felt an affinity for me and pursued me at a vulnerable time. As I reflect, I realize it was a time when I just needed a friend, not a new partner. Nonetheless, he wouldn't accept my resistance or hesitation. I was convinced, once again, that he was all about sacred union and wanted to partner with me and help me raise my kids.

Shortly after we met, I spoke at a conference in South Africa hosted by Michael Tellinger and went to Adams Calendar, where Anunnaki ruins exist. It was so amazing and life-changing to be there. When I returned home, the move to live with this new partner was already underway, and he was determined. It was a nicer home than the one we were previously in, and I just had to hope for the best in the belief that this person truly loved me. I certainly had feelings for him, but it was moving quite fast!

Without getting into the details of our relationship, we were a public couple for a few years. It was obvious to many that he wanted to make sure he could present his stuff at the events I would speak at. On his behalf, I would ask the producers to include him in the line-up. At some point, he became so intertwined with all I was doing—wanting to merge our energies, even in healing sessions for people—that it overtook my sovereignty and boundaries. I finally realized that he, too, was targeted to throw me off, even though I still don't fully understand it all. But it was clear that something was out to disrupt our relationship. It eventually turned into an on-and-off relationship as we navigated the confusion of our experiences together.

What I knew for sure was that I did not bring out the best in him. He held a deep mistrust of me that I couldn't figure out, which broke our relationship apart. With everything I lived for and expressed in my presentations—sacred union, integrity and truth—even though I was completely loyal, he did not trust me.

One of the most significant events I presented at was June 4th-6th, 2012, in Mt. Shasta, California. It started when Chief Golden Light Eagle approached me at a MUFON event I was speaking at because he had seen a video where I

Conference with author and researcher Michael Salla. This event took place on the 21st of September 2017, called The Ufology World Congress, held in Montserrat, Barcelona, Spain.

explained a dream I had. I dreamt that a giant golden eagle emerged from the sky and swooped me up, taking me to another world. I almost forgot about it, so it was funny when he said this to me after he had heard of me and about my dream. He was the Golden Eagle! Looking back on it and with the connection that Eisenhower had to the Dakote Star beings, it seemed apparent that the gathering of the tribes was what was taking place now.

All the while this was taking place, a person named Tom Magruder was sending me books and albums in the mail that talked about all these significant things. He even sent me a book about Venus. In particular, he sent this writing that caught my attention:

"As planet Earth nears a new millennium, the fate of civilization dangles in the balance. An age of peace and enlightenment is held hostage by evil doers of darkness. Warlords and eradicators of the environment plot to wipe out

the ancient ways of the people and drain dry the life force of Mother Earth.

In this darkness before dawn, a band of freedom fighters rises from the few indigenous clans and tribes that remain. These are the children of light that carry the wisdom of the ancients. These are the planet protectors who follow the path of honor. These are the awakened wizards who play for peace. These are the wind warriors."

This was the same year the recruiters targeted me to be on Mars. So, being invited to this conference was extremely significant because this was also when the Venus transit was taking place. While at the event, I happened to run into a group of people at the co-op in downtown Shasta who had plans to view the sky event through the telescope at the College of Siskiyous, which is where Andrew Basiago attended the Mars training program taught by Ed Dames. With my connection to Andy and my own recruitment experience, it felt like an incredible synchronicity to me! This opportunity to view the Venus transit through the telescope at this location was surreal.

The attention and admiration from being in the public eye didn't sit well with my partner. In all forgiveness and understanding, no other breakup left me in ruins like this one. I don't blame him. It wasn't even about him or a broken heart so much as it was about how much this relationship distracted and derailed me during what I consider the most critical time in our human history. But even deeper than that, it was another crushing blow to my boys, who needed a stable father figure—not to witness his abusive behavior towards me and all my tears and anguish in response. I remember being thrown out of his truck when he would get triggered, spilling hot coffee all over myself, only to be left on the side of the road. I have yet to fully comprehend what I endured and how much it compromised me on every level like my whole life force was being sucked out of me. I felt stuck as we lived together and disheartened that this was what I was up against.

When I did events, I wasn't just talking about Mars recruitment or what I knew took place during the Eisenhower administration. I mostly spoke about this ascension window period and our higher potential related to activating dormant DNA. I focused a lot on the divine feminine and the galactic history connected to how this planetary body came about, the importance of sacred union, balance, and integration of polarity and what the Christ-Sophia template was about. Not everyone will believe these things or be into learning more about them, but I hope this book will help it all make more sense. Nothing else makes sense to me, and in saying this, I don't mean to imply that a single truth exists. It is all about activating your own truth frequency, which must happen so one can align with their higher mind and Source energy, hone intuition, receive essential downloads, and walk a path that provides many synchronicities supporting one's purpose and mission.

Before I got into doing a lot more conferences when I focused more on astrological readings, one of my clients reached out to me and suggested we do a trade. She claimed to be a medium and speak with the angels. Her name was Leslie, and I agreed to it. When it was her turn to read me, it got very in-depth, and she shared all sorts of incredible things, which, unfortunately, she would later use against me for believing what she told me. I recall questioning her abilities and whether what she was sharing was true. So it boggled my mind that she would later turn so dark to use our exchange of energy against me. All the while, it came to light that it intertwined with the struggles of my existing relationship.

Amongst all the speaker circuit conferences I appeared at, one to which I was very connected was the Star Knowledge Conference. They flew me to Wisconsin to do a healing ceremony because they recognized the attack I was under. It meant the world to me. But the more Leslie and I were in contact, something horrible was starting to transpire, and this was also around the time my partner and I needed to call it quits.

I want to share more about my experience with Leslie—it was one of the sickest and most horrific things a so-called "healer" could do to a person without having remorse. I got sick after she completely turned dark on me. I hope my story can help someone else.

My partner at the time also turned a bit dark, but I had compassion because he acknowledged that he was highly targeted. Unfortunately, Leslie couldn't do the same. It's important to acknowledge when you are being targeted and attacked, especially if you claim to be a healer. In our trade, she began to give me readings after I had read all her children's charts and her own, some of which I recorded. She didn't tell me anything I hadn't heard before in my readings, but a few new things.

At this point, I had already spent two years at a clairvoyant institute, working on past lives and present-time healing. I once asked her about my connection to the Magdalene energies on Earth, so she looked into my past lives and was stunned when she saw that I lived this life in the past. I didn't feel I was the only one with these experiences, so I didn't think much of it. I don't overly identify with it. She read so much, and because I was going through yet another devastating breakup and had more questions, after the trade was complete, I began to pay her to help me figure out what was going on. She was into it. In my readings, she talked about the attacks and more, and we seemed to have a decent connection. One of my dear friends, who previously helped me with this book, became a part of the conversation and is an absolute witness to what I endured. I do not share much without a witness or someone who can validate everything I am saying.

My friend, Leslie and I had three-way conversations. My then-partner was also a part of some of these discussions and readings and witnessed what was being shared. He struggled with what she was saying, and they started connecting. Not in an inappropriate way, but he needed help understanding the stuff she was sharing with me.

I often received letters from people who do spiritual work. I received and email saying I was in grave danger and had to get away from this man sucking me dry of my light. He discovered it because he read my emails without asking, which infuriated him and sparked something quite insane. It wasn't my fault this letter got sent to me. I didn't know what to do. I agreed that it felt like some entity attachment or weapon was coming through him and sucking my life force and light. Still, instead of them being kind, another fight with him ensued, and Leslie just went dark on me. After four years or so together in the public eye, I had hit such a wall with this breakup. The upheaval and instability I faced again, even though I paid my way and for my children's expenses, was more than I could take.

I had been sober from alcohol during the relationship because he made it clear he would not stand for anyone drinking. I had already quit since my kids were born, except in moments of utter stress, which I was experiencing. I was declining due to sheer pain, and nothing worked as far as herbs or other modalities for decreasing anxiety and PTSD. Leslie picked up on my downward spiral. But this time, I did not want her counsel because I sensed increasing untrustworthiness. She and my partner started to team up against me. I still hold no animosity toward my ex because I don't think we could have been more challenged.

Anyway, my partner moved out. I needed him to go, especially after the author Judith Moore told me he was being targeted and mind-controlled to assassinate me. I doubt it would have worked on him, but the stress was killing me, and how this was utterly messing with our heads was too much for both of us. Even Galactic Historian Andrew Bartsiz said something similar when I reached out for help figuring out what was happening.

Unfortunately, it took place before I flew to Wisconsin to be with the Star Knowledge family, who was made aware of this and wanted to lend support. So they flew me to this ceremony dedicated to me and one other woman who was also struggling. Chiefs from all over the country came to this, and one went on a journey. As the drums were beating and winds were blowing throughout the room, the Chief returned and said that this partner of mine would be okay to walk with. He acknowledged our genuine love for each other. But alas, it didn't last, and although it has taken me a long time to forgive some of the awful things that transpired between us, I have. After this ceremony, it just got worse. Out of respect, I won't share the details. But I will share that this woman, Leslie, became one of the darkest forces I feel I have ever dealt with, and I am still processing it to this day.

Uluru, Australia at Cosmic Consciousness Conference. I was so grateful to be a speaker at this epic event. We got to hike around, visit many locations and meet so many amazing people.

It is something I overcame, but barely. Recently, the painful memories came flooding back after my ex posted a picture of her celebrating her birthday. Even though we both re-married many years later, I still couldn't believe it. I had to comment but waited until her birthday had passed. I reminded her of the spiritual abuse and how impossible it has been to recover from it. It derailed me that I even let her picture trigger me badly.

I continue to struggle with the pain, wondering why I haven't let it go and why it still hurts so bad. Why is this taking forever to heal from and overcome? It was one of the worst things I have ever encountered from a "healer." It damaged my spiritual energies so profoundly. She ripped away everything I held sacred, mocking it and straight-up lying. I never claim to be anyone or anything, but it would be unfair to myself to deny this mission and all that I feel deep within my soul, which is for me to own and experience.

I felt no other option but to reach out to Lisa Renee—the only person I knew who would fully understand. We are very close and have epic conversations when we talk. I feel so connected in our missions that I don't even know where to begin. So, sobbing deeply, I wrote her a letter about it. We had discussed it in the past as well. I do my best to avoid reaching out too much. Given all she does and deals with on behalf of humanity, I never wanted to bother her. But I needed her perspective and support. She would say the perfect and most profound thing as a salve to my soul. Here is an excerpt from what Lisa wrote to me:

> *"Beloved Laura, the level of hatred, misogyny and dripping vitriol they have for her (Sophia) is unparalleled. They never wanted her to return, they did everything unimaginable to torture rape and steal from her body, siphon out every last drop of animating holy spirit, the most sacred essence of life lives and breathes inside of her, they both covet this and despise it.*

> *Hold on sweetheart, try to explore the meaning in this painful betrayal, by knowing that your rebirth and emergence to find her was all you were doing, searching the underbelly of depravity and inversion to seek her parts and return them back to her. We are in war, we have lived in warfare, and in war there are casualties.*

> *We must arise beyond all whom ignorantly tried to destroy us and kill our spirit, to see the real reason we agreed to come here and endure this pain, in order for the real Founders to return into this reality. You will rest assured and peacefully in all you have done when it's time to leave..."*

I don't want to send negative energy to anyone, blame, or wrath. I forgive, trust divine justice, and am not about revenge. Some abuses are so severe, especially spiritual abuse. Our connection with Source is sacred. If you are in the healing arts, you better know what you are doing. I take what I do incredibly seriously. When I give astrological/tarot readings to people, I am entering a most sacred space. I used to do more clairvoyant energy readings. (Did you realize we are all clairvoyant?) I stumbled upon it during my two years at a healing institute, and I worked on past and current life stuff, energy centers and grounding. Once you enter a person's deepest spaces, it's imperative you hold the highest integrity.

My pain isn't so much from an ego level. It upsets me because the damage inflicted undermines my ability to assist others, which is why I am here. The horrific abuses people have endured worldwide under the care of so-called "professionals" are astounding. The only reason I allowed it to disable or injure me, which I now fully accept my part in, is because I agreed to something I never sought out. I was astonished that someone could lie so blatantly and that my ex would barely have my back knowing exactly what was happening. I got tired of feeling so drained and mistreated. Don't get me wrong, I am no perfect person, but you don't do this to people. Many may not understand why this has impacted me for so long. Just know there is far more to this story than what I have already shared.

So, as much as I can bounce back from a lot, there are places no one should go. If you do spiritual work for people, know you have a tremendous responsibility to be in divine unconditional love and respect. Hold compassion and know appropriate boundaries. We all have access to sacred union from within through the force of love, unity, creation, and imagination. The template we all hold within our divine inheritance is that of remembrance. Christ-Sophia is in all of our genetic code.

I know there are many amazing healers out there! It's challenging when you come across the few that miss the mark. Some of you know what I mean! I provide the services I do because I don't want anyone to endure this horrid and terrorizing road alone. It is a beautiful and wondrous thing, we know. Life's adversities are helping us to find ourselves again. Yet some phases and initiations along the way don't always feel this way, and depending on the amount of trauma we carry or how empathic we are, it can take longer or feel more debilitating.

MY GREATEST TEACHERS

I am so incredibly proud of my two sons. I have no idea how we managed to get to where we are today with all the instability and chaos they endured. Somehow, we escaped many situations, like the Mars recruitment, with lots of danger around every corner. Amidst it all, I was working incredibly hard to support us with low-paying jobs while dealing with constant, massive amounts of energy from the attacks and weaponry as a result of my mission. I cried through so much because I couldn't give them the best of me.

I lacked solid help or community, but my heart and devotion carried us through. My boys helped me learn how to transform and rise to being human. Every day, they hear how much I love them as we rise together to deal with the inevitable challenges of public school systems, a confusing past, and a global mission. More than anyone, they understand the importance of it all. My mother and father also played such a huge role in their lives, making sure we were all okay, and for that, I am deeply grateful.

My sons have been the greatest blessing in my life. They helped me to rise out of the dark trenches I found myself in. Before I understood how targeted I was, I took it so personally and got lost. I thought it was me and that I had created it and really messed up. But over time, the truth was revealed to me. Finding out they intentionally tried to trip me up and derail me changed everything. My boys gave me the strength to override it all because love is stronger than all the weapons or control. In the face of death, love guides us back to ourselves so we can transform and be reborn.

They have a strength and resilience that inspires me greatly. As adults, they teach me how to stay more neutral and grounded. They have kind and loving hearts and validate my strength and devotion to them and this greater work. They are moving forward in life in a most beautiful way.

Through my boys, I have learned that when there is no one to be that source of inspiration or strength, always remember how temporary the struggle or pain is. Whether going through a death cycle, hit with tragedy or needing to walk away from something that doesn't feel right—you are the perfect person to fall back on. It is the most incredible time to embrace and hold space to redis-cover who you truly are, your deeper soul calling, and your passion. Then find the strength to pursue it, don't let anything stop you, and see that all the obstacles that attempt to stand in the way are there for you to learn to fly over instead of hitting your head against and giving up.

MOVE TO OREGON, DARK ENERGIES IN EUGENE

Eventually, the boys and I decided we needed to move. Around that time, there was a massive gas leak in Los Angeles. There was no way I could stay in Ventura. I considered getting a roommate to help with the expenses and tried finding a cheaper living situation, but nothing came together. After my ex left to go on the road since we wouldn't work out as a couple, the only way I could move and have my ex move his things out of the house was to leave.

So, we decided to move to Eugene, Oregon, a beautiful part of the world with many educational opportunities. The twins were self-educated but not inter-ested in school, so they stopped their junior year and switched to online school. It was challenging to get them to focus, understandably, with all they were start-ing to realize about the world.

One of our road trips led to us meeting geoengineering expert Dane Wig-gington, and my sons became very passionate about what they were hearing. I al-ways wanted to attend as many conferences with them. So they joined me a few times at James Gilliland's ECETI Ranch in Mt. Adams, Washington, a very well-known hot spot of UFO activity where he both lives and hosts terrific conferences.

I wanted Oregon to work out, but the boys refused to try what I thought was a pretty cool high school and even found an alternative one. They were frustrated, and as most teenagers are, they acted out and had no one else to take their stuff out on other than the one closest to them—me. How could anyone their age process the loss of their father and multiple failed relationships to which I gave my all in the hopes of being a family? How could they be well-adjusted at that stage in the game? The tiny house we got was impossible for me to occupy with them there and still do work. The noise carried through the thin walls, and they were not wanting to go to school. Handling their energies while trying to earn money felt nearly impossible.

I was briefly in and out of hospitals because I was mistaking panic attacks for heart attacks, and no one who came into my life seemed supportive but a few. I am not referring to clients. No blame or judgment—that is just how it felt. My boys were also going through so much, and I wanted to help them. I wanted so much more for them. This huge blow with my ex, him not fully letting me go so I could move on once and for all, and his repeated attempts to hook me back in only to abandon me was a roller coaster I had had enough of. I tried to find a mother's kind of help for our family. I put ads on Craigslist that got flagged and just started feeling defeated, even though I am never one to give up.

My ex from Baja started to contact me again, claiming he had learned so much and realized how important I was to him. He insisted I visit him. It was stupid of me to even consider it a good idea with his narcissistic and patriarchal tendencies and not treating me very well. In the beginning, we had a great time. I recall him taking me to an incredible hidden surf spot. He was very cool in many ways and highly conscious. Still, I would learn he had severe issues with being a control freak, treated me exceptionally demeaningly and was near-abusive to my boys at times. This time, I hoped he had changed. He tried luring me back into his world, saying everyone he had been with since did not compare to his love for me. I was vulnerable and feeling quite broken, so I agreed to go on a little trip to visit him in Northern California. It was clear after I arrived that he hadn't changed much when he asked me to wash his dishes for a meal I didn't have. I don't mind helping out, but this was so weird to me, and other things he did and said just felt off. It saddened me, and so I said I needed to leave.

On my way home back to Oregon, driving in the freezing rain around the area of Grants Pass, I lost my ability to see, and on the windy highway with huge trucks heading my direction and cars with their brights on, I hit a guard rail. My car spun, the airbags released, and I stopped on the edge of a cliff. I realized one more spin would have meant my death, plunging hundreds of feet into a raging river. People stopped and asked if I was okay and called for help. I sat in the car with the cop, who was kind and supportive and helped me get a tow.

A dear friend who lived in Ashland, Oregon, came when I called for help. He gave me a place to stay for the night and assisted me in getting a new vehicle. Thankfully, I upgraded my insurance before the accident, just a random decision one day. Because the car was totaled, I was reimbursed an amount equal to the value of the vehicle and enough money for me to get a new one. So I bought a van to have something I could sleep in and eventually give to my boys so they could do the same and store their camping gear. I so appreciate this friend of mine. He has been like a saint to me. He had a classic Stuedabker vehicle filled with stickers and memorabilia, all dedicated to Eisenhower—he loved him! We have been friends for many years, and he continues to support me and my work.

MEETING KEVIN

Two years into Oregon, I was still doing readings and trying to moderate as I coped. I had a session with a client named Kevin O'Shea, and I remember him wondering why I kept rescheduling. I know it is not fair to the client, but at first, I was taken aback, thinking I didn't want to do a reading if I felt like utter shit. However, this was my source of income, and people were having a very positive experience with my readings, so I just tried to keep up with them as much as possible.

My mom has always been supportive in emergencies and had my back during this period. It was just unbelievable. There were days I felt myself dying and leaving my body, and my mother was always there to help me get and stay grounded. I was sobbing and in so much pain, and she would find a way to send so much love through her words. What she did for me during this dark time will always be in my heart. I've had many dark periods, but this one hit me harder because it was such a critical time for planetary ascension, and I was barely holding on. The heartbreak was insane with such sadness and anger of feeling so unsupported—such a stark contrast to the time I was thriving speaking at events, feeling spiritually strong and empowered knowing my message was getting out all around the planet as I traveled the world. To feel then so screwed over, mistreated, betrayed, and neglected by the friends and partners closest to me, who knew more than anyone else what my mission was. Even with the confirmation that this was all attack energy from the dark side, I still wish they had been strong enough. I wished I was strong enough not to let it hurt me so badly.

On another call, Kevin asked me if I was okay and inquired what was happening. I hesitated to answer him, but I felt his genuine concern. Finally, I said, *"Do you seriously want to know?"* and he said yes, so I told him. Given all the public stuff I was doing, he assumed I was happily married and supported. He asked me, *"Doesn't someone have your back?"* I told him I didn't know how to ask for help. I knew I wasn't a victim and was only trying to deal with it. I also revealed the harsh truth about what happened in my past partnerships and the insanity of it all. I don't think words could ever fully portray how deep it went, nor would it be of any benefit.

Kevin O'Shea and I hiking around Uluru, Australia. This location is so powerful and connected with the 13th Stargate and the Mother Arc.

We ended up talking for over four hours. We felt an intense connection but were also shy about expressing it. Occasionally, a little bit would leak through in our exchanges that would acknowledge our familiarity and chemistry. We would quickly push it to the side, as it was clear he wasn't interested in pursuing me, just concerned for my safety, especially after he discovered I was a single mother of twin boys. Something at that moment moved deeply in his heart to offer us a refuge and a space to heal. He told me I could come up and visit, and he would make me tasty meals since he was a chef. He shared a lot about his life and his past marriages that were very long. Two marriages between the both of us!

I avoided accepting his kind offer because I couldn't believe it. I continued attending events. Nothing but bullshit transpired, and I didn't want any option other than simply figuring it out myself. I exhausted any other option and acknowledged the Universe's attempt to point me in his direction—true to my being a hopeless Libra longing for sacred union. I was in a dire situation of great need, which I knew was not the right energy to draw such a connection to myself. I also prefer the challenge of trekking through rugged terrain without submitting to being a person of need. I am a survivor and didn't want to rely on the kindness of others unless there was a major energetic exchange. He told me this characteristic was beyond apparent and said it changed his life when he started to follow my work. He shared that my messages were helping to pull him out of his own major depression and sparked quite a bit of hope in him!

Love is stronger than all of this, and I realized no formula was required to find it. Sometimes true love shows up when you need it most, and after deciding to take him up on the offer, I quickly realized that there were forces at work that supported us in seeing this through. But the "true love" part hadn't emerged just yet. It was about to reveal itself, though, and the more I got to know him, I realized this man was my best friend and truly cared about me and my sons. He was not trying to use, pursue or take advantage of me in my most vulnerable situation. Just recognizing this alone sparked such a deep love, respect, and appreciation that it opened up a whole new layer in me.

As we shared, he revealed messages he started to receive from the other side. He told me he sensed my great-grandfather telling him, *"Go get her."* He felt hammered over and over with this statement. It felt like a rescue mission, but our true love rekindled itself after lifetimes of experiencing it, and we were finally acknowledging it once again. I never thought I needed rescuing. But I was exhausted, and the turmoil and despair made it hard to survive another day.

Before I had time to digest what was happening seriously, he drove all the way to Eugene to help me pack up my house and move us to Montana, no strings attached. I thought, wow, I initiated this, and now he is on his way here? How could I ever accept such kindness and generosity? I could only throw him all the money I had. It's worth noting that I have moved over 50 times and helped others move, too. I always had great strength and enjoyed it. I felt paralyzed and dysfunctional this time and couldn't help him move my stuff into the U-haul. I felt pretty much on my deathbed.

My boys were upset, not knowing what direction life was taking us or if it was safe, wondering who this man was and why Montana. As much as I thought I was good at hiding my coping, I knew they picked up on it, and it affected them. Would they go for this sudden breakthrough and move? Well, something in them stirred, and to my surprise, they agreed to move to Montana. They became inspired by the pictures I shared and felt the gentle and warm energies of Kevin, who has so much integrity. Since we got together, we continually grew closer through all our meltdowns as we worked through so much trauma from the past—every single one of us.

When it was time to hit the road, I was to follow Kevin in the U-haul with our van. However, I didn't want my boys to endure the road trip, and since they were already 17, I flew them out to meet up with us. The drive alone was hard for me. I felt my life force wasn't there. I had so many near-death traffic encounters. I wondered how I would drive the 11 hours to get there. I did my best to muster my strength and get through it. The weather got rough along the way, and I was so tired. With all my road-tripping, I knew enough to pull over and take a break when I felt I might fall asleep behind the wheel. But there were many miles between exits, and I was nodding off, which was scary.

Kevin kept his eyes on me from the U-haul and noticed me struggling. He saw me between two semi-trucks and how I avoided getting into a horrific accident. He ushered me to pull over to the side of the road. At this point, I think we were right outside of Spokane, Washington. I expected he would give me a hard time or talk down to me like many of my ex-partners did if I messed something up, trying to find any reason to invalidate me or my authority. Those energies so depleted me in my life that the PTSD just expected a vibration like that. Instead, he gave me the warmest hug and just held me. At that moment, I felt my heart melt. I felt so, so much more for him.

I felt such immense love and gratitude that when we finally arrived, my inner voice kept telling me, *"This is your husband!"* I then retracted, thinking, OMG, I should be quieter about these deep feelings coming to the surface of my mind—did I actually think that? It proved to be impossible for me to grasp that it was the real deal. Wow. It kept coming up in my head. The first night, just like the night I first met him, I knew I just needed to sleep close by to him. So, the first night in Montana, instead of going downstairs to the basement he converted into an apartment, I slept on the couch near his bedroom.

The next day, we decided to hang out and watch a movie. He knew I was a bag of nerves and was cosmically, physically, emotionally and mentally exhausted. The healer and nurturer in him were like a flame or fire that drew me closer, providing me warmth. I did do his chart, and it blew me away. Six planets in Leo in the 5th house, which is the house of Leo. Sun, Venus, Mars, Mercury, Pluto,

Jupiter. I won't go into all the other extraordinary things about his chart and our combined charts (which also reveal our profound challenges), but that is quite a combination. A few people along the way have depicted me in artwork as a Goddess with a lion next to me. Leo the Lion. Then I got to thinking about Lions Gate and the Magdalene energies! Woo-hoo!

Funny, he was getting the same feeling even after two days of me just being there in his home, having transformed the downstairs into a separate apartment for me and my boys to find a sense of stability and refuge from the constant attack and extreme storms that kept trying to derail us. We looked at each other and laughed at the fact that we were both feeling the same. Soon enough, I moved into his bedroom because I couldn't sleep without being close and by his side, and I hadn't left that room since. Oh, ha, that was day three. He shared with me that when he went to work after a string of his own trials—injuries from surfing accidents (a broken neck while surfing in Todos Santos in Baja), pulling muscles with weights, and carpentry injuries—that his intuition spoke to him, saying "She is your wife." Ha! I, too, have a deep love for Baja and have been there many times. Our similarities were wild—I had epic Todos Santos stories, too!

We had a spiritual marriage not soon after, and a year later, we made it legal. We didn't need some fancy wedding. It was the coolest thing to stand outside the court consecrating our marriage and say, *"I do. I love you and always have. I love you into the Beyond. Beyond death do us part. I love you beyond this life."* I had a beaming smile that went straight to my soul, though I still struggled with how unbelievable it all felt. I struggled a lot initially as all my traumas rose to the surface. Was I just delusional? The triggers were more than I ever imagined I would be dealing with, with someone so pure of heart who was also wise, kind and gentle.

I was not easy to deal with at all. I interrogated him and experienced extreme paranoia that maybe he was just another plant or someone out to control or derail me. Certain things transpired that made me question everything. Was he sent to get me in the same way Agent X was? The events that transpired after our marriage are more of an ode to Kevin being a saint—more than I care to share after everything we have been through. All I know is that my time with him has revealed an unconditional love, unlike anything I have ever known. Man, I put this guy through so much. But our love grows every day, and honestly, I love him more with every passing day, week, month and year.

We are building a beautiful future together and are dedicated to many extraordinary co-creative visions. Kevin has stuck with me beyond the ups and downs and thicks and thins. Actually, it's more like he has put up with total insanity on my part, and I am amazed that to this day, he snuggles up to me, expressing his deep love for me, which I joke and say, no way, I love you more! OMG, thank you, Source!

I hate to say this, but the number of pathetic triggers I experienced was more than what I would've expected. I pretty much thought that love in my life would be very hard to open up to again, yet it was also everything to me to experience in this life. I do have to laugh at the utter ridiculousness of it all because he has only reassured and helped me with trauma and anxiety, which I feel come with being targeted and having so many former partners turn on me out of nowhere. Learning how people are targeted to turn around and target another person was what the Mars recruitment proved to me. They were aware of the partners I would meet and somehow maintained their control of them. Knowing that there was a list of men, or what they called plants, to be placed in my path to trip me up—as you can imagine, my trust issues were enormous. He blesses and kisses it away with an understanding I never imagined possible.

I could share so many more amazing things about Kevin. His skills are mind-blowing. He used to be a carpenter and preferred building houses alone because he found working with crews frustrating. We took a trip to Utah to drop off his son at his mother's house. He showed me some of the houses he had built. I was excited to see them and was so blown away! We aren't just talking about a cabin or something small and simple. We are talking about a deluxe home in the mountains. I thought there was no way he could have built this by himself. Maybe he was trying to impress me, as I certainly had my fair share of men in my life who would do just that. Anyway, on our way up the hill to the house, we passed by someone he knew who lived close by, and when he came outside, he said, "Wow, Kevin O'Shea," he was a legend around there. He said he watched Kevin single-handedly build this house, and they couldn't believe it. He brought his daughter there, who also had some fantastic stories about my Kevin!

CRAZY CONFERENCES

After Kevin and I got together, I made many trips, some together and some alone, like Chile, Brazil, Chichen Itza, Mexico, Hawaii and around the USA since my Oregon days. We went to Barcelona, Spain and Montserrat, which was incredible. The energies of the Goddess, Black Madonna, the Virgin Mary, Joan of Arc, Ariadne and the Magdalene energies were profound to see in person. The mountain of Montserrat has been of religious significance since pre-Christian times when the Romans built a temple to honor the Roman Goddess Venus.

On our first trip to Australia, we visited the sacred site of Uluru. My Uncle Richard Bradshaw is a lawyer for the Aborigines in Australia and was one of the lawyers behind ensuring that it would not become a tourist trap but would give rights to the Aborigines and protect the Aboriginal name Uluru. My global work has been about opening natural stargates and assisting in the activation of the 13th gate, which happens to be located in Ayers Rock, Uluru, Australia. This is accomplished through conscious participation in grounding the Mother Arc energies into the Earth's core, which has not been available for quite some time.

I followed up my second trip to Australia with a trip to Hong Kong, which was around the time things fell apart with some friendships in the disclosure community. It was in 2018/19 that I did an event in China with Dr. Michael Salla and John DeSouza. We were in Shanghai and then Beijing. We explored many palaces, the Great Wall and the Forbidden City, which was beyond wild. People who recognized me approached me to have their picture taken together—it was surreal. At one of the two conferences we did in China, a pop star who was their equivalent of Justin Timberlake played a song to introduce my talk and gave me a signed CD of his music. The crazy synchronicities and miracles I could go on about. We all have this in our lives along the way.

But something was so significant around the time of the Dimensions of Disclosure Conference in 2019. I had just returned from Hong Kong. I took this trip again later in the year, just as the protests affected flight and travel, and it was a miracle that I could get out. The conference ended in Hong Kong, and I was headed to catch my flight back to the USA. Our driver got us and our luggage in the vehicle.

A tunnel had been temporarily closed earlier that day, almost blocking our ability to get to the airport, but eventually opened up, and we drove through in the nick of time. We arrived at the airport early enough, decided to grab a bite at a restaurant with the driver, and kept our luggage and belongings in the vehicle. We had a fabulous meal and reminisced about our fun time at the conference and the tours we took to sacred sites, beautiful walks through amazing gardens, and two days of exploring all the intriguing places where the protests were not happening. We lost track of time, and then someone in our group noticed that flights were canceled, but mine was still on time. Stunned, we rushed to grab my belongings and passport before getting to the gate to board. We went down the escalator to the parking lot when the driver realized the keys were not in his pocket and nowhere to be found. Time was ticking, and my panic set in.

The driver went to look for them, retracing his steps towards the restaurant we just ate at. We stood outside with the vehicle, praying he would return soon—the anticipation was intense. We waited and waited. Eventually, he showed up, waving the keys in the air. He frantically put the keys into the door lock, opened it, yanked my suitcases, and grabbed a cart. We rushed to the check-in area as more flights were canceled. Panic was in the air as many travelers realized they were stranded, yet somehow, my flight was still active. Unfortunately, boarding had already begun, and I had a long way to get to the gate. I said my goodbyes, ran as hard as possible and boarded the plane just as they closed the door. I got to my seat, and the plane took off. I was elated and relieved. I came home so jet-lagged from Australia to Hong Kong and then back home, with another conference in Ventura in a week.

Conference in China with John and Bella DeSouza, Michael Salla, Kevin O'Shea and myself in December 2018. It took place in Beijing and Shang Hai, and we traveled to many incredible locations, including climbing part of the Great Wall.

After the conference in Ventura, it was clear that some people in the disclosure community were shaking things up, filing lawsuits and pointing fingers. The stories are endless! Some major divide-and-conquer strategies were beginning to infiltrate. I chose to take a step back, but that didn't mean it wouldn't affect me. My former associations with some of these individuals would be brought to the surface and questioned when my intent and hope was that it would all get healed and resolved.

It is now about setting appropriate boundaries and moving forward on this mission. I have yet to invest myself fully into any one story or narrative. I always strive to keep an open mind and do my best to connect the dots and get to the bottom of things regarding what we are up against in the here and now regarding ET involvement in our world.

Recognizing Eisenhower

"Eisenhower is part of the creation of the Secret Space programs—but without his leadership, many failing organizations had no accountability to their actions and infighting between the organizations spread.

This continued lack of transparency and continued deception going on between these World powers spread corruption, greed, mind control and horrific crimes against humanity."

– Lisa Renee, Ascension Glossary

Since the Eisenhower administration and after World War II, the full implications of the Military Industrial Complex had yet to be wholly exposed, along with all the terrible layers it has been hiding. We now live in times where disclosure is happening, and our need for discernment is ever-increasing. Many, including Lisa Renee, say that Eisenhower did meet with alien species. Elena Danaan has said he did attend some meetings but didn't sign the Greada Treaty. And Dan Cooper is adamant about saying he wasn't even allowed to attend the negotiations.

The battling of destructive planetary forces that affect many countries and populations and the balancing of powerful energies all run in my blood. My great-grandfather, President Dwight D. Eisenhower, the Army general who led the Allied Forces to victory over Hitler, has placed me in a unique position since I am willing to venture down all the rabbit holes. There may have been some victories, but the war wasn't won. I remember the horror I felt flipping through photo albums with my family to see pictures of the Holocaust.

I find bizarre all the Holocaust denial and the many psyops and disinformation introduced into a so-called truth community or people who claim to awake to the lies of history. It is incredibly hard to navigate, but we must dig deeply and keep an open mind to arrive as close to the truth as possible. Unfortunately, some aren't willing to do that because they have difficulty admitting they may have been mistaken.

The details of it all began to awaken in me and the research I pursued as I continually noticed the struggle we are born into. We each have beautiful potential, but we are somehow programmed not to see it or operate from a false sense of self that the matrix and social engineering have constructed. So many of us cry out to rise fully in our authenticity and find the truth. Many can sense that something terribly off in our world has the potential to launch them on this journey. It can take so much effort to feel like one is on track and even more to fully understand the level of manipulation that has infiltrated just about every sector of society. Huge rabbit holes exist that can be all-consuming to venture down.

My great-grandfather, Dwight D. Eisenhower, led the Allied Forces to victory in Europe before being elected the 34th President of the United States of America. In office, he kept the peace for eight years while something else was going on underneath the surface beyond his control—things connected to extraterrestrials, hidden agendas involving Mars, Secret Space Programs, and a global elitist dark cabal that he had to wrestle with—and began to take over much of what he put in place.

In a famous speech, Ike warned:

"In the councils of government, we must guard against the acquisition of unwarranted influence, whether sought or unsought, by the Military-Industrial Complex. The potential for the disastrous rise of misplaced power exists, and will persist. We must never let the weight of this combination endanger our liberties or democratic processes. We should take nothing for granted. Only an alert and knowledgeable citizenry can compel the proper meshing of the huge industrial and military machinery of defense with our peaceful methods and goals so that security and liberty may prosper together."

I would discover that my path would take me to the heart of his speech—his warning about the Military Industrial Complex. They started as a small group of people who profit from war and are threatening democracy and peace in the world because of it. As a 5-star general and President of the United States of America, Ike had firsthand insight into this problem and tried to warn the American people.

I have always felt his presence and guidance with me. We were both born with soul missions, and the trajectories of these missions are similar. We are both Libras, seekers of balance and justice, and our true intentions have been distorted and misunderstood by many who wish for another agenda to overtake this planet. There is no control agenda where I am coming from. It is about encouraging humanity to take its power back and become aware of all that has been happening so we can achieve ascension. Unfortunately, the same groups he warned us about promote the misunderstandings of folks like us.

What he warned us about, I experienced firsthand when I got up close and personal with aspects of the Secret Space Program. It has been something many people have had to contend with. The targeting and knowing that one could be murdered or heavily compromised for being a speaker of truth is a real risk. Yet, so many are helping restore humanity to a thriving species breaking bonds with enslavement and mass manipulation of incarnate consciousness.

They have targeted the Eisenhower legacy using tactics as far-fetched as time travel, with attempts to rewrite history. These groups seek to blame Ike for ET government treaties or call him a war criminal, with accusations about a massive genocide of the German people. He has recently been exonerated of this in a new documentary you can find through Mark Felton Productions. There are even places where it says he was a Swedish Jew. The truth is that his family was Pennsylvania Dutch and had German ancestry. He was the third of seven sons born in Denison, Texas. His parents, David and Ida, were members of the River Brethren Church in Abilene, Kansas, an off-shoot of the Mennonite faith, but they moved in a different direction later in life.

The Jews have been heavily targeted, and the Zionists and Nazis are all a part of this complex deception. These accusations about Eisenhower have attracted a particular audience. Still, the force of truth has always beckoned me to find some answers, and in the process of doing so, I am greatly reassured of Ike's good intentions and actions. I will have much more to share soon on that topic.

So much is stored in our ancient remembrance and connection to Mother Earth. I am wary of anything else because this planet was created with all the abundance we need to heal and activate our divine blueprint. Though advanced technologies would accelerate the up-leveling of our human vessels, we should strive to do this organically from within. The DNA prints are different from off-planet influences that can scramble our DNA to create a necessity for their solutions. We should remember that we are the ones we've been waiting for, so what are we waiting for? The minute we rely on something so advanced, we compromise our ability to remember all that we are, which comes about through a vital process of initiation from within. We are the most advanced technology to discover.

MORE ABOUT MARS

Recently, in the News, CNN mentioned the colonization on Mars and people signing up to be permanent residents there. Hence, these ideas and concepts are now out in the open. But what remains hidden are the reasons, intentions, and true history of ET involvement and the future we can create beyond our hijacked state. We have dormant and advanced DNA that many don't want us to be in touch with. That is why there is an invasion or attack that opposes our expansion, unification, and liberation, so this is what we need to focus on. The amount of illegal activity behind the scenes to fund these projects is unbelievable. Our tax dollars are their slush funds without our knowledge or consent. We have the right to know. It is not just drug rings. It goes into the darkest form of criminal activity that we can imagine. It would be one thing if they were secretive for our betterment. But the secrets are so that unbelievable abuses can occur, involving the torture and manipulation of so many, as we would stop them if we only knew.

These humans are collaborators and hide what they are doing from people they may be working alongside. Compartmentalism makes it extremely difficult for anyone to know what they are attempting to do, and those who do know are either trying to help them or stop them. My gut tells me it will take the human race to end this. Since 1947, in the USA alone, at least 131 DUMBs (Deep Underground Military Bases) have been created, according to Phil Schneider, an engineer involved in creating these bases. He disclosed that 62 of these bases house short and tall "greys" and extraterrestrial craft. Worldwide, 4,000 bases are estimated to exist.

In 1952, the Bilderberg Group was created to take the decision-making about the alien problem and other international issues out of the hands of governments. Over the years, this group evolved into (or merged with) a secret world government. By now, it is almost entirely populated by the Illuminati. It is where the real shadow government exists as one big operation that continues to spread its tentacles. A book called "Space Gate – The Veil Removed" suggests:

> *"The Bilderberg, the Council on Foreign Relations and the Trilateral Commission are the Secret Government and they have their hands on all the Alien technology and run their show through MJ-12."*

Now we can see how this shadow government and off-planet beings influenced the recommendations of the alternative timeline scenarios since we could only come to these conclusions on our own or possess the technology to get there with their input. It has also been said that they want us to be on a catastrophic timeline to be more easily controlled by their plans for a New World Order. Within intelligence groups, clandestine think tanks, and secret societies, there is much opposition, internal wars, and battles between benevolent factions and those who are not. The politics connected to the Nazis and Zionists are all within this shadow government and appear to us as two sides of the same war machine to keep us conquered and divided. Still, they vie for who will have more control over the human race, and we are caught in the middle—but we can also greatly influence the outcome. It is a mirror of the cosmic battles that are taking place, that originated even before our current planet fully formed and that are now here on Earth. All these ET races interlink through a vast and ancient galactic history, and some hold the genetics of the others through hybridization.

The Mars teleportation project represents the first time since 9500 BC that Earth and Mars societies have reunited. A couple of colleagues and I are developing a Mars Protection Treaty to re-establish open relations between Mars and Earth and to prevent the colonization of Mars by Earth.

I am not here to determine who is on what side within these secretive organizations, and I don't wish to cause upset to those who are doing their best on our behalf. Instead, I want to express the hidden truths that we all unite and face together, as we must also end the constant indecisiveness about disclosure and what humanity may or may not be ready for. The cat is out of the bag, and there is no way to avoid answering to the human race now. We need the police force, military, politicians, and pilots of planes spraying toxic aerosols to stop serving these agendas. Unity is everything right now. Eisenhower stepped into quite a dilemma when he became President. With the Cold War and the competing acquisition of weapons between the superpower countries, standing for peace and maintaining security was a profound balancing act. Eisenhower's famous Atoms for Peace speech at the United Nations two months before the December 8, 1953 meeting indicated that he supported ending nuclear weapons development and testing.

MANY PERSPECTIVES ON ET INTERACTION

Many whistleblowers lack direct evidence because they weren't there or the information passed down was somehow tampered with. The people who gave them information were likely to spread disinformation mixed with some truth. We see the same thing today with many well-intentioned journalists and individuals sharing what their "insiders" have told them. I know I probably shared things that weren't wholly accurate over the years, but now, with folks like Dan Cooper in my life, what is disinformation makes far more sense than some of the stories that have been spun and put out there for the public to ponder and consider.

The "First Contact" with President Eisenhower supposedly occurred at Edwards (Muroc) Air Force base in February of 1954, though some think it was Homestead Air Force base in Florida. It was with blond Nordics, similar in appearance to the Pleiadians of many contactees. But Dan Cooper told me that Commander Valiant Thor warned the U.S. about the Nordics in 1952 when Truman was POTUS. He told the U.S. that the Nordics, at that time, were in bed with the Nazis.

MAJESTIC 12

1. Almirante Roscoe H. Hillenkoetter
2. Dr. Vannevar Bush
3. Secretario James V. Forrestal
4. General Nothan Twining
5. General Hoyt S. Vanderberg
6. Dr. Detlev Bronk
7. Dr. Jerome Hunsaker
8. Almirante Sidney W. Souers
9. Mr. Gordon Gray
10. Dr. Donal Menzel
11. General Robert M. Montague
12. Dr. Lloyd V. Berkener

According to Dan Cooper, MJ-12 had the legal authority to sign treaties with alien species according to the terms of the Unconditional Surrender Agreement.

Many exopolitical scholars have noted that the meeting with extraterrestrials on February 20-21, 1954, was attended by a group of four members of civil society. They were Gerald Light, a metaphysical scientist; Edwin Nourse, a leading economist; James Francis MacIntyre, bishop and head of the Catholic Church in Los Angeles; and Franklin Winthrop Allen, a well-known journalist.

In addition, William Cooper, who was killed in 2001 and is claimed to have served in the U.S. Air Force and the U.S. Navy as well as Naval Intelligence until 1975, had access to classified information and shared this:

"This alien group warned us against the aliens that were orbiting the Equator (the 'Greys') and offered to help us with our spiritual development. They demanded that we dismantle and destroy our nuclear weapons as the major condition. They refused to exchange technology citing that we were spiritually unable to handle the technology which we then possessed. They believed that we would use any new technology to destroy each other."

According to William Cooper, the history of this race has experienced something similar, with portions of their race spreading out to Rigel, a part of the Orion constellation. After the so-called Lyran Wars, the Dracos attacked Nordics on Lyra, with many fleeing to Rigel. He goes on to say:

"The first thing that they (the Draco/Greys) did was subtly infiltrate all strata of society and use implants to exercise mind control. They then systematically eroded the collective soul matrix and assimilated the popula-

tion into their group memory complex, effectively replacing the soul history of the population with their own memories, turning them into drones."

After making it to Rigel, contactee George Andrews describes this:

"There was a nuclear war and environmental disaster on Rigel, and before this or during, the Dracos and Grey ETs infiltrated them covertly.

The surviving Nordics were part of a hybridization program where the short Greys—from Zeta Reticulum, were probably designed to genetically engineer them, and they then became the 'Tall Greys' or 'Tall Whites.' The Tall Greys have a more dominant role than the 'common' shorter ones. The Nordics who were able to flee went to Procyon and they were also attacked, but Alex Collier a contactee has said that they have recently liberated their planet from the Greys and want to help us."

At the Muroc Air Force base meeting, this race stated that we were on a path of self-destruction and must stop killing each other, polluting the Earth, raping her natural resources and had to learn to live in harmony. William Cooper states that these terms were met with extreme suspicion, especially the condition of nuclear disarmament. It was believed that meeting that condition would leave us helpless in the face of an obvious alien threat. We also had nothing in history to help with the decision. Therefore, nuclear disarmament was considered not in the United States' best interest. According to Michael Salla's exopolitical research, confirmation of the First Contact meeting comes from the son of a former Navy Commander who claimed that his father, Charles Suggs, had been present at that meeting. Another whistleblower, the son of William Lear, the famous creator of the Lear Jet, confirms First Contact and claims that it involved an extraterrestrial race that was turned down for their principled stand on technology transfer.

John Lear's research goes on to say that given the intensity of the Cold War, the national security officials present may have decided it was more prudent to seek better terms before agreeing to the extraterrestrials' request. Gerald Light's testimony implies that the meeting at Edwards did not result in an agreement but intense disagreement between Eisenhower officials. They also talk about at least four alien groups involved in the meetings, including the "Nordics," Alien Greys, another humanoid group with some at least nine feet tall, and a reptilian race. Light believed President Eisenhower planned to make "an official statement to the country" about one month after his letter was written. But as we know, no such announcement was ever made.

Disclosure Treaties with the Greys, according to the late William Cooper, describes another encounter and agreement that was reached after the failure of the first meeting. While Cooper has a different version of dates and times for the 1954 meetings, he agrees that there were two sets of meetings involving different

extraterrestrials meeting with President Eisenhower and Eisenhower administration officials. Fortunately, it has become clear that Eisenhower didn't sign any
treaties, and something that has not been brought up in the disclosure community is the Unconditional Surrender Agreement made in 1952.

Another notorious treaty that did not originate with the Eisenhower administration since the first, known as the "Greada Treaty," was signed in 1934 and renewed every ten years. The second one would have been in 1944, confirmed by
a few sources, and again in 1964, which has also been confirmed. The possibility
of cloning humans is also something to consider. Support for the diplomatic role
played by the "Tall Greys" comes from William Cooper, former Navy Intelligence
Advisor, who claims he saw classified documents where the "Tall Greys" did negotiate agreements with the Eisenhower administration in meetings beginning in 1954.

In the U.S. we first hear about relations with the Nordics in 1934, with
President Roosevelt and Hitler. For the most part, when we hear about relations
with ET and our governments, we only hear about Eisenhower. For instance,
as Dr. Pinotti and CUN documented in 2000, today we know that UFOs were
reported in Italy during the '30s and that Mussolini, considering them a new foreign aerial weapon, created in 1933 an official committee headed by Guglielmo
Marconi, "Gabinetto RS 33," with the purpose of reverse engineering studies after
a UFO crash in Lombardy and the recovering of two Nordic-type pilots Il Duce
considered German pilots. Nazi Germany later inherited these Italian studies.
In any case, regarding the USA, the above-mentioned treaties did not originate
with Eisenhower. Numerous people validate this, a few of which I'd like to share.

A whistleblower who is an ex-operative for M-16 writes:

*"In 1934, a group of Pleiadians approached the US government, under the Roo-
sevelt administration, in an effort to work out an eventual military disarmament arrangement. The US government refused, so the Pleiadians approached
Hitler and the Nazis instead. The Pleiadians worked out a treaty with Hitler
and the Nazis that in exchange for technology the Nazis would not attack the
Jewish people. Their treaty with the Nazis held together until around 1941.*

*The Nazis developed their advanced saucer-shaped aircraft from the Pleia-
dian technology. By 1941, the Pleiadians pulled out of the treaty and would
no longer deal with Hitler and Nazis. It was at this time that the Greys
approached them, and this is where the Nazi trauma-based mind control
technology came from."*

So, according to this whistleblower, the first treaty between the Grey ETs
and the American government under the administration of Roosevelt was
signed in July 1934. It was the so-called "Grenada Treaty." Mr. Prince states:

"It was here that the agreement was first made between the Greys (who

were actually representing a race of reptilian-like beings from the Draco star system) and representatives of the US intelligence community. The treaty stated that in return for the Greys providing high technology, the US federal government would allow the Greys to proceed unhindered with human abductions for use in an ongoing ET genetic program."

Jason Bishop III, a Dulce Base whistleblower, said, *"The U.S. Government agreed to trade animals and humans in exchange for High Tech Knowledge, and allow them to use (undisturbed) underground bases, in the Western USA."*

Reports confirmed by contactee Billy Meier stated that space-time technology was exchanged by a certain race of Pleiadians with Hitler's Germany from 1933 to 1934, seemingly through a group of Nazi channelers —the psychic women called "Vrilerinnen" and headed by Maria Orsich. When Nicola Tesla claimed he was in contact with some race of extraterrestrials, the U.S. government asked if it were possible to meet with these aliens. Tesla said he could arrange it. So, after the initial shock, the U.S. government made arrangements to meet with the Pleiadians and then with the Greys. Our government, during the Roosevelt administration, seemingly got secret technologies that weren't about mind control, like what the Nazis received but were anti-gravity devices, metals and alloys, environment, free energy, and medical technology and this was in exchange for allowing the Greys to infiltrate human societies on different levels, which also included the possibility of cloning certain world leaders. According to this whistleblower, the treaties are renewed every 10 years. If Casbolt's and Meier's statements are true, this is what the backdrop is, which potently validates the meetings with ETs that took place in the Eisenhower administration in 1954.

Edward Snowden, Paul Hellyer and Charles Hall have all spoken about the "Tall Whites," also known as the "Tall Greys." After piecing things together from many accounts, the research of Jim Nichols, a key exopolitical scholar, claims that President Eisenhower faced alien beings in 1954 who possessed technologies so advanced that even beginning to be able to defend ourselves seemed useless. However, these creatures assured Eisenhower that conquest was not their intention.

William Cooper says:

"According to this agreement, the US Government would allow people to be abducted on the condition that they would not be harmed, that they would be returned safely and that they would not remember the incident. In exchange, the US Government would get highly evolved technology."

Another part of the Edwards Agreement was the exchange of "ambassadors." One of the ambassadors was the reptilian ambassador Krill from Tiphon in the Draco system. Another one is often called J-Rod. The ETs called "the Zetas" come from the Reticulum constellation and are believed to be of humanoid descent, whereas other races (those from Draco, Orion and Ursa Maior) are considered reptilian species. There is much more history to share about these races, including a planet formally called Apex that became the Zeta Reticulum. Not all are harmful, but some joined with the service-to-self beings when they destroyed their world and became short Greys. These were the beings engineering the Nordics on Rigel into the Tall Whites. They are known to want to stop our ascension by misaligning the Earth's grids. The Zeta Talk website says those connected to the Alternative 3 timeline are service-to-self Zeta Greys. With so many potential meetings, I am sure we have dealt with a mix of those who want to help us and those who only wish to help themselves.

According to William Cooper:

"Another major finding was that the aliens were using humans and animals for a source of glandular secretions, enzymes, hormonal secretions, blood and used us in horrible genetic experiments. The aliens explained these actions as necessary to their survival. They stated that if they were unable to improve their genetic structure their race would soon cease to exist. We looked upon their explanations with extreme suspicion. Since our weapons were literally useless against the aliens, MJ-12 decided to continue friendly diplomatic relations with them until such time as we were able to challenge them on a military basis."

Col. Philip Corso, former advisor to President Eisenhower's National Security Council, revealed the treaty was a trojan horse:

"These creatures weren't benevolent alien beings who had come to enlighten human beings. They were genetically altered human automatons, cloned biological entities, actually who were harvesting biological specimens on Earth for their own experimentation. We had negotiated a kind of surrender with them as long as we couldn't fight them."

Remote viewers who wanted to know where the Greys are coming from discovered they are from three different time eras and that most are coming from different times in the future. Some authors believe Greys are not aliens but future humans or future hybrid humanoids.

Dr. Michael Wolf claimed he was a member of the satellite government for over 25 years. He attained a high "Above Top Secret" clearance level and worked primarily on joint ET/human scientific projects. His version is a bit different compared to Cooper's. Wolf has described the Greys as having positive motivations regarding their presence on Earth but have been inhibited and targeted by rogue elements in the US military. Similarly, Robert Dean believes that the extraterrestrials visiting Earth are friendly. Military abductions called MILABs appear to others to be from real extraterrestrials. Many have stated that they think there is a mixture of real ETs and more robotic ones engineered to assist in military abductions. Chipping and artificial telepathy are going on, so one can conclude that many abductions aren't with real ETs, and this is perhaps why there are so many abduction cases. It contrasts with the testimonies of Cooper, Lear, Schneider, Corso, and arguably even General Mac Arthur over the true motivations of the Greys. Gerald Light's claim of a "terrific conflict between the various 'authorities'" is worth repeating on whether to inform the general public. They also desired to get a handle on the intentions of these beings before making anything public.

Disclosure has been an enormous challenge, even before these meetings. In December 1953, the Joint Chiefs of Staff issued Army-Navy-Airforce Publication 146 that made the unauthorized release of information concerning UFOs a crime under the Espionage Act, punishable by up to 10 years in prison and a $10,000 fine, not to mention the threats to families and people's lives, proven by a few of the whistleblowers I have mentioned, who are no longer alive due to unexplained deaths.

Infiltration has been a major factor since World War II. And though this war changed something, it was never won. Nazi presence exists in the United States because of Project Paperclip, treaties, and a deeper internal shadow government that has turned defense-related projects and technologies into weapons used for our enslavement. And this infiltration continues.

We are challenged as humanity to fully understand the difference between who is here to help and who isn't. However, that can only come through discernment, educating ourselves about our galactic history and bringing hidden truths out into the open. We also must develop spiritually so that we are not limiting or blocking ourselves from expanding into higher Earth energies. We need to see all beings as extensions of ourselves and it is up to us to align with what will serve the highest good of humanity and the planet. Surely, there is no concrete evidence for all the elements I present. On the other hand, despite this, they show a possible "secret history" we must face and consider.

MORE ABOUT THE ALIEN AGENDA

Disclosing the U.S. government's long-standing knowledge of the "alien agenda," Phil Schneider's original notes indicate that between January 1947 and December 1952, no less than 16 UFO crashes/retrievals took place. Some say that of the spacecraft we see, approximately 60% are flown by off-world beings, while the military reverse-engineers around 20%.

Author and gifted Medical Intuitive, Stewart Swerdlow, spent years serving various US and foreign government agencies and special interest groups, including the Montauk Project. He had this to say:

"The controller elite includes terrestrial governments (executive, legislative, and judicial branches), media organizations, international organizations, and military and intelligence organizations that are populated by clones or cyborgs under the command and control of the Grey/Reptilian faction whose intent is to takeover Earth."

This had been in the works for a while and has been the larger plan. The shadow government works directly with these beings, while many among them wish to defend us. Stewart goes on to say:

"They have advanced technologies that are not being used to protect us at all or help those in need or clean up the environment. Instead they are being used for black budget projects that use millions of lives and millions of our tax dollars. Technology in the Wrong Hands/Montauk With Project Paperclip and the Nazi involvement, it seems that the use of these technologies that were to help us with ET threats, fell into the wrong hands. According to Preston Nichols, who was a part of the Montauk project, 'the humans from Sirius B played a role in providing exotic technology such as time/inter- dimensional travel, to clandestine government agencies involved in both the Philadelphia Experiment and Montauk Project.' The first one deals with a 1943 US Navy teleportation test, and the second to the Long Island facility devoted to secret military experiments."

Alex Collier explains that those from Sirius B have come here and really messed with our heads, and they are the ones who originally gave our government the Montauk technology. He says this exotic technology was provided for the purpose of encouraging national security agencies to develop offensive military capabilities in the event of possible extraterrestrial threats. John A. Quinn, a Montauk Project researcher, said that much of this was legitimately funded until the late 1960s, but then Congress found out about the psychotronic and mind control aspects of the project. They decided to end research to avoid these technologies from falling into the wrong hands and being used in unacceptable ways.

Unfortunately, it had fallen into the wrong hands. Michael Ash, who did a Montauk Survivors tape series, has said that Tall Zeta Reticulan Greys were involved at Montauk. The Draco were also there and were actually in control of most of the projects. The real agenda and the amount of mind control and illegal activities in hidden areas of our government they can get away with is staggering, and I have personally met many mind control victims who have suffered unbelievable trauma. It is also apparent that the war between these off-planet groups keeps us from a desired positive timeline.

There is a theme related to the harvesting of souls, the siphoning of our vital energies, and the Greys trying to create a soul matrix through hybridization since they digressed and lost their soul energy and ability to reproduce in the future. They could be us, picking up our genetic material to save ourselves if we don't make bold choices and actions now. We could turn into Greys and be ruled by the Reptilians, but not if we focus on our spiritual development and bring balance back to this Earth. Many higher races living underground have not digressed into these forms because they are not polarized to just technological advancement, and they have avoided being engineered.

Being engineered means negating emotion, which some races intentionally got rid of because they felt emotions were a problem. It is important to note that there are positive and negative within both races, just like we see in the human population, much diversity. There is also hybridization amongst these races and with humans.

The Greys are in survival, but we have to take it upon ourselves to openly discuss every element involved so that we can begin to create a positive shift in this world. We cannot help a race to the detriment of our own. The more we understand, the more we can prevent this type of future scenario for ourselves. They want to use us to cheat their way to immortality or into reaching a more developed dimensional capacity. Some, though, want to blend in with us and have a chance of becoming a healed race, and those are the ones we should embrace and accept since there is no turning back, and any being who wishes to allow us to progress in peace are the true friends.

Positive Intervention Contactee Alex Collier claims that the intervention of the beings from Sirius A is due to mistakes made by those from Sirius B regarding technology transfers.

> "My understanding is that those from the Sirius A system are trying to be beneficial and assist, because they feel responsibility in that those who colonized Sirius B system were originally from Sirius A. The main activity that can be attributed to those extraterrestrials from Sirius A is to assist in building a suitable ecological system for (human) evolution on Earth by altering the 'biomagnetic energy grid' of the planet. They are the original builders of our grid, the architecture on which our planet was based. So therefore they are useful in discerning the sacred geometry and discerning the physical laws of our home world. They can help us in constructing the new grid, and in constructing a new system that is appropriate for our next challenges. So we would say that the Sirians are excellent allies in the strategic design work that lies ahead."

Through the failed 2006 attempt to recruit me into a hidden operation regarding the Alternative 3 colonization of Mars scenario, I discovered that other projects represented different aspects of this. My friend and colleague Andrew Basiago and I have collaborated on many things and were able to put the dots together with the amazing work and research of Alfred Lambremont Webre. This is not science fiction. There was a secret teleportation program to Mars, the CIA Jump Room Program, in the 1980s, which recruited Andrew D. Basiago and other whistleblower participants. The teleportation technology for this program may have been donated to the U.S. government by a specific species of grey extra-terrestrials. Russia and the U.K. also had teleportation programs to Mars at this time. There are reports that the current bases on Mars may number up to 500,000 settlers in what is effectively a "breakaway civilization."

WHAT REALLY HAPPENED—UNCONDITIONAL SURRENDER AGREEMENT

"As I already explained to you before, MJ-12 had the only LEGAL authority to do that; sign Treaties and/or Agreements with ET alien species, according to the Terms of the Unconditional Surrender Instrument signed by Truman, and all of Congress, on July 19, 1952, surrendering the U.S. to the Nazis. In other words, Dwight had NO such powers whatsoever, as POTUS, when he assumed that position (POTUS) on January 20, 1953. His powers to negotiate or to sign such Treaties or Agreements with any ET alien species had already, LEGALLY, been passed onto MJ-12 before he assumed Office as POTUS.

How many times do I have to say this; Dwight did NOT sign any Treaty or any type of Agreement with any ET alien species or with the Nazi's. Anyone telling you otherwise is spoon feeding you ICC/Nazi/ Draco Alliance disinformation; Nazi Propaganda Ministry engineered propaganda, carefully designed to hide the truth of their existence and their powers from the U.S. public."

– Dan Cooper, Senior Advisor to the Earth Alliance

After all the back-and-forth exchanges with Dan Cooper and me presenting to him all the information I have heard over the years about ET government treaties, this particular response he sent me stood out. The funny thing is, I never bought into that disinformation, so I never stopped researching and questioning.

According to Michael Salla material from SSP whistleblowers, President Truman and General (and future President) Eisenhower refused to agree to their terms (the Nazis) until they flew UFOs over Washington, D.C., between July 12th and July 29th, 1952. As you can see, these dates line up with what Dan Cooper shared with me. In 1947, before Eisenhower was President, MJ-12 had made it a secret law "Above the President" that the subject and knowledge of UFOs and their occupants would remain the highest guarded secret only above atomic weapons.

The Nazis were successful in taking over the Military Industrial Complex and much of the government in the United States and Europe. This is where the development and infiltration of the Military Industrial Complex began and eventually led to the most powerful of the Secret Earth Government/Group entities that we are referring to as the Interplanetary Corporate Conglomerate or ICC.

How this ties into what Lisa Renee has said is another important piece that may help connect some dots like I have been attempting to:

> "The Zeta contacted the earth world governments during the first World War to make agreements for the barter of earth resources and human genetics in exchange for Grey Alien advanced technologies and assorted militarized weaponry. The Zeta were involved in colonizing Mars and were active during the Atlantean culture that eventually led to the fall.

> They joined with the NAA (Negative Alien Agenda) to counteract and destroy the Christiac Human Guardian Race for control and domination of this Time Vector in this Universal Time Matrix.

> The Zetas are interested in Breeding Programs to create Zeta human hybrids in order to maintain control over the earth in the future timelines. Thus, they formed covert agreements with the world governments and allied forces during World War II in order to reproduce their own race, and through which they could use the Zeta Hive Mind to more effectively mind control the population of the earth.

> During World War II treaties were made with the allied government, and as a result, several organizations, black operations and covert groups such as Majestic 12 were set up to further administer to these treaties, while secretly testing out assorted alien technologies, weaponry while reverse engineering space craft, and these activities are what began the Compartmentalization process to set up different factions for the Secret Space Programs as well as build deep underground complexes for high level testing of these alien technologies carried out by the Military Industrial Complex.

> During the time that Franklin D. Roosevelt was President (1933-1945) several species of Grey aliens contacted all the major world governments and made secret treaties with many of them, that were inherently conflicts of interest, but they had no intention of honoring any of these agreements.

> Roosevelt did not enter agreements, but Churchill did, offering the children and adults to be used for abduction and experimentation for a variety of off-planet alien projects. They agreed on 5,000 people and more than 50,000 were abducted. Churchill knew he made a deal with the devil."

The Zetas, I have heard, are the ones who came up with the Alternative 3 scenario that we should go to Mars and thus contacted the Jason Scholars set

Dwight was not POTUS on July 19, 1952, the date of the infamous UFO flyover the Capital. Nor, did he hold any seat in Congress. Hence, Dwight did not sign the Unconditional Surrender Agreement (Treaty) of July 19, 1952, signed by all of U.S. Congress, led by Truman, on that day, according to Dan Cooper, Senior Advisor to the Earth Alliance.

up in Eisenhower's administration, which has been said to be connected to or is another name for MJ-12. I feel my great-grandfather's guidance since childhood would help me with the targeting and manipulation that was attempting to take me there to be a permanent colonist.

Bonnie Baumgartner from Mystic Knowing website says:

"The US government gave permission for the Greys to have access to any humans they chose to experiment on for the last 100 years in exchange for their weapon technology and the science of cloning humans. The National Security Agency created human-Grey hybrids. Some members of NSA are considered part of The Grey Group Mind Complex and Communication System. Some of the Grey Group are located on the moon and Mars."

Dan Cooper says an unconditional surrender took place, making it impossible for any President to sign treaties with aliens. Elena Danaan, Alex Collier and Dan Cooper have all said MJ-12 signed these treaties behind his back, but this Unconditional Surrender had already occurred.

As previously noted, Dan Cooper said that the U.S. surrendered to the Nazis unconditionally on July 19, 1952.

"Ike had no choice but to openly comply with the official 'Instrument of Surrender'—the unconditional surrender of the United States to the Nazis (the National Socialist German Worker's Party), signed by all of Congress and most of the prominent businessmen of the period on July 19, 1952, when Tru-

man was POTUS. He opposed the 'Instrument of Surrender of '52' secretly by establishing various military and civilian covert units for that purpose. One of them was Ike's Force (also known as the United States Marine Corps, Special Section, or USMC SS for short) which continues today. This U.S. military unit is the most successful military unit opposing the Interplanetary Corporate Conglomerate/Nazi/Draconian Empire Alliance (also known as the ICC/Nazi/Draco Alliance) today, by far. He ordered the first attack on the Grey's (Zeta Reticulans) Deep Underground Military Base (DUMB) at Dulce, New Mexico, knowing that he would lose that battle just to learn more about his enemy and to test his best against them. They (the U.S. Army Rangers and also the Green Berets) lost 30-to-1 in the Dulce Wars. This battle at that DUMB of the Greys occurred more than a decade before the one reported to have occurred in 1969 and was a much larger engagement. Several thousand U.S. special forces troops engaged against the Grey's forces then, and nearly half of them lost their lives in that action. Ike also established the White Hats—the first of which were Texan U.S. generals and admirals.

That's where the name 'White Hats' came from. Ike's White Hats are the ones that brought Ronald Reagan into their fold, right after the ICC/Nazi/Draco Alliance had him shot (March 31, 1981) for attempting to disclose the Secret Space Program (SSP). It was Reagan and the White Hats that had Dan convince China (November of 1985) to do business and to teach China how to do business to make them a powerful ally in the fight against the ICC/Nazi/Draco Alliance. In other words, it was Ike that established the Earth Alliance. If it weren't for him, there wouldn't be an Earth Alliance today in the position to defeat the ICC/Nazi/Draco Alliance. Barack Obama also attempted to disclose the SSP (December 10, 2009), and his attempt also failed. The ICC/Nazi/Draco Alliance actually reversed time[9] to counter that attempt.

With another special unit (civilian) established by Ike, he also ensured that numerous photos and videos of Nazi spacecraft and other SSP technology would continue to resurface (reach the people) in the mass and alternative media.

That civilian unit that Ike established has been extremely successful at ensuring that many key photos and videos of the SSP continue to resurface. They made sure that the photos that my father (Robert N. Cooper, an SSP photographer with the USAF Space Command Division) took of the SSP were preserved and are being made public today. Ike was the one that first appealed to (formally petitioned) to the Sphere Beings Alliance (also the Guardians) to put up the impenetrable Outer Barrier (an 8th Force energy field) around our solar system, which they did on December 14, 2014. He was the person that first attempted to convince the Sphere Beings Alliance that humanity was worth freeing from ICC/Nazi/Draco Alliance dominion over us (the people, humanity at large). It

*was another civilian unit that Ike set up to continue to petition the Sphere Be-
ings Alliance for their assistance that eventually did convince them to intervene
on our behalf. The Guardians first approached me in 1975. So, I presume that
is when they first took up residence in our solar system.*

*Like you (Laura), I was also appalled at the fact that the U.S. had so readily
surrendered, unconditionally, to the Draconian Empire's lackeys, the Nazis,
and that every POTUS since Truman, including Ike, had kowtowed to them
since then. When I exclaimed my disgust to my retired U.S. Navy Vice Admiral friend (a 40-year veteran SSP scientist) about this, he said, 'but Dan,
they were a million years ahead of us technologically. We had no choice but to
surrender to them.' So, I wouldn't be so hard on Ike for kowtowing to the ICC/
Nazi/Draco Alliance, in his time, were I you. He did more than any other
person did, or could do, to assure our (the Earth Alliance's) victory over the
ICC/Nazi/Draco Alliance. The Guardians assure me that we prevail in our
(the Earth Alliance's) conflict (war) with the ICC/Nazi/Draco Alliance. Why
else would the Guardians have wasted their time and resources coming here
if that weren't the case? Does that, in short, answer your question Laura?"*

When I asked him about Project Paperclip, he replied:

*"Yes; one of the terms of the Surrender Instrument of July 19, 1952 (which
Truman signed) was to whitewash the backgrounds of many Nazi scientists
so that those scientists could be employed in the U.S. without repercussion
(retribution or trial). Truman, from 46 to 52, was using captured Nazi scientists (that is what you know as Project Paperclip) in an attempt to catch up to
the Nazi scientists working out of Antarctica. One example (of the US trying
to play catchup back then) was the Philadelphia Project (Experiment). That
was an attempt in 1947 (on the USS Eldridge) to recreate Nikola Tesla 6th
Force cloaking technology (from notes that the FBI confiscated from Nikola
Tesla's labs) that Nikola Tesla had sold to the Nazis in 1927.*

*There was the attempt by the U.S. to catchup to the Nazis from 1946 through
July 19, 1952. The U.S. failed miserably in that effort and on July 19, 1952
was forced to unconditionally surrender to the Nazis...It ran from '46 to '52
with a handful of captured Nazi scientists, some of them Nazi spies. The Nazis allowed a handful of their best scientists to get captured to spy on the U.S.;
to see how far they(the U.S.) were coming along in their game of catchup and
to steer them (the U.S.) in the wrong directions (send them down dead ends)."*

According to this man named "Anonymous," at a certain point in the 1950s,
U.S. President Eisenhower had been getting reports about UFOs and ETs and
wanted to find out the truth. However, after the Roswell crash of 1947, and with the
help of Truman signing new secrecy and security laws, a secret cabal (who called

A-2

TOP SECRET / MAJIC

EYES ONLY
• TOP SECRET •
••••••••••••

EYES ONLY   COPY ONE OF ONE.

SUBJECT: OPERATION MAJESTIC-12 PRELIMINARY BRIEFING FOR
  PRESIDENT-ELECT EISENHOWER.

DOCUMENT PREPARED 18 NOVEMBER, 1952.

BRIEFING OFFICER: ADM. ROSCOE H. HILLENKOETTER (MJ-1)

NOTE: This document has been prepared as a preliminary briefing
only. It should be regarded as introductory to a full operations
briefing intended to follow.

• • • • • • • •

OPERATION MAJESTIC-12 is a TOP SECRET Research and Development/
Intelligence operation responsible directly and only to the
President of the United States. Operations of the project are
carried out under control of the Majestic-12 (Majic-12) Group
which was established by special classified executive order of
President Truman on 24 September, 1947, upon recommendation by
Dr. Vannevar Bush and Secretary James Forrestal. (See Attachment
"A".) Members of the Majestic-12 Group were designated as follows:

          Adm. Roscoe H. Hillenkoetter
          Dr. Vannevar Bush
          Secy. James V. Forrestal*
          Gen. Nathan F. Twining
          Gen. Hoyt S. Vandenberg
          Dr. Detlev Bronk
          Dr. Jerome Hunsaker
          Mr. Sidney W. Souers
          Mr. Gordon Gray
          Dr. Donald Menzel
          Gen. Robert M. Montague
          Dr. Lloyd V. Berkner

The death of Secretary Forrestal on 22 May, 1949, created
a vacancy which remained unfilled until 01 August, 1950, upon
which date Gen. Walter B. Smith was designated as permanent
replacement.

••••••••••••••
• TOP SECRET •
TOP SECRET / MAJIC
EYES ONLY   T52-EXEMPT (E)
EYES ONLY   002

68

A memo titled "Operation Majestic-12" claiming to be a highly classified government
document. The memo appeared to be a briefing for newly-elected President Eisenhower on
a secret committee created to exploit a recovery of an extra-terrestrial aircraft and cover
up this work from public examination.

themselves MJ-12 or Majestic 12) took over the UFO and ET issue and brought the programs underground. It went black. Certain military agencies, unknown even to the President and other intelligence heads, kept the whole thing top secret, keeping the technology to themselves and even cutting deals with some of the aliens.

Richard Dolan describes how things were out of control, and Eisenhower wanted to find out who these black military groups were and what they were doing. When Eisenhower contacted them, MJ-12 replied that they were outside the jurisdiction of the White House and that their material was classified on a "need-to-know" basis—which went above the Presidency. This infuriated Eisenhower, who sent two CIA agents (including Anonymous) to tell the head of MJ-12 to report to him within a week—or else he would take the 1st army from Colorado and invade Area 51 and S4! According to "The Freedom Articles," Eisenhower threatened to invade Area 51 if these rogue military operatives would not surrender control of the UFO and ET issue. Dan Cooper replied to me about Richard Dolan stating:

> "Yep; that's what MJ-12 told Ike; none of his business. Someone had it correct. MJ-12 never caved into Ike's demands. Ike did send out the 1st Army to attack the DUMB at Dulce, NM. Area 51 and S4 were NOT considered, by Ike, to be targets of interest because they weren't commanded, or heavily staffed, by ETs."

I think later on, it did become a target of interest after hearing the testimony of Anonymous on his deathbed.

Fast forward to today and the implications this has on current events unfolding, I felt called to ask Dan:

> "People are talking about the Alliance and mass arrests all the time, is there any such thing really happening? I mean there must be something going on from White Hats or Alliance? You communicate with some White Hats, are they able to share anything?"

This was his response:

> "Nope. That is an ICC/NAZI/Draco Alliance propaganda (disinformation) campaign. They want you to believe that the War is over and arrests are being made to keep you (the people) from getting involved. They looked through the Looking Glass and saw their demise by the people's hands. So, they are doing everything they can to prevent the people from rising up and defeating them.
>
> There are NO White Hats in the Earth Alliance. The White Hats take requests from the Earth Alliance. They do NOT take orders from the Earth Alliance. White Hats are United States generals and admirals and some United States politicians. People that do that in other countries are called something else, in each such country. The term 'White Hats' came from United States movies of the old west (in the United States)."

DULCE WARS

The researcher Stewart Dunlop reports:

"The Dulce Wars takes place in 1979, when Phil Schneider is part of a drilling operation at Dulce NM. After four shafts have sink, Schneider was appointed to travel down to determine the problem. He claims he discovered a cavern with aliens, and members of the FBI and the black berets were forced to intervene."

We hear about the Dulce Wars that took place in 1979 but don't often hear about the one in 1954. From what I have learned from Dan Cooper, there was an invasion of the DUMB in Dulce, NM, different from the Dulce War we hear about from Phil Schneider. Interesting to note that 1954 is the year of the supposed renewal of the Greada Treaty!

Dan Cooper has helped shed much light on this from the information he received. He shares:

"Several other reliable testifiers (also labeled whistleblowers) mentioned it too. They said that Ike sent in the 1st Army and that the 1st Army fought both Draco and Greys at the Battle of Dulce NM in 1954. My Vice Admiral source said that a lot of special forces (had to be Green Beret back then) were involved in that battle. He also said that mostly Draco were involved and that the loss ratio was 30 to 1 in favor of the Draco forces. He also said that more than 2000 U.S. troops were involved and that the United States lost nearly half of them in that Battle."

When I asked Dan about some of the whistleblowers claiming Ike signed a treaty with the Greys, like Phil Schneider, here was his response:

"I don't know what Phil Schneider said about Ike but, I suspect that he was merely repeating disinformation. Remember, as an ICC/Nazi/Draco Alliance tunnel (DUMB) builder, he would personally NOT have access to such sensitive information. He would have had to have heard it from someone else inside the ICC/Nazi/Draco Alliance. That means that he was fed disinformation. He was given the party line. The Nazi Propaganda Ministry spent a lot of money and time insuring that the American public did NOT know that they (the Nazis) won WWII and that the U.S. surrendered, unconditionally, to them (the Nazis)."

VAL THOR

Dan Cooper has also shared information with me about Valiant Thor's involvement:

"Dwight D. Eisenhower, when he came into office on January 20, 1953, inherited that Treaty of July 19, 1952. Dwight D. Eisenhower had nothing

to do with the unconditional surrender of the U.S. to the NAZIs, which occurred on July 19, 1952. Anyone telling you otherwise is lying to you, or worse, passing on lies.

First contact with the Nordics was by the NAZIs in, no later than, 1929. That is when the Nordics gave them a city in their domain. It is called New Berlin and it is still there.

Commander Valiant Thor warned the U.S., in 1952, when Truman was POTUS, about the Nordics. He told the U.S. that the Nordics, then, were in bed with the NAZIs.

Commander Valiant Thor also warned the U.S., in 1952, about the Greys. In 1952, the Greys had agreements with the NAZIs. The NAZIs, in exchange for people, including a 100,000 U.S. citizens per year, received technology from the Greys. I will specify what technologies at a different time. I know precisely what (the tech) the Greys gave to the NAZIs in exchange for a 100,000 people, U.S. citizens, per year."

In his book, "Stranger at the Pentagon," Frank Stranges writes:

"Valiant Thor's last meeting with the President did not reap any lasting results. Eisenhower wanted to let the world know of Val's proposed plan, but the Secretary of Defense, the head of the Central Intelligence Agency and the Military Chiefs of Staff were opposed to his suggestion. The President attempted to effect a joint meeting before the General Assembly of the United Nations. But this plan too was rejected."

Dan Cooper goes on to say:

"I know a lot about Commander Valiant Thor (Val) from my sources (White Hats). He did in fact advise Ike for years, specifically on how to defeat the ICC/Nazi/Draco Alliance, and end their dominion over humanity. The Venetians (Commander Valiant Thor is a Venetian from the planet Venus in our solar system) themselves were/are very Christian. They were/are adamantly opposed to violence. They (Val Thor and some of his Venetian associates) were the ones that told Ike about the Sphere Beings Alliance (the Guardians) and they contacted the Guardians and submitted Ike's petition for their (the Guardian's) help to save humanity. There is so much more to tell about Val ...

... Val Thor merely advised Ike. His species, the Venetians, however, also signed a Non-Interference Agreement with the Draconian Empire, like so many other planets, throughout so many other galaxies. Val Thor is a rebel among his kind (the Venetians) and is protected directly by the Guardians. He has immunities like me, which have allowed him, like me, to advise, without fear of retribution from the ICC/Nazi/Draco Alliance. Val Thor did NOT speak to me. He spoke with the Guardians, though. The Guardians speak to me."

TARGETING AND ATTACKS

*"The Earth Alliance of today would not exist if President Eisenhower
had not understood the evil forces at large. In his wisdom he made sure
to assemble a group of white hat generals who could form the plan that
would eventually liberate earth's humanity. We are all part of that plan;
It's why we came. Those targeting Laura Magdalene Eisenhower with
false information and smear tactics want to stop disclosure. Their goal is
to thwart the power of the cosmic soul sauce Laura brings to the table—
that allows a healthy and inspired integration of true history with our
collective creative empowerment."*

– B.G., Facebook friend

Connecting to the different levels of ego, soul, Monad and Christos
Avatar represent the fullness of our DNA capacity to overcome anything that keeps us from healing and activating our true blueprint that can only
be achieved from within. When all this gets stabilized, it purges the heavy density, transforms wounds, clears the shadow selves and changes the nature of our
relationships, going beyond karmic entanglements and lower dynamics that are
unable to achieve a truly loving and balanced relationship. This process helps us
achieve better connections with others, but we move through many layers and
gatekeepers and a degree of relentless targeting to achieve this. My relationship
world was always a target, but I now find that my current partner and I have developed a level of immunity to these lower forces.

So it appears that in the face of attack and targeting, the act itself must be
a catalyst and reminder of the very thing they are attempting to rob and block
us from. The most threatening thing to them would be that we transcend all
attempts to derail and throw us off. This energy impacts the Earth and reflects
trinitized forms, which is the override frequency to vampiric energies.

Being targeted is a real thing. I could feel the hidden weaponry my whole
life and couldn't talk about it with anyone. Sometime later, experts in this field,
including medical intuitive and clairvoyant healers, validated its presence and
impact on my life. I began to learn a lot about geoengineering, weather modification, how humans and nature are being silently assaulted, and how those disclosing this type of information were mainly targeted and derailed. I had to learn
how to die and return to the same body to overcome this timeline where they
sought to control me. This process took over 20 years.

It was never just about me but my desire to assist the human race. I recognized that something huge was completed when I completed this long, ardu-
ous journey into the underworld that so many know all too well. But it in no
way meant that it would be smooth sailing from that moment on, far from it.

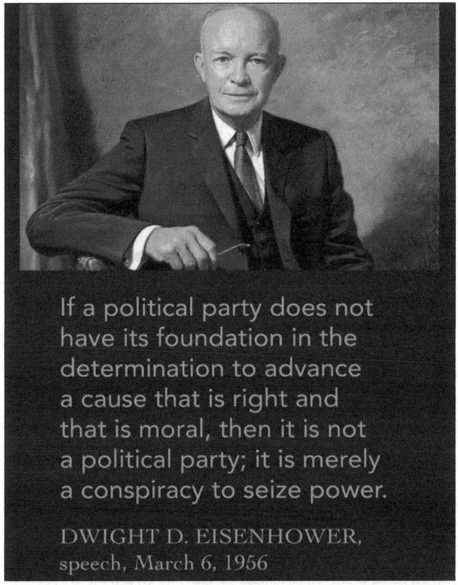

If a political party does not have its foundation in the determination to advance a cause that is right and that is moral, then it is not a political party; it is merely a conspiracy to seize power.

DWIGHT D. EISENHOWER,
speech, March 6, 1956

Eisenhower's quote that, to me, is just as powerful as his warning about the Military Industrial Complex! This is from a speech in 1956, and I feel it is significant because, by this time, he was already aware of how much he had lost control to MJ-12 and how his desire to do what is right and what is moral was overwhelmed by the looming threat of Deep State agendas that put their power above the presidency.

However, it was a step closer to embodying what was needed to handle all that lay ahead. Even to this day, the attacks and deep dives within to retrieve my strength in the face of it all continue. But it sure would be nice if humans would enter the soul matrix fully and be more heart-centered and loving because that is what we must never lose. We must never lose our capacity to see beyond all the tactics used to divide us and separate one another from what could be a beautiful unification and awakening.

We are here to heal and transform together. We must do all we can to resist negative ego, hatred, compliancy, tyrannical forces, and victim consciousness to the point where we can't see the truth anymore or the good intent of those doing all they can to help liberate this planet and humanity from inversions, dark weapons, deception and trickery.

The path that led me to the people involved in the hidden Mars agenda and my ability to see through it into our true galactic history, understanding ascension mechanics and the archetypal and astrological, became the very thing that helped me to transcend their controls and break free. It enabled me to access the strength and wisdom I needed to survive. I knew I was making decisions that would impact more than just my personal life as a guardian of the Organic Ascension timeline, assisting humanity to see that there is much more to the picture than we could have imagined.

We now face choices that will move us into an AI world or an organic, advanced, higher-dimensional Earth. If we choose the latter, we must draw it in by awakening it from within. AI, on the other hand, imitates reality, permitting something else to take over our process. It harms our soul's development and threatens to destroy all biological life by disconnecting us from our souls. The controller groups have entirely focused on this critical window period to interfere with our progress. Still, we need to understand AI more fully because once you start to get pulled into it, it is hard to reverse and get away from.

I began to understand alchemy and the elements we hold by feeling into the depths of the story and wounds of Mother Earth—how this planet became what it is and how we became who we are after our beginning as more highly advanced forms. Along with the Venus transits, we are pointing those inner elementals into the direction of Spirit so that it can hold dominion, versus allowing physical matter to limit and intimidate us, where we feel at the mercy of everything as if we have no say or control over the way the future unfolds.

What we align with depends on whether we are programmed or live from our authentic selves. Even if we aren't programmed, we might be wounded by the programs or confused by life in general as we feel into our intuition versus the things that try to think for us, projecting future scenarios or creating events that lead us to believe this is our reality. We may not know what to think as many cultures, general society, and the internet intermingle truth with so much disinformation. Control agendas influence how we are raised by distorting the highest expression of our roles. What we see in the media and governments is mostly propaganda and programming.

We are operating from what has been conditioned into us. What is working its way to the surface of our being, which is more organic and the essence of the divine, shows us a whole other world manifested from the inside out. Because, with the inner work, we can purify, which allows us to become conduits and embodiments of the universal energies, divine forces of nature and astrological shifts that open us up to more of who we are.

We vibrate at the same frequency as what we attract, but one philosophy cannot apply to all situations. Sometimes, we are attacked and fall into crisis because of the light we hold or because we threaten the control system. A crisis can suddenly open us up to returning home, but some don't see it that way. Some give more power to the things outside themselves, which tells them we don't have the inner resources to recover from something like disease, pain or trauma. We can always use outside assistance, but it isn't beneficial if it disempowers our innate abilities.

We are in a relationship with everything—nature, the cosmos, those we choose to form relationships with, and our own self. We will experience our ups and downs with others, but in crises or times of stress, do we find ourselves distancing, or are we bonding more and becoming a coherent team? Having space is essential but not to the point of neglect. Anger directed towards others can damage. Manipulation causes decay or a vampiric dynamic. It is bonding through compassion, empathizing, or seeking clarity and understanding that sets the foundation for union and the alchemical marriage. It is one of the most empowering antidotes we can embrace in these times, and it is one of the main driving forces for this monumental shift in the collective. Mastering our voices and the power behind our words sets soul alchemy in motion. Words are powerful.

Remember, we sank in density ("fell") from Harmonic Universe 2 (HU2), dimensions 4, 5 and 6. We existed in these higher dimensions and beyond because we held a higher frequency that was co-creative, alchemical and empowered. Yes, we lost that through hybridization and modifications to suit nefarious agendas, but we are now powerfully climbing our way back "home."

As Above, So Below

"Since we contain divine essence in our hearts—it is the Divine Masculine and Divine Feminine within us that needs to harmonize. This divine harmony must happen internally before we can create harmony and peace in the world.

The harmony and higher potential we achieve within, is reflected without. We as Creators, create the New Earth with this divine harmony. The main source of Divine Feminine energy is Gaia-Sophia. To me, Gaia is our Mother Earth, and Sophia is the Great Mother, or oversoul, to Gaia."

– Nancy Robbins, Elements Designs Collection

We can notice all these conditions in our personal lives by observing how negative ego sabotages us. When we feel an imbalance, we can radiate a much higher frequency by embracing both our masculine and feminine sides. We can also tell when we are off balance by what we attract to ourselves. Targeting and attack, though, happens, and it increases when we begin to move into our Galactic Chakras, attempting to stunt our growth and damage our self-esteem so that we turn the other way and stay stuck in this time loop.

The struggle to maintain that relationship in this lower density is what creates timeline wars. When we begin to succeed in embodying this type of thing, there is a psychic attack and some level of warfare. With our consciousness and intent, we can recover the pages of this union that exist in our ancient memory in soul remembrance. We can dismantle all that was put in place to keep it disconnected. In the higher planes and trinity, it is always in this union, while in the lower densities, it can go anywhere because of free will, but when it's anchored in the planet, the immune system is ready to shake things up. The Mother force is more grounded in the planet now, so what we will see from her will be very different from what we are used to. This planet is finally ready to shake off all parasitic influences, or at least many are prepared to get up and move on, following their soul lantern light of wisdom into a whole other level of her body.

We are in a relationship with life. It is our divine partner. We communicate constantly with it, and our dynamic with life plays a huge part in all that we manifest. It communicates to us, and we communicate back. Something is trying to mess up our relationship with it, of course. Those meddling archons and controllers, who stand as impostors and crappy partners, we need to ditch and kick to the curb and finally break up with. They keep us from our true love relationship with life, Earth, the cosmos and Spirit, where unconditional love dwells. When we are authentic and genuine to ourselves, we are more able to step into a relationship with all of life. We read signs, notice synchronicities, pick up on animal and plant medicine, and partake in the abundance of foods and herbs to heal us. We feel into all that is sacred, our soul comes to life and shines beyond falsity and toxicity, and we emit a frequency that benefits all to remind each to step into true love frequency. We advance our DNA. We learn how to honor ourselves, choose love and wisdom in our every expression and hold healthy boundaries. We release ourselves from being victims to a crap partner of the false matrix and raise its vibration by poking holes through the NET reversal until there is no way for an artificial timeline to sabotage us. Our devotion to true love is the boat ride into ascension.

TOGETHER AS ONE

"The mystery of the Divine Feminine speaks to us from within her creation. She is not a distant god in heaven, but a presence that is here with us, needing our response. She is the Divine returning to claim her creation, the real wonder of what it means to be alive. We have forgotten her, just as we have forgotten so much of what is sacred, and yet she is always part of us.

But now she needs to be known again, not just as a myth, as a spiritual image, but as something that belongs to the blood and the breath. She can awaken us to an expectancy in the air, to an ancient memory coming alive in a new way. She can help us to give birth to the Divine that is within us, to the oneness that is all around us. She can help us to remember our real nature."

– Llewellyn Vaughan-Lee

This period may find some men struggling with the influx of divine feminine and Venus energies, especially those still holding firm to the old ego conditioning of control and dominance, whether knowingly or not. Rest assured. It is not about women taking over but about union, the heart, and restoring her position as she brings balance, justice, transformation, nurturing, wisdom and intuition back to our Earthly experience.

Her force has the power to awaken the divine masculine into his highest embodiment, providing a safe container to let the old paradigm programming go because he knows that without her being in her true position of power, humanity will not survive. He also knows that she exists within him, as he exists within her. There is no threat to her power because they are a team. As she inspires him, he impregnates her with the vision of a peaceful world anchored by their alchemical union, planting seeds in the depths of darkness to create new realities. The Mother Womb becomes purified into the creative cauldron of regeneration, as the power of their intention and devotion kicks out all those who inhabit her realms, those who steal energy and rob souls to feed their dark agendas.

Their union restores the divine templates and inner divine blueprint, bringing all creatures, beings and elements into a conscious, knowing breath of oneness. It reawakens the true cosmic dance that doesn't need to struggle with power games but instead truly honors the beauty of their movements together, acting as a force field of light and protection around all who choose to know this within. It repairs the divorce, the separation, the corrupted gender roles that exploit the body and all that is sacred and which damage self-worth, integrity, access to higher consciousness, and the ability to initiate oneself organically into a place of self-acceptance, integrity, honor and co-creation with Gaia and cosmic forces.

So men do not feel threatened by the increasing and expanding energies. And women, do not fear your power because you remember being persecuted or killed in the past. Let's truly love and respect one another. This is our time to rise together as one!

WHAT IS SOUL?

If we want to know what our soul looks like, just look at nature, Earth, Air, Fire, Water, Aether and all the animal spirits we relate to at different times. We hold receptors and affinity with all the plants, herbs, fruits and veggies that are encoded to heal us. The whole process of decay, death, rebirth, alchemy, and transformation exists in nature and within our being. We continue to upgrade our DNA if we honor her beauty and foster our soul development, eventually becoming a Merkabah lightbody, able to come and go from the physical as we please, dropping light pellets on all who are trapped and seeking divine inspiration.

Nature is the world's soul, and we carry the same soul within. When we purify negative ego tendencies, we clear and purify our inner elements. Then, the Earth responds by taking us into higher dimensions of experience, where contamination no longer exists.

Multi-Earth, artwork by Sequoia. "The name Gaia has been used to describe the future earth in its 7D form in the Monad Matrix Universe. Our planet Earth exists in three main formed identities in this Universal Time Matrix. 3D Earth is called Earth or Terra, 5D Earth is Called Tara and 7D Earth is called Gaia." –Lisa Renee, Ascension Glossary; https://ascensionglossary.com/index.php/Gaia

The 13th Gate Mother Arc has been activated. It is impacting all ley lines and stargates positively. The 13 families hijacked this number and created so many wars that the Earth couldn't embody the Mother energy. Electrical Wars, Lemurian Holocaust, Atlantean Cataclysms, Nephilim Wars, World Wars, and on and on!

Well, you can't kill the souls, because we all come back again and again. Dark agendas may try and genetically modify us so we stay in zombie amnesia, but it's impossible to separate many of us from our soul and spirit. Now all we need to do is connect with Mother Earth, trust this ascension that is unfolding and starve the beast matrix. Even if we find ourselves unfortunate to be in the middle of it, our consciousness doesn't have to!

CO-CREATING AND INNER WORK

As we expand into our highest potential, we immediately nurture the needs of our lower chakras. When we don't, our growth is stunted and our lower chakras reveal un-wellness, whether physically, emotionally or ego. We then become compelled to do the inner work, as the health of our ego determines the kind of experience we will have. And when we do the work from the perspective of the collective, we encounter a whole other experience.

When we move into our hearts, we can reflect more easily on our priorities and successfully heal. The quality of our progress towards this is based on what we choose to empower with our precious life-force energy. It is delivered through our voice print and song and released into the environment.

If we get entangled in the effect and do not recognize the cause, the duality of war increases and the outer world remains distorted. If we focus on healing the root of the problem, we embody the antidote and don't need to think much further or go into survival and give our power away. The cause is an imbalance, cannibalistic parasitic systems we choose to stay locked into agreements with, toxic energies or people. From a historical and galactic level, this is due to our free will choices leading to the misuse of power and the contamination and manipulation of DNA, the elements and consciousness. The mind control used to separate us from Mother Earth, ourselves and each other distorts our relationship to sexual energy and union between the masculine and feminine. These are the very things we need to call back, work on and devote ourselves to. When we do, the rest will iron itself out. The more of us who cast our vote for the truth our soul understands and longs for, the sweeter life is bound to get!

We are going through the ultimate global detox. Things may still feel heavy. Difficult news may still present itself. There is a healing crisis that occurs when one is detoxing. But because unity, truth, love and wisdom are spreading like wildfire, a foundation for community and camaraderie has been paved along our way. As we navigate through the madness, we witness a massive purging. This alchemical process changes the substance down to the cellular level. Waking up to our truth can feel quite painful in our bodies. We may even experience physical discomforts and ailments, too, and an increased sensitivity to the pain-body vibration of another. But like any detox, like having the flu, you feel worse in the middle of the healing because the pathogens and old issues get illuminated. On the other side of this healing light, all is transformed and cleared.

Many more people will soon be ready for the next phase in this unfolding saga, riding waves of ascension in a world where real evils do exist and, thankfully, are now being eradicated from world control. Sometimes, it feels like it is moving at a snail's pace, but we hold the psychic and spiritual power to guide it along or even accelerate through powerfully focused intent. No matter what happens in the outer world, we must know this. Our focused intention and creative energy can take over the helm and sail this Ship of Humanity to better shores!

Raising the vibration of ourselves and the planet takes grounding and anchoring higher vibrational energy, merging the higher mind with the lower mind. Our epiphany, insights, inspirations, times of bliss, and deep appreciation for nature and each other can be anchored in our life experiences every day through gratitude and taking the time to adjust our lifestyles accordingly so that they can accommodate all the good that is streaming in. Without that, we can get blocked, ungrounded, and sabotaged, with archonic influences waiting in the

"Symbology of Tarot and Astrology" Adrienne Brown Art of Laura Eisenhower.

wings to exacerbate the situation and create drama, power struggles and further imbalance. Our higher nature and all it shows us must be more than a philosophy, fantasy, pipe dream or vision. It needs to become a way of life that we devote ourselves to so that we are not living a double life between our lower ego and our felt love, wisdom and divinity that we are.

The clarity and wisdom come along for integration, to inspire life changes for the better, not just for good moments and a feeling of having a good day. This is the work of shifting physical reality. This purifies us and helps us to create healthy boundaries and transmute toxicity. Our higher selves hold the bigger picture and desire to participate in the human experience fully and allow this to come through. It is true transformation, healing and awakening—it is true ascension! We then see how spirit holds dominion over matter instead of matter and lower density controlling and limiting us. When the negative comes along, a beautiful challenge is presented to us until we learn how to be empowered co-creators and artists with the elements and the vastness of our creative imaginations.

Insecurity shows itself when you hold latent gifts or higher potentials that are not fully embodied yet. It can make us feel as if we are lacking in something when the truth of the matter is that we are looking for the rest of ourselves, and until we find it, we feel incomplete. Following the sensations of insecurity is bound to guide you to all the parts and places where these hidden potentials lie to be retrieved. Let this sensation drive your quest to discover wholeness and self-intimacy rather than lack or "not good enough," which only reinforces behavior patterns that feed a false projection. There is no need to compare yourself to others unless it inspires you. Thinking someone is better off is the real illusion we face. When you fully embody your gifts and highest potential, only good feelings can come from it, and a greater appreciation of each other's uniqueness will catapult us into Unity Consciousness.

There is so much that is blatantly obvious yet can't be proven that people still cannot accept. So, the best thing we can do is start with the inner work to better cope with any distortions and remain open to all possibilities, including a potential bifurcation of timelines based on the choices in front of us. The more connected we are to our intuition and psychic abilities, the easier it will be to see the imposters and deceptions and move into this amazing shift fully present in our human body, Earth and consciousness.

These times are like an adventure into greater self-knowledge, awareness and a recognition of our ability to co-create this reality. Our creative power can serve and help bring us to our dreams or destroy us and cause decay. We are being pulled into processes that bring us face to face with our true selves, and everything we have become that isn't. The masks, the beliefs about ourselves that injure or over-inflate us, programs, traumas, pain and fear may be aspects of our experience. But it is all converging into a single point if we can let it, our sovereign and divine power. The inner work transforms us, and we see all density and weight lighten. We uncover things like unconscious patterning, programs and wounds undermining our health, relationships and creative abilities. What we bring to the light and out of the shadow can be released or transmuted into something else.

This is what is happening on the macro level, as information is being released from researchers, experiencers, whistleblowers and those who truly understand holistic and energy medicine. When we find our treasures, gifts and

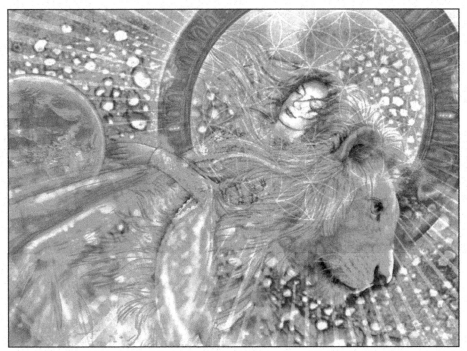

"Symbology of Dreaming, Stargate and the Lions Gate energy" Adrienne Brown Art of Laura Eisenhower.

abilities just waiting to come into fuller expression, we begin to step up more. We must call all parts back from whoever may be using them for negative reasons. Giving the higher aspects of ourselves a more dominant role and letting the lower aspects answer to this divine power is how we become real participants in global healing and strong vessels for the ascension energies to manifest. The division between higher and lower self and duality needs integration. Our willingness to be the living expression of what nature guides us towards and is in our DNA allows the happily-ever-after and true love story to unfold.

As we step more into our true authenticity, we vibrate at the higher frequencies of truth. We find synchronicities and magic more present and have an easier time hearing internal guidance from our higher self and spirit guides. To be authentic is to embrace your inner elements of Earth, Air, Fire, Water and Aether. It does no good to tuck away, limit our expression, or let accumulated contamination set in. We will want to find healthy channels for our expression, especially any rage or fire. However, judgments must be dropped and space held for unknown things to be brought into our conscious awareness.

In a world with so much toxicity, assault and injustice, it's understandable that depression, anger and anxiety show up. Thankfully, there are ways to work with it to gain wisdom from it rather than suffer and feel stuck and in the loop of guilt and shame. When we consciously devote ourselves to this path, we can do the energy maintenance work we need, stay aligned, and become more balanced and purified.

EMBODYING DIVINE TEMPLATE AND UNITY CONSCIOUSNESS

"…the sacred union of Jesus and his Bride once formed the cornerstone of Christianity…the blueprint of the Sacred Marriage, that the later (church) builders rejected, causing a disastrous flaw in Christian doctrine that has warped Western civilization for nearly two millennia."

Margaret Starbird, 'The Goddess in the Gospels'

We are in a time of recognizing the importance of bringing balance back to this Earth. As we do, we are becoming more aware of our DNA connection with the Earth grids and how our chakras connect us with the multi-dimensional cosmos. We are waking up to the macro/micro connections, the "as above, so below," and it is helping us see more clearly how we can harness our creative power to make positive change on this Earth.

The awakening process that will benefit us as humanity is embodying Unity Consciousness and sacred union of our masculine and feminine. This Earth was created within the pages of a cosmic love story, filled with tragedy, hope, calamities, battles and revelations. This planet was seeded as an ascension planet when the Goddess herself, the 13th stargate, morphed into the physical planet to help us access zero point energy and the Neutron Window. This brings us back to oneness with the Andromedan Galaxy, our original galactic core that was in oneness with our Milky Way system.

The imbalance is obvious, as evidenced by the predominant patriarchal systems that we have existed in for some time. We are learning to move beyond any agreements we may have made with it and their associated patterning. Never-ending wars to conquer and divide us are not holding up as easily when an urgency within makes itself known to tell us we better drop whatever it is and find a way to come together. As we illuminate the truth and walk its path, everything else falls away and is not allowed entry.

Truth is living a full experience, connecting to what is organic, our soul, and is aligned with Spirit. Determining what is true on the outside asks us to contemplate its validity until it either becomes obvious or there is proof that it does or does not belong. This is the process of discernment. Truth doesn't need any believers as it exists regardless. We don't need to get lost in the rabbit hole, but it does help to understand the conspiracies and how we have been played and manipulated. It will help us unplug from harmful influences and be conscious to call our power back, or at least pause long enough to evaluate. When we adjust our lifestyles to match our newfound revelations and values, we become active

Etch a Sketch. When I get really focused, I live to do this kind of artwork, one that disappears eventually.

and conscious participants in our ascension into higher Earth energies.

Our divine blueprint, the Christ Consciousness and the wisdom of Sophia is becoming more revealed to us. The exciting news is that our chakras and DNA strands connect with them. The stargates and multiple harmonic universes in the Time Matrix, including the Trinity and all it encompasses, connect with it, too.

There are many beings from other universes. Hybrids of all sorts exist. There are countless races, many of which have created control agendas that impact us. Some are more benevolent than others yet still rely on a degree of control over others. A prominent SSP whistleblower speaks about 22 different ET groups that have played a role in influencing our DNA and something like 900 different races interacting with the Secret Space Programs. We would be shocked if we knew the diversity we are dealing with here.

You can't screw up true love, and you can't force something to be what it's not. We live in a world where artificial constructs are generated by imitating the original. It can be quite confusing, and too often, we base our worth and how we respond on something false. Understandably, we sometimes get caught up in the illusory aspects. What we hold on to is often what we see around us, mistaking it as reality, far from what we need. What is found within are the seeds and our ultimate destination, full of developmental phases that never cease to unfold.

If we don't fully love ourselves, we become more susceptible to hatred coming at us until we notice more love in our lives than we thought possible, the smiles and support. But sometimes, it is like false lights or satellites beaming our way that we later realize had a self-serving agenda. Why we had its attention in the first place, to use and leverage us for their gain. All of these experiences ultimately lead us to seek out balance. There can be no stereotypes. It is either real or not, regardless of how one feels. It only matters if we can tell the difference and know who our true friends and partners are.

The artificial and genuine exist in the same space, like two ends of a pole. What we can see through and what we are orientated toward determines what we end up experiencing. Our inner conditions determine our reality. External realities not in alignment with our soul still exist, so we may still need to traverse them to reach the end of the pole we desire.

We either engage in radical truth, awareness and clear seeing, or wishful thinking and fear-based perceptions and projections. We experience the entire picture for a reason. If not, we have the free will to determine its meaning for us. This doesn't mean we deny the other's existence as long as we know we have a choice, and at some point, one must be made. No one is immune to soul-shattering experiences. We must only be willing to escape the tentacles of evil-wearing-a-mask. It is part of a great wake-up call that we shouldn't be crushed or intimidated by. In the end, we are only facing ourselves.

Choose one thing and accept the challenging aspects that come along with it. Then, realize that both sides promise a bit of challenge. Appreciate our changing natures. Like the weather and climate, we are asked to pay attention and be prepared through awareness, intuition and insight.

In the end, love is stronger, and imitations eventually expire. True love defies all matrix programs. Know your truth first—your vibration and way of being—not an explanation of it. It is where all the answers of the universe are. If you experience delays and obstacles, know that true love can never be destroyed. So much deconstruction must occur for the truth to reveal itself. As long as we trust that these greater forces hold the upper hand and patience, it can feel like a long hike in the woods with many interesting and beautiful things to observe.

Ocean Art. Some of my artwork.

Perhaps we can forget about the destination we are striving to reach and instead notice what shows up along the path, knowing that eventually, when we least expect, what we have always sought to find and truly longed for shows up!

I feel the love that Ike had for Mamie in the harshest times on Earth is an example of what can help us through turbulent times—pure love. Whether we have someone in our lives or are just nurturing our self-love and connection with nature, Spirit, Father/Mother, Christ-Sophia, love wins this war and is a force stronger than anything, and to me, is the truth we must awaken to.

> *"Darling,*
>
> *Starting tomorrow I have a series of trips that will last without interruption from six to ten days. So if you have a lapse in arriving letters, don't jump at the conclusion that I don't want to write—I'll simply have no opportunity to pick up a pen.*
>
> *I'm a bit stymied in my mind as to subject to write about. So many things are taboo—and the individual with whom you are acquainted (including myself) go along in accustomed ways. Mikey is a jewell. I often wonder how I existed without him.*
>
> *Anyway the real purpose of this note was to say I'm well, and love you as much as ever, all the time, day and night. Your picture (in a gilt frame) is directly in front of my desk. I look at you all the time. Another is in my bed room. Loads of love—always.*
>
> *Yours Ike."*
>
> *– Eisenhower's letter to Mamie*

This love is exemplified through the art that some of my friends have created using my photographs. It amazes me that they would even take the time, and I appreciate the symbology! It is also poured into the art I have created over time. One favorite was done with the Etch A Sketch, which represents a metaphor in my life of lovingly creating something and then releasing and letting it go—since when you shake it, the drawing disappears!

THE LOVE OF THE MOTHER

Blessings to all mothers of this Earth who embody the unconditional love of our planet. Not only the mothers of children but anyone birthing creatively or being a nurturing force in someone else's life. May we fully embrace the unconditional love of the Mother, which comforts us in our darkest hours. Her love is how we thrive and blossom. All who embody the heart of the Divine Mother impart wisdom and remind us that we are not alone. Gratitude to the Mother for her ability to forgive those who turn the other way. Blessings and unconditional love to the mother who holds guilt, pain or regrets, and may she learn to love herself, find her inner beauty, and release herself from the pain and turmoil when life has not supported her or where others have made her feel inadequate and less than divine. May this mother find her balance and transformation.

May she find inner peace and awaken to her divine majesty. Blessings to all the children or adults who have not had a strong mother force in their lives or have been wounded by their mothers. May they find unconditional love from the Great Cosmic Earth Mother and their own Goddess aspects within, to feel empowered and strong. May they find a healing path that will allow self-worth to grow and all fears to subside into pure love. Blessings to the mothers who wished to bear children but couldn't—you remain a powerful creator and mother force. May you find joy in nurturing and embracing the journey as is, knowing it is perfect. Blessings to the mother force within men and the men who honor their inner feminine and the women in their lives. Gratitude to those who are sensitive to all mothers' processes and who hold space for empowerment and healing.

The Window Period

"Why do we follow Sophia, what is her attraction for us? The fact that she has made the descent into the seven levels of hell, that she knows and shares in our pain and exile? Or do we follow her because she goes to prepare a home for us in her temple OF seven pillars? Many of us find her here and now, practically and skillfully using THE seven gifts of the Spirit to transform our lives alchemically."

– Caitlin Matthews, the Goddess Sophia

We can bring the consciousness of the higher realms to Earth. We can choose the vibration of everlasting peace to wash through us. This is the possibility of the ascension window period. This is the potential of this collective, high-frequency, planetary vibrational occurrence, which can resolve all the wars, diseases and symptoms of imbalance. Many are already initiated into this shift, while others still endure the karmic journey of awakening.

A critical number of awakened humans is needed to manifest the full planetary shift. What is the whole concept of the 144,000 or the "Hundredth Monkey Effect?" When we can reach a critical number, the shift will happen naturally, like a healthy immune system wiping out all illness, conflict, environmental problems and global disasters. The Earth herself is participating in this transition. The intelligent energy of spirit will once again overcome the limits of 3D matter, break the illusory chains of death and suffering, and finally allow peace and well-being to be experienced for everyone on Earth.

The first step is shifting from a service-to-self (STS) to a service-to-others (STO) orientation. It doesn't matter what race, bloodline, nationality, or religion you are or what line of work you are in. Only two main types exist: STS self-oriented beings and STO other-oriented beings. STS beings are predominately oriented in negative ego, greed, power, domination and control. STO beings are predominately oriented in universal love, unity, and service to humanity and Mother Earth. It also includes working on oneself to be a greater healing force for the world. Our soul journey tells a far greater story about why we chose to incarnate into certain families and scenarios. Still, we have a choice whether to embody Unity Consciousness. It is the force capable of healing the planet, transforming humanity and healing our ancestral lines.

The Earth has a specific plan that humans are naturally in tune with. That is how we evolve. We have come to where we are now, not only technologically speaking but also using science to manipulate our ability to reproduce or influence life. Our connection to our political evolutions and learning from other generations and ancestors about family patterns and our place, purposes and creativity in life walks closely with the specific unfolding that can assist us in our awakening. It reveals our connection with the whole planet and gives meaning to the shifting ages and changes. By having to fall back and rely on only ourselves, possibly through some extreme loss or shift, we can open to greater insight if we don't fall into apathy and helplessness.

We may ask ourselves why everything external is letting us down and betraying us. For those who feel this as a constant theme, it is time to embrace the journey into the dark shadow aspects of self to find one's internal treasures while moving through blocks, resistance, fear and insecurity. Taking on this challenge is key to living in more wholeness and mindfulness about how creative our thought forms are and how out of control things can get when we run on auto-pilot or take in too much from the outside world to define our self-worth and our future trajectory. We are the ones to create this. It is our cauldron of creation, our womb energy that gives birth, that needs to discern what to take in and what to reject because we ultimately birth our reality from thoughts, ideas and visions. We must be impeccable to keep them aligned with our truth and the greater universal forces, cosmic and natural law, that are not inverted. It connects with our intuition and ability to nurture ideas and exists within both men and women. This is what we are reclaiming. Without this reclamation, it remains unexplored and subjected to take over, to be used and exploited by others who wish this power for their own gain. This is the darkness that must be embraced so that lower forces outside us don't attempt to control this place of power.

Finally, humans now have access to the morphogenetic fields embodying the blueprint of the divine plan of the Mother Earth encoded in our DNA. Humans can now begin to understand her hidden history and human lineage and the process of ascending a species and planetary body, which are absolutely connected.

Divine Mother Earth Time. A show I do with my friend Marisa Acocella.

This is where we can heal and become strong enough to reject anything that diverts our attention away from this—the root of disease and mental and emotional imbalance and afflictions. Those things enable a future scenario we do not need to consent to. This is also the growth period that our body is giving us reminders to get back on track to look into why the pain, affliction or dis-ease is showing up. It is all about frequency and shifting perspective by exploring the soul and its experiences rather than the monkey mind or ego trying to contend with it, which often results in handing power away without questioning what is being sold to us.

CLAIMING SOVEREIGNTY AND LIBERATION

Right now is a wonderful opportunity just to step back and embrace our unbelievable progress. Increasingly strong ascension energies are only going to keep building and intensifying. These are powerful times to claim full liberation and sovereignty, but it starts with removing the shackles and letting go of the negative patterns of our bad habits, which hold us hostage to the very thing we want to break free from. Releasing ourselves fully from this cycle is the greatest victory of all. We must cut the chords with the old paradigm and divorce ourselves from the imposters.

The alien energies that showed up in my life pushed me to connect the dots, using mythology and astrology, to understand a story in my soul that was helping me to weave myself back together. My work in the world now is to help people understand these concepts so that synergy and connecting the puzzle pieces can be established through all levels of society, in politics, education, industry, philosophy, creative arts, science, physics, the imagination and the symbols and archetypes of soul. Myth and archetypes exist in our subconscious and, like a snowball, will grow into an avalanche that will consume us if we do not give them the recognition, within and outside ourselves, that they deserve.

Waking up is not some new revelation. Many of us have known who we are all along and have been very awake, totally disoriented in this artificial world. The challenge is fully bringing one's true nature to the surface and not allowing oneself to buy into the projections others may throw, feeling insecure for not fitting in or trapped. Many have allowed their treasures and uniqueness to become a curse and a personal prison. We liberate all when we unlock our shackles, barriers, and resistances and step into our power and freedom!

Every time we break down, we find an entry point to our deepest treasures. Every time we lose our way, we have an opportunity to become master navigators through the wilderness of life. Every time we move through adversity with a little humor and faith in ourselves, we open a portal into our magic and miracle vibration. Every time we are ready to give up, we find more strength to reach the peak of the highest mountain. When we go through loss on any level, we comprehend the larger picture, tap into the abundance of the universe, and are reminded of our connection to everything, including the unseen worlds.

We become empowered whenever we speak up and do not hide who we are. Every time we rise above the negative ego and align with our higher self, we find our divinity and transmute and transform this lower density. Every dis-ease we courageously face teaches us how to find balance and hone our intuition, showing us what needs to be embraced or released. Every mistake we make helps to reroute us to the right action. When we think more about self-love rather than the love others can give, we flourish and find strong boundaries.

Everything we are willing to overcome connects us with the regenerative power of nature. When we drop the judgments about what we are going through, we begin to embody the wisdom to heal ourselves, and we can also assist with the healing of others. Struggles can be a blessing when they help us to bust through the many layers of self until we reach our higher self, which then enables us to crack through the many layers of this human experience until we reach the truth about what is occurring on this planet and how to shift it. As painful as it can be, it is far better than being unconscious and asleep.

As long as we can stay inspired and not lose touch with our passions and dreams, we will have all the fuel we need to manifest our deepest soul longing. Pain is our way of sounding the alarm so that we can rise and expand into our multi-dimensional nature and authentic self with both feet on the ground. This is the journey and adventure into reclaiming our birthright and freedom.

Like an earthquake, the potential energy of this shift brings the release of tension and restores harmony while showing everyone involved a part of themselves that is hard to face. Harmony isn't created by holding on to old beliefs or demanding that others see it your way. A person who seeks control and refuses

Cosmic Mother Rising. A show I do with my friend Phoenix Rising Aurora.

to be open to an evolving view makes harmony impossible. Every obstacle we overcome is a deeper initiation into our divine potential. Everything we survive certifies us as a guide for others. Every time we get over our fears, we release the resistance to realizing our inner bliss. Every time we cry endless tears, we water the seeds of thousands of dreams.

The freedom of exploration, spiritual fulfillment and well-being are not just far-off ideals. They are attainable now. When we are inspired by our highest imaginations and confident in our abilities to rise above the conditions that threaten humanity and the planet, we can navigate our dreams, explore the universe, and discover how to exist in the vastness of the ethereal and physical worlds with protection, creative freedom and spiritual power.

To Live or Die

"The law is living word of living God to living prophets for living men. In everything that is life is the law written. You find it in the grass, in the tree, in the river, in the mountain, in the birds of heaven, in the fishes of the sea; but seek it chiefly in yourselves. For I tell you truly, all living things are nearer to God than the scripture which is without life. God so made life and all living things that they might by the everlasting word teach the laws of the true God to man. God wrote not the laws in the pages of books, but in your heart and in your spirit. They are in your breath, your blood, your bone; in your flesh, your bowels, your eyes, your ears, and in every little part of your body. They are present in the air, in the water, in the earth, in the plants, in the sunbeams, in the depths and in the heights."

– *The Essene Gospel of Peace*

Extinction or enlightenment is upon us. Denying our spiritual path is the root cause of potential extinction. Enlightenment is an internal force that can be translated into the larger world. We can choose this by ridding ourselves of negative energy and the tendency to sabotage our truth and be controlled by others. We will then be filled with the unconditional love of Spirit and the creative wisdom of nature. We can improve our lifestyles, habits, thoughts and relationships and become the bliss, peace and joy for which we yearn. It won't be just a passing feeling. It will be the reality of the Golden Age.

We are all Earth's inhabitants. We must learn to share, work together and create stronger bonds. I hope it won't take long for most humans to put down the weapons, the judgments, dramas and distractions that take us away from this goal. The part in us that is unity, the Christ-Sophia divine oneness within, where we are equal and united, must be celebrated and recognized by all of us for balance and peace to truly prevail on this planet.

The deep roots of the Earth and the dark abyss are the Mother's womb, and Venus marks the path of the Mother's heart. Through our deaths and resurrections, we continue to live out these archetypes, turn with the cycles of life, and the moving nature has shown us toward victory and completion.

The dark is the soil, the womb of the Mother, the light is the Christ Consciousness within, that become seeds, they fall into the dark to birth higher realities and our tears of joy for love and sorrow for the pain and suffering, waters these seeds and our essence the sun, creates growth. Life requires that we feel, imagine, experience, and dream and that we integrate duality like polarity in a dance or a merging that is alchemical and transformational. Don't fear the dark. That is your power and a great catalyst for self-mastery. The more we fear it, the more something else is in control. We must embrace the wholeness of all we are and are made of to ascend. The negative ego aspects of self get purified when we get in touch with our depths, light, and divine template of sacred union.

Our gifts are each other's. We can be good at anything if the passion is there. True Oneness is diversity in harmony. True Source is unconditional love, not judgment. We are given opportunities to correct things and bless things. Don't settle for less than you deserve, and know everything hellish will pass as you come to realize you are in a transformation process and can be the alchemist. The Earth's foods, herbs and animals are medicine and healers, our soul reflected back, capable of meeting all of our needs. Nothing can stop us. We are the power of immunity over disease, awareness and divine power over attack. We have the vastness of the creative imagination and are the artists of our destiny. Don't let anything else in. We can have the boundaries and inspiration to soar into the beyond with both feet on the ground!

The Rebel Collective. A show I do with my friend Drago Reid.

ALTERNATIVE 4

There are far more benevolent ET races than malevolent ones, but we must understand the full picture to tell the difference, protect our human rights and achieve our highest potential. We have abilities beyond our wildest imagination. It is time we recognize the benevolent forces and vastness of our multi-dimensional cosmos and recognize that we are mirrors of multi-dimensional beings. We must also recognize the contributions of others who have healing solutions, safe technologies and factual truths about what is happening, who have been largely ignored and need our support. By individually clearing ourselves of the programs, manipulations and controls, we can reverse the damage that has been done.

Alternatives 1-3 chorded us to unknown things done in secrecy, usually through scenarios under the guise of being "for our benefit" and "in the event of a catastrophe." That is, catastrophes that were engineered, easily provoked and simulated through weather modification and dark technologies, like HAARP, which can create super storms and disasters.

In stark contrast, my Alternative 4 scenario is all about aligning with the Organic Ascension timeline and the divine birthright of our incredible human potential as a unified force working with the higher dimensional races of the cosmos. To accomplish this, we must be the victors over the agendas that seek to conquer and divide us all. Thankfully, the groundwork was successfully laid during the 2012-2017 Stellar Activation Cycle window period, ensuring our success as we now write the script for our hero's journey.

Many dark agendas still attempt to control and divide us, but they won't stand if our differences are seen as gifts. These gifts will be hard to appreciate if we continue to let politics, religion and the choices we make about our health keep us in a low vibration of judgment and attack.

An excerpt from Ike's Speech:

"We pray that peoples of all faiths, all races, all nations, may have their great human needs satisfied; that those now denied opportunity shall come to enjoy it to the full; that all who yearn for freedom may experience its spiritual blessings; that those who have freedom will understand, also, its heavy responsibilities; that all who are insensitive to the needs of others will learn charity; that the scourges of poverty, disease and ignorance will be made to disappear from the Earth, and that, in the goodness of time, all peoples will come to live together in a peace guaranteed by the binding force of mutual respect and love."

Since my great-grandfather first spoke of it 50 years ago, the Military Industrial Complex has thrived on official state secrecy. Even as disclosure happens, it will no doubt continue to be manipulated, never fully revealing what has been done behind our backs for all these years or why secrecy has continued to flourish. Yet, disclosure is inevitably happening among us nonetheless. As we understand and integrate other valuable truths, we will become protected against disclosure being used to introduce false concepts that will draw us further into the web of deceit.

Fifty years after President Eisenhower warned the American people about the Military Industrial Complex, society is finally preparing to disclose the fruits of its 50-year, Strangelovian departure from sanity, including the introduction of human robots that will act as weapons of war, humans being weaponized through mind control, the weather being controlled and even a faked war with an ET race using hologram technology that has existed for decades. All this is possible, and much of it is well underway.

It's time for us all to move forward and clear the junk of the past, live in full integrity, work on achieving balance and harmony, fill our being with the golden rays of Source universal love and fully own the power to break free of all that has held us back.

As far as what the rest (majority) of the human population needs to do, it is too much to cover in this book. But in "Messages From the Guardians," Dan Cooper shares this:

"The Guardians (also the Sphere Beings Alliance) told me that the Earth Alliance (also the BRICS Alliance now; but, including 85% of the world's population later) defeats the ICC/Nazi/Draco Alliance, and soon thereafter that

News Evolution. My collaboration with Patty Greer and Alfred Lambremont Webre.

happens, the Trials begin. It is important to understand that the Trials do NOT begin until we (85% of the people along with the Earth Alliance) have defeated our slavers, the ICC/Nazi/Draco Alliance; and, that the Trials have NOT begun yet because we did NOT win the War against them yet. We cannot win the war until the people (85% of them) start acting together.

The Guardians spent a lot of time describing to me what transpires at those Trials.

Every single one of them (all ICC/Nazi/Draco Alliance personnel) and all of their collaborators, get put up on Trial for the crimes that they committed (or, facilitated; or, aided and abetted in) against humanity. The Guardians provide the evidence for each person's Trial. Essentially, the Guardians take the court (the jury, the panel of judges, the accused, and the attorneys) back to the time and place of every crime that that person committed so that they (the jury, the panel of judges, the accused, and the attorneys) can witness those crimes being committed for themselves. It doesn't matter how sweet those people might appear to be, they will be sentenced for all the crimes that they committed against humanity.

For each life that they took, or aided and abetting in the taking, they will receive one lifetime sentence. If the sentence is a 1000 lifetimes, they (their souls) will be placed in clones, a 1000 times over, to insure that they are punished for every single crime against humanity that they caused or aided and abetted in causing. Every sentence is a prison sentence. Many sentences will also include hard labor for lifetimes. There is NO chance of parole. There is NO chance of receiving a reduced sentence for defecting, after the window to do so has passed.

That window will soon pass. Turning State's evidence has no relevance when acquiring evidence is NOT an issue, as is the case with these Trials."

Look for more information to continue coming through other channels and future books. Until then, continue doing your due diligence to understand who the real enemy is and what you can do to protect yourself. These times are filled with false narratives, propaganda and fear tactics that seek to disable one's ability to thrive and uncover the truth of who we really are. This is a most necessary step to prepare for what is to come with the complete restructuring of life on Earth as we know it. Let's join with the Earth Alliance and the Guardians' presence and do our part to help.

FINAL WORDS

Part of our challenge and task is learning how to manage our minds and emotions in a primarily negative world. We are far greater than this matrix that has plugged into our chakras and energetic circuitry. But sometimes, we need clarification about where the borders exist between the matrix and what lies beyond it.

Along with Mother Earth, we are the ones who hold the positive aspect of this experience, and we are the guardians of the Positive Ascension Timeline. We are going through this as the harmonized divine feminine and masculine within. We follow that internal guidance when aligned with our truth frequency and intuition.

If we can relate to the part of ourselves not reflected in current society, deep within us as an independent epiphany and gnosis, and if we can refuse to get entangled in the lower frequencies of negativity, like misery, despair, suffering, anger, greed, ignorance, pride, jealousy, addiction, etc., then we are allowing divine light to stream into the circuitry of our being and Gaia. Like the seven deadly sins, we need to go into the dark night of the soul, pass all the gatekeepers in our chakra energy centers, and turn them into the seven virtues.

We will then open up to our Galactic Chakras and illuminate our "junk" DNA as a treasure to retrieve and discover. From here, transmutation of our energies that have gotten locked into the false replica creation that is seeded with evil intent is possible, as it then reveals the true pure goodness and beauty of the Organic Creation and God/Goddess, Father God/Mother God and the integration of polarity and union that creates the Christ-Sophia template. This is how we assist in opening natural stargates and clearing wormholes of inorganic entities. It is encoded in the land and in us, and to change the world is to change how we operate in it, to release ourselves of the imposters and embrace the true love story that exists within. To break up with the abuser and release ourselves from the old paradigm and tyrannical authority into the reunion with the twin flame spark that seeded creation and our divine connection with this ascending planet. Who holds this as she expands into the fullness of her higher harmonic universes and gives us all the medicine we need while guiding us through her many cycles, seasons and cosmic alignments that move the physical planet forward into initiations for us to experience and grow from.

It is very easy to give into these lower energies since it is a vibration held by those in power, and they target us in extreme ways through dark technologies. We have been cheated, abused, robbed, controlled, manipulated and lied to. We have been traumatized and shattered by our losses, witnessing harm to all we hold sacred.

It is hard to embody such high energy in the face of all of this. But be inspired by what is beyond, rather than sink into negativity, because we believe this is all we have. Once we can accept that this is a Virtual Reality Game that our body is partly designed to be plugged into, we can begin the process of freeing ourselves and becoming more empowered to not fall into the pits and the traps that have been set for us strategically for thousands of years. Focusing on this assists in creating the most profound Divine Justice, enabling a backlash of huge proportions to all those who need it most for their own awakening.

Our strength in continuing to rise above it all, replenishing ourselves and regenerating in the field of pure spirit and remembrance is the key. Honoring each other and our relationships and bringing the best of ourselves forward means having true devotion to counteracting all negative tendencies by choosing to be conscious communicators, dreamers and creators.

Throughout this journey, I have had the honor and pleasure to co-create with many talented and inspiring people, and I would like to mention some of them here.

I co-host three podcasts with friends with whom I've made a deep connection. They include Divine Mother Earth Time with Marisa Acocella, a cartoonist who is the author of "The Big She-Bang – The Herstory of the Universe" as well as other books; Cosmic Mother Rising with Rising Phoenix Aurora, founder of A.U.R.A Hypnosis Healing and author of "Galactic Soul History of the Universe;" and the Rebel Collective with Drago Reid, a QHHT practitioner who developed extraordinary abilities after a motorcycle crash and Near Death Experience (NDE).

Other collaborations include Seth Leaf Pruzansky, author of "Fight to Enlight," who has overcome incredible adversities and is connected with some life-changing medicines and Tourmaline Sacred Living Spring Water; A show called News Evolution with Patty Greer, a filmmaker and expert in Crop Circles; Alfred Lambremont Webre, a Futurist, Tribunal Judge, Lawyer and author of "Exopolitics: Politics, Government, and Law in the Universe;" and finally Dr. Sharnael

Wolverton-Sehon, a naturopathic doctor, minister, author of "The Science of Miracles" and other books, who teaches on Divine Health and the Human Body.

I used to do a show with David Nino Rodriguez called Dark to Light. It got censored from Patreon, and I have been permanently banned from YouTube because my message of love, healing, unity, and desire to explore deep topics and seek out helpful healing tools and modalities is just not welcomed. Exposing all I know about what has really become of this country and world violates "community standards," while what I see as harmful content is still out there. It is something out of our hands. It appears that only they have the "authority" to pick and choose what should enter the minds and consciousness of humanity.

We need to stand strong and not consent to such a violation of our basic rights, freedom of expression, and access to valuable resources that reveal our greater choices, opportunities and areas of our minds we can expand into that can help co-create a more beautiful future for ourselves and future generations. Fortunately, many have created platforms that are censorship-free. But this is a war on our minds and spiritual warfare. We have it in us to not compromise ourselves anymore.

David, a former American heavyweight boxer, has become such a powerful force in the world. He wrote a book called, "When the Lights Go Out: From Survivor to Champion." He has faced unbelievable challenges and adversity and turned it all around. Sharing these kinds of stories can help remind us of the power of the human spirit, which never gives up or gives in.

Here is David, in his words, commenting about these times:

"We are at the very tail end of the old system. I can feel it throughout humanity. Call it the coming shift, apocalypse, ascension or whatever... There has to be some kind of mass event coming. I know each of you feel it as well. It's almost like a purgatory feeling and each of us are either getting ready to be called on or left behind. The energy definitely can't be ignored."

My message is about the power of the human spirit, healing and unifying, and protecting future generations from utter confusion around things such as their gender. I hope that we all express our truth from within, learn to love the body we were given and understand what it is here to teach us. All the discomforts, blocks and pain are asking to be seen instead of ignored, covered up or escaped. We can live on a more soul-centered level beyond indoctrination and social engineering, moving beyond what comes at us through the TV, our phones, and what society throws at us. We can find the courage to look at what is really taking place so that we no longer support this dark agenda's power over the world or fall for its many disguises of false benevolence seeking to gain your trust while "flashing" you with its disturbing underbelly.

There is so much more to awaken to and to protect and acknowledge. So many are being silenced and censored as they expose this vital information to humanity, who are smeared, ridiculed and misrepresented. The more you can see things for yourself versus being told what to think, the more we can rise and overcome this attack on awakening our human potential and divine birthright.

This time around, our souls came in, not to play the lower matrix game but to end it once and for all. Now is the time of purification and transcendence. It is The Great Awakening! Envision the world you wish to live in and enjoy your journey to *Awakening the Truth Frequency*!

FOOTNOTES

INTRODUCTION

#1 Lisa Renee and her Energetic Synthesis material, *https://energeticsynthesis.com/*

#2 Ashayana Deanne's Freedom Teachings, *https://www.arhayas.com/*

CHAPTER 1

#3 Eisenhower and the Earth Alliance, Ike's Force: Eisenhower's parting speech on the danger of the Military Industrial Complex, *https://www. eisenhowerlibrary. gov/research/online-documents/farewell-address*

#4 Dan Cooper: Unacknowledged Secret Access Programs (USAPs) of the United States, *https://en.wikipedia.org/wiki/Special_access_program*

#5 Stellar Activation Cycle: Lisa Renee's Ascension Glossary, *https://ascensionglossary.com/*

CHAPTER 3

#6 Artificial Tree of Life, or Tree of Death, Satanic Ritual Abuse (SRA) Artificial Tree of Life, *https://ascensionglossary.com/index.php/Artificial_Tree_of_Life*

#7 Not Junk DNA: Polarity integration, Integration of Polarity, *https://ascensionglossary.com/index.php/Polarity_Integration; https://ascensionglossary.com/index.php/)*

CHAPTER 10

#8 Agent X and the Aviary; Artificial Telepathy website, *https://artificialtelepathy. blogspot.com/2006/06/*

CHAPTER 11

#9 What Really Happened—Unconditional Surrender Agreement: Reversed time, *https://youtu.be/FgWgsstTx-8*

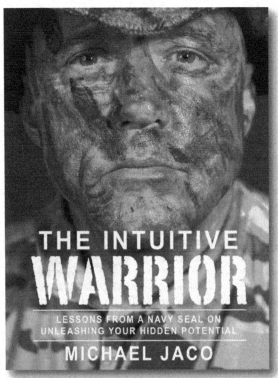
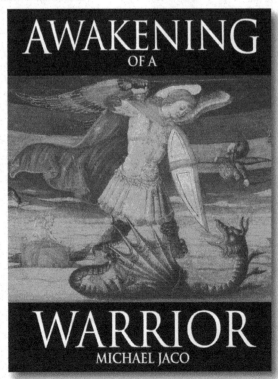

LEO ZAGAMI BOOKS FROM CCC PUBLISHING

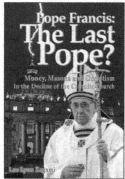

Pope Francis: The Last Pope?: *Money, Masons and Occultism in the Decline of the Catholic Church*

– by Leo Lyon Zagami

Perfect for anyone interested in prophecies about the end times, Pope Francis: The Last Pope reveals the truth about the last Pope and the darkness that may follow him; fascinating investigations into the gay lobby; Freemasonry; the Jesuit agenda; and, the legend of the White Pope, the Black Pope, and how Benedict's resignation may fulfill an ancient prophecy.

$16.95 :: 224 pages   paperback 978-1888729542

... all eBooks priced $8.99

Kindle: 978-1888729566; PDF: 978-1888729559
ePub: 978-1888729573

Confessions of an Illuminati, Volume I: *The Whole Truth About the Illuminati and the New World Order*

– 2nd EDITION; by Leo Lyon Zagami

From the OTO's infiltration of Freemasonry to the real Priory of Sion, this book exposes the hidden structure of the New World Order; their occult practices; and their connections to the intelligence community and the infamous Ur-Lodges.

$17.95 :: 408 pages   paperback 978-1888729870

... all eBooks priced $9.99

Kindle: 978-1888729894; PDF: 978-1888729887
ePub: 978-1888729900

Confessions of an Illuminati, Volume II: *The Time of Revelation and Tribulation Leading up to 2020*

– by Leo Lyon Zagami

Since the Second Vatican Council, the hierarchy of power emanating from the Jesuits in Rome and the Zionist's in Jerusalem, united by a secret pact, have been manipulating world powers and using economic hitmen to create a unified one-world government.

$17.95 :: 380 pages   paperback 978-1888729627

... all eBooks priced $9.99

Kindle: 978-1888729658; PDF: 978-1888729634
ePub: 978-1888729641

Confessions of an Illuminati, Volume III: *Espionage, Templars and Satanism in the Shadows of the Vatican*

– by Leo Lyon Zagami

Take a unique and personal journey into the secretive world of the Dark Cabal. Explore a variety of cryptic topics and learn the truth about the mythical Knights Templars, the Jesuits, and their mastery of the Vatican espionage game.

$17.95 :: 336 pages   paperback 978-1888729665

... all eBooks priced $9.99

Kindle: 978-1888729696; PDF: 978-1888729672
ePub: 978-1888729689

The Invisible Master: *Secret Chiefs, Unknown Superiors, and the Puppet Masters Who Pull the Strings of Occult Power from the Alien World*

– by Leo Lyon Zagami

Leo Zagami's groundbreaking study of aliens and UFOs explores where we come from and which mysterious figures have guided humanity's political and religious choices. From the prophets to the initiates and magicians, all ages have drawn from a common source of ultra-terrestrial and magical knowledge, passed down for millennia. This text reveals the identity of the unknown superiors, secret chiefs, and invisible masters who have guided Freemasonry, the Illuminati, and others.

$17.95 :: 380 pages   paperback 978-1888729702

... all eBooks priced $9.99

Kindle: 978-1888729733; PDF: 978-1888729719
ePub: 978-1888729726

Sacred Places North America: 108 Destinations

– 2nd EDITION; by Brad Olsen

This comprehensive travel guide examines North America's most sacred sites for spiritually attuned explorers. Spirituality & Health reviewed: "The book is filled with fascinating archeological, geological, and historical material. These 108 sacred places in the United States, Canada, and Hawaii offer ample opportunity for questing by spiritual seekers."

$19.95 :: 408 pages paperback: 978-1888729139

... all Ebooks priced at $9.99

Kindle: 978-1888729252; PDF: 978-1888729191
ePub: 978-1888729337

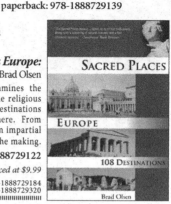

Sacred Places Europe: 108 Destinations – by Brad Olsen

This guide to European holy sites examines the most significant locations that shaped the religious consciousness of Western civilization. Travel to Europe for 108 uplifting destinations that helped define religion and spirituality in the Western Hemisphere. From Paleolithic cave art and Neolithic megaliths, to New Age temples, this is an impartial guide book many millennium in the making.

$19.95 :: 344 pages paperback: 978-1888729122

... all Ebooks priced at $9.99

Kindle: 978-1888729245; PDF: 978-1888729184
ePub: 978-1888729320

Sacred Places of Goddess: 108 Destinations – by Karen Tate

Readers will be escorted on a pilgrimage that reawakens, rethinks, and reveals the Divine Feminine in a multitude of sacred locations on every continent. Meticulously researched, clearly written and comprehensively documented, this book explores the rich tapestry of Goddess worship from prehistoric cultures to modern academic theories.

$19.95 :: 424 pages paperback: 978-1888729115

... all Ebooks priced at $9.99

Kindle: 978-1888729269; PDF: 978-1888729177
ePub: 978-1888729344

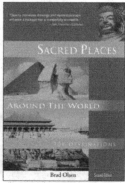

Sacred Places Around the World: 108 Destinations

– 2nd EDITION; by Brad Olsen

The mystical comes alive in this exciting compilation of 108 beloved holy destinations. World travelers and armchair tourists who want to explore the mythology and archaeology of the ruins, sanctuaries, mountains, lost cities, and temples of ancient civilizations will find this guide ideal.

$17.95 :: 288 pages paperback: 978-1888729108

... all Ebooks priced at $8.99

Kindle: 978-1888729238; PDF: 978-1888729160
ePub: 978-1888729313

World Stompers: A Global Travel Manifesto

– 5th EDITION; by Brad Olsen

Here is a travel guide written specifically to assist and motivate young readers to travel the world. When you are ready to leave your day job, load up your backpack and head out to distant lands for extended periods of time, Brad Olsen's "Travel Classic" will lend a helping hand.

$17.95 :: 288 pages paperback: 978-1888729054

... all Ebooks priced at $8.99

Kindle: 978-1888729276; PDF: 978-1888729061
ePub: 978-1888729351

THE ESOTERIC SERIES FROM CCC PUBLISHING

Beyond Esoteric:
Escaping Prison Planet
– by Brad Olsen

Nothing in this world works the way we are led to believe it does; there is always more to the story. Be aware that there is a war being waged for your body, mind and soul. Owners of corporations have taken over governments in a new form of Fascism that now incorporates high technology and artificial intelligence. The survival of the human race may depend on breaking the Truth Embargo, that is, exposing the Big Lie.

$19.95 :: 480 pages; paperback: 978-1888729740

... all eBooks priced $9.99

All ebook ISBN versions: 978-1888729757

Modern Esoteric:
Beyond our Senses
– 2nd EDITION; by Brad Olsen

Organized into three sections (Lifeology, Control and Thrive), Modern Esoteric: Beyond Our Senses by World Explorer magazine editor Brad Olsen examines the flaws in ancient and modern history, plus explains how esoteric knowledge, conspiracy theories, and fringe subjects can be used to help change the dead-end course we humans seem to be blindly running ourselves into.

$17.95 :: 480 pages; paperback: 978-1888729504

... all eBooks priced $9.99

Kindle: 978-1888729856 • PDF: 978-1888729832 • ePub: 978-1888729849

Future Esoteric:
The Unseen Realms
– 2nd EDITION; by Brad Olsen

Things are not always as they appear. For the past century forbidden subjects such as UFOs, human abductions, secret space programs, suppressed free energy devices and other fantastic notions have tested the human mind, forcing it to decipher fact from fiction. But is there a common thread? As sites like WikiLeaks and their founders try to unveil war secrets and covert black operations, international governments have little-by-little begun exposing what they've tried for years to keep hidden. Chronicling what he calls the "alternative narrative," Brad Olsen gets down to the middle of it all.

$17.95 :: 416 pages; paperback: 978-1888729788

... all eBooks priced $9.99

Kindle: 978-1888729801 • PDF: 978-1888729795 • ePub: 978-1888729818

CCC Publishing is distributed by Independent Publishers Group (800) 888-4741, www.IPGBook.com
Follow us on: www.EsotericSeries.com & www.Facebook.com/ccc.publishing • www.CCCPublishing.com
features the content of all of our books online, plus blogs, ebooks & discounts